DATE DUE

DEMCO

PSYCHIATRIC PROBLEMS IN OPHTHALMOLOGY

PSYCHIATRIC PROBLEMS IN OPHTHALMOLOGY

Edited by

Jerome T. Pearlman, M.D.

Associate Professor of Ophthalmology
Jules Stein Eye Institute
UCLA School of Medicine
Los Angeles, California

George L. Adams, M.D.

Associate Professor, Department of Psychiatry
Baylor College of Medicine
Houston, Texas

Sherwin H. Sloan, M.D.

Assistant Clinical Professor of Ophthalmology
Jules Stein Eye Institute
UCLA School of Medicine
Los Angeles, California
Chief of Ophthalmology
Veterans Administration Hospital
Sepulveda, California

CHARLES C THOMAS • PUBLISHER
Springfield • Illinois • U.S.A.

Published and Distributed Throughout the World by

CHARLES C THOMAS ● PUBLISHER

Bannerstone House

301-327 East Lawrence Avenue, Springfield, Illinois, U.S.A.

© *1977, by* CHARLES C THOMAS ● PUBLISHER

ISBN 0-398-03596-2

Library of Congress Catalog Card Number: 76-23301

With THOMAS BOOKS *careful attention is given to all details of manufacturing and design. It is the Publisher's desire to present books that are satisfactory as to their physical qualities and artistic possibilities and appropriate for their particular use.* THOMAS BOOKS *will be true to those laws of quality that assure a good name and good will.*

Printed in the United States of America
R-2

Library of Congress Cataloging in Publication Data

Main entry under title:

Psychiatric problems in ophthalmology.

   Bibliography: p.
   Includes index.
   1. Eye--Diseases and defects--Psychosomatic aspects.
2. Blind--Psychology. 3. Eye--Surgery--Psychological aspects. I. Pearlman, Jerome T. II. Adams, George L., 1942- III. Sloan, Sherwin H. [DNLM: 1. Eye diseases--Complications. 2. Mental disorders--Complications. WW100 P974]
RE912.P79   617.7   76-23301
ISBN 0-398-03596-2

CONTRIBUTORS

George L. Adams, M.D., Associate Professor, Department of Psychiatry, Baylor College of Medicine, Houston, Texas.

Leonard Apt, M.D., Professor of Ophthalmology, Chief of Pediatric Ophthalmology, Jules Stein Eye Institute, UCLA School of Medicine, Los Angeles, California.

Morris C. Beckwitt, M.D., Assistant Clinical Professor of Psychiatry, UCLA School of Medicine, Los Angeles, California.

Michael P. Gross, M.D., Adjunct Professor of Psychiatry, UCLA School of Medicine, Los Angeles, California.

Jarvin Heiman, M.D., Assistant Clinical Professor of Psychiatry, UCLA School of Medicine, Los Angeles, California.

Sherwin Isenberg, M.D., Resident in Ophthalmology, University of Illinois Eye Infirmary, Chicago, Illinois.

Jerome T. Pearlman, M.D., Associate Professor of Ophthalmology, Jules Stein Eye Institute, UCLA School of Medicine, Los Angeles, California.

Paul J. Schulz, M.A., Consultant in Psychology, Braille Institute, Los Angeles, California.

Sherwin H. Sloan, M.D., Assistant Clinical Professor of Ophthalmology, Jules Stein Eye Institute, UCLA School of Medicine, Los Angeles, California. Chief of Ophthalmology, Veterans Administration Hospital, Sepulveda, California.

Donald W. Verin, M.D., Chief Psychiatrist for Los Angeles County Mentally Ill Offenders Unit, Los Angeles, California.

Charles W. Wahl, M.D., Clinical Professor of Psychiatry, UCLA School of Medicine, Los Angeles, California.

PREFACE

It has been said that, because of its preciseness, ophthalmology escapes the multitude of psychosomatic patients who deluge the general practitioner's or internist's office. Nothing really could be farther from the truth. As a specialty, ophthalmology has its great share of psychiatric and psychosomatic related problems. However, they are frequently missed or ignored by the ophthalmologist.

This compilation of articles on selected psychiatric problems for the ophthalmologist is not intended as a sweeping review of psychosomatic ophthalmic problems. Instead, we have gathered together topics which we feel are relatively common, often exasperating, but important for the ophthalmologist to be aware of and to add to his interest and abilities as a diagnostician.

The Editors

CONTENTS

PSYCHIATRIC
PROBLEMS IN
OPHTHALMOLOGY

Chapter 1

THE EYE AND "I"

Sherwin H. Sloan, M.D. and Charles W. Wahl, M.D.

Sherlock Holmes, in one of his stories, described a way in which a person can be made to reveal his most treasured possession. "Yell 'fire'" he said, "and a mother will rush to save her children, and a maiden her jewels." You may recall that he solved a puzzling case in this way.

Similarly, when man is faced unexpectedly by the threat of physical injury, he instinctively covers his genitalia with one hand and shields his eyes with the other. The "balls" and the "eyeballs" are thus linked together in the unconscious mind by more than a play on words (Fig. 1-1). For the eyes are our most precious and valued physical possessions, being as they are, our windows into the world. It is therefore not surprising, as numerous studies have shown, that most people would rather sustain any injury or loss than endure blindness. This being so, it is not hard to understand why the eye therefore occupies a place in our body-image and internal conception of ourselves that is unique and unparalleled in psychic life.

The eye, in all times and all ages, has been very central in man's interests in, and awe concerning, himself and his function. This archaic primacy is evident today in the way a schizophrenic child will draw a fixed and central eye into the inchoate and formless deliniation of a sketch of the human face. He shows through this and other evidence that the eye is the seat and essence of the person and even with the loss of every other aspect of the body-image, the "eye" is equated with the "I" or the self. In this he shares a belief with the ancient Egyptians who in their Eye of Horus formed a concept of an apotropaic power that protected against all evil and magically ensured success, a talisman which the physician uses even today each time he employs the symbol R_x from which it is directly

3

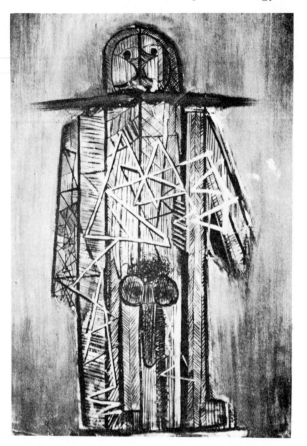

Figure 1-1. A figure of a man by Victor Brauner showing the artistic link between the "balls" and the "eyeballs".

derived (Fig. 1-2). In the mythopoesis of races, in the concepts of a schizophrenic child and the unconscious of all of us, we learn that the eye is envisioned not as a receptive organ but a protective one (Fig. 1-3). Vestiges of this concept are evident in our speech. We speak of a "darting, withering or piercing glance," or "transfixing with a stare". All readers of the comic strip Lil' Abner© know of the effect of the "double whammy". This paleological concept is used by the hypnotist who has learned that asking the subject to fixate upon his eye is more

Figure 1-2. The Egyptian Eye of Horus.

likely to induce a rapid hypnosis than having the patient stare at a pencil eraser. And are we all not somewhat influenced by the popular belief that a steady gaze and a clear eye are prime indicators of inner strength, honesty and steadfastness of purpose? Even today, the Italian peasant shuns the individual with ophthalmia since, as a rheumy eye indicates the *mal occhio* or "evil eye", such a person is to be feared and hated (Fig. 1-4). Edgar Allan Poe, in his story, "The Tell-Tale Heart", describes a man who kills another and who gives as his reason, "I think it was first his eye that made me hate the old man."

To the ophthalmologist, knowledge of the symbolic representations of the eye becomes indispensable to the understanding and evaluation of various eye symptoms. The general ophthalmologist's office has its large share of patients with symptoms from the nonspecific itchy burning eye to the patient with a profound depression following an enucleation. Submerged beneath the obvious and accessible complaints may lie the more symbolic and unconscious conflicts and associations

Figure 1-3. Redon's depiction of the great all-protective eye.

that contribute to or make up the total etiology of the symptom.

There is a saying: "A beautiful eye makes silence eloquent; a kind eye makes contradiction an assent. This member gives life to every part of us." What happens when this member no longer sees or when this member is removed? To a patient undergoing the possibility or accomplishment of one of the above the loss can be equated with death. In fact, to the

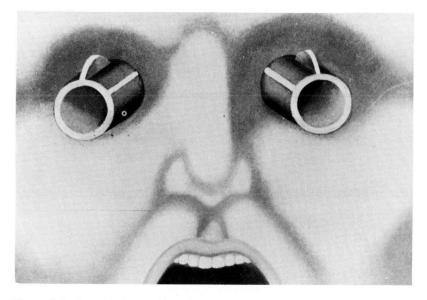

Figure 1-4. An artistic manifestation of the power of the evil and destructive eye.

ophthalmologist, blindness becomes equivalent to ophthalmic death. An internist loses the battle when the patient dies. The ophthalmic patient lives but he, as well as his ophthalmologist, may react violently to this ophthalmic death.

The image one has of his body or his worth may be analogous to the image one has on his retina. The total lack of a retinal image or a greatly diminished one may produce equivalent feelings of diminished personal worth. A "dead eye" may mean a dead man. Universally, primitive peoples have looked upon the eye as having a very special and mysterious quality and the primitive concepts of the eye and its relationship to death are numerous. It is almost instinctive for members of the medical and paramedical fields, as well as relatives of one who has recently died, to close the deceased's eyes as soon as the pronouncement is made. There is an old Jewish custom of covering the mirrors in the home of a person recently deceased lest that person look back at us from previous reflections.

Artists, philosophers and psychologists long have envisioned various ways in which the eye may represent aspects of our psychic lives. To illustrate the preceding comments, let us look at what has been evident to artists regarding the symbolism of the eye.

The concept of the "evil eye" has been with the human race quite a long time. A masterful dissertation on this subject is presented in Gifford's book, *The Evil Eye*. There is virtually no culture studied without some traces of the evil eye concept. The thought that the eye is capable of projecting the evil thoughts of its owner is one of the most ancient and universal ocular superstitions. An evil mind, most likely, must have an evil eye. St. Matthew (6:22, 23) expressed some of the thoughts of Jesus as: "The light of the body is in the eye: if therefore thine eye be single (that is sound), thy whole body shall be full of light. But if thine eye be evil, thy whole body shall be full of darkness."

One might imagine that concepts in the belief of the evil eye have greatly diminished with modern technology and the space age. If one takes another look at the great increase recently in the occult, astrology and the devil, it is evident that these ideas have not disappeared from modern society.

Diverse and miraculous are the effects which have been attributed to the evil eye. The belief in the evil eye has undergone fascinating elaboration through the ages. The imagination of man, reasoning from an original false premise and motivated by fear of harm and hope of protection, developed a core of belief which is still with us in nearly all parts of the world. The power to inflict evil has been ascribed to entire races or religious sects, to animals and mythical creatures, to demons and spirits. This myth contains a profound truth because the difference between animal and human aggression is that man is able to plan to inflict evil on his fellow being.

The evil eye could sometimes be recognized as an inflamed or squinting orb, and this superstition was downright dangerous for any person who happened to be cross-eyed, or had inflamed or reddened eyes. It is not surprising that endless fantasies have been woven around the first organ of influence and fascination

Figure 1-5. Magritte's view of the eye as the totality of the human soul.

— the eye as a mirror of the soul (Fig. 1-5). Witches, demons and devils use fascination to full advantage in casting an evil spell (Figs. 1-6, 1-7). There are schizophrenic patients who are firmly convinced that they can kill with one terrible look. Jean-Paul Sartre once remarked that if man's gaze could fertilize women, they would all be continually pregnant. Certainly, the eyes betray what we are thinking and feeling.

That the eye can exude and impart evil does not mean that it cannot also embody a symbol of protection from evil.

As much as the eye has been associated with evil, it has also provided comfort, solace and protection against evil.

Primitive man, faced with the difficult and uncooperative forces of nature, created gods to whom he could appeal to preside over the uncertainties of his life. The Egyptians created the eye god Horus to provide comfort and answers. This Egyptian god, who once suffered the loss of an eye, symbolizes and

Figures 1-6 and 1-7. Two representations of the devil with multiple evil eyes.

instills a sense of the renewal of growth and fertility, of healing and cure. In Syria ancient eye temples and eye goddesses have been unearthed and probably played a significant role in the everyday lives of the inhabitants of that time long ago (Figs. 1-8, 1-9).

In the Christian religion St. Lucia has a unique position as patron saint of the eyes (Figs. 1-10, 1-11). In Asian culture, an imaginary omnipotent eye, sometimes called the magical third eye or urna, is often described as the organ for direct intuitive exploration, attack, conquest, penetration, and all-knowing wisdom and protection (Figs. 1-12, 1-13).

That the eye, as one of its many symbolic manifestations, might be associated psychically with the genitalia may be surprising and even upsetting to some. Evidence gathered from artists and cartoonists indicate that this indeed is true for some patients, and perhaps, for all of us in the unconscious. Indeed,

Figure 1-8. Eye amulets from the Syrian temple of the eye.

Gifford devotes two entire chapters in his book to the Masculine Eye and the Feminine Eye.

In the very first paragraph of this chapter it is stated that the "balls" are somehow equated psychically with the "eyeballs". There is evidence that this is indeed so. Victor Brauner, not long ago, attended a party given by Salvidor Dali. Somehow at this party Brauner lost one eye in an accident. His drawings from this date dramatically exhibit the artist's association of the

Figure 1-9. Altar of the eye temple of Tell Brak (Syria).

eye with the genitalia (Figs. 1-14, 1-15, 1-16).

Stepping somewhat "lower", Figure 1-17, obtained from a pornographic magazine, demonstrates the association of the eyes and the genitalia even at this level of human endeavor.

The female breasts do not escape psychic symbolism with the eyes, as shown in the drawings and cartoons that follow (Figs. 1-18, 1-19, 1-20, 1-21).

It is not only because of its primacy and uniqueness of function that the eye is a focus of a special psychic investment and

Figures 1-10 and 1-11. Artistic examples of St. Lucia, patron saint of the eyes.

interest. A further large reason lies in its function of sight itself. The developing child uses the eye and the tactile senses as the primary agents of gratification of curiosity. He soon learns however, that some things are forbidden to touch and other things forbidden to see. In psychic development, as in Greek mythology, some things cannot be looked upon without the fear of being turned into stone, or the consequence more exactly in the Law of Talion, to be struck blind or to be castrated or killed. The child's sense of sexuality is initially far more visual than it is tactile. The wish to look and the wish to touch

Figure 1-11.

are very early components of sexual exploration and our phrase, "a good-looking woman", is a reminder to us of this period of life when looking was everything. The voyeur, for reasons of guilt and punishment, never progresses beyond this pregenital stage and the story of "Peeping Tom", who was struck blind for his forbidden look at the nude Lady Godiva, has its exact counterpart in the child's unconscious. Hence, it should not surprise us to learn that a strong repression of an incestuously motivated voyeuristic wish when deeply repressed can sometimes be at the root of occular difficulties of many

Figure 1-12 and 1-13. The urna, or third eye of protectiveness, in the Oriental religions.

diverse kinds such as psychogenic amblyopia or amaurosis.

What does all the preceding mean in relationship to ophthalmic patients in our day-to-day office practice? Even if it only adds a minute comprehension of the complex psychic significance of the eye to each individual, it is thus worthwhile.

In the evolution of our understanding of all factors that effect human life physically and mentally, the concept of the eye's psychic and symbolic significance is just an infinitesimally small component. Yet, for the ophthalmologist, an appreciation of subtle factors involved with each patient may be a significant advantage for both doctor and patient. Let us not separate the "eye" of our patients from their total being. Remember, the eye is just a small organ but nonetheless a most powerful, and at the same time fragile, component of the "I".

Figure 1-14. Victor Brauner's depiction of accident causing the loss of his eye.

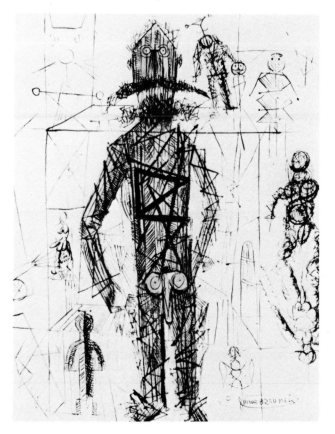

Figure 1-15. Once again, the "balls" and the "eyeballs" interlinked by Victor Brauner.

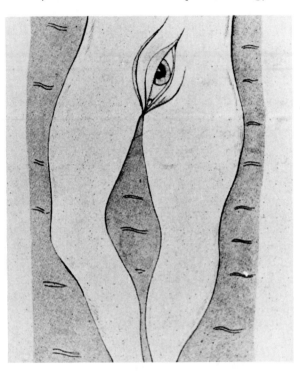

Figure 1-16. The genital eye of Victor Brauner.

Figure 1-17. What more can be said!

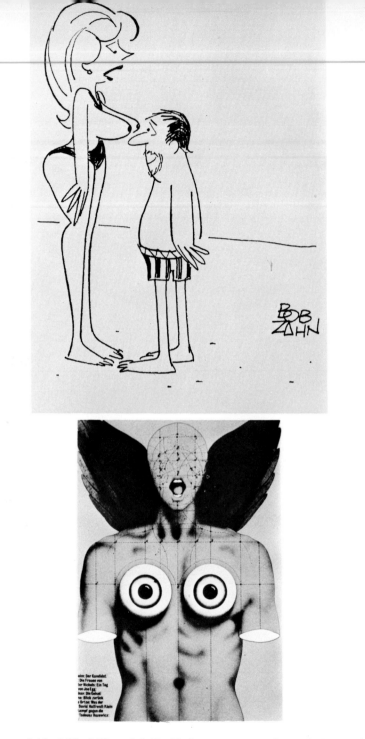

Figures 1-18, 1-19, 1-20 and 1-21. Various representations of the symbolic association of the eyes and the female breast.

Figures 1-20 and 1-21.

REFERENCE

1. Gifford, E. S., Jr.: *The Evil Eye*. Macmillan, 1958.

Chapter 2

PSYCHIATRIC EVALUATION OF THE OPHTHALMIC PATIENT

Donald W. Verin, M.D.

THERE are numerous areas where the paths of psychiatry and ophthalmology intersect. The ophthalmic patient can, as occurs with patients treated in other specialties, fail to improve with treatment. He may develop uncommon complications as the result of interference on his part. Failure to take medication, overdosing or erratic use of prescribed drugs suggest some psychiatric process in operation preventing the patient from following the ophthalmologist's instructions for dealing with his eye problem.

It is important to have some idea of how a patient will react with one eye patched and poor vision in the other while confined to a darkened room recuperating from eye surgery. Will the psychiatrist's assistance be required in managing a patient who has a neoplasm of the eye where enucleation is contemplated? What are feelings of the patient with rapidly declining vision? Is he psychologically strong enough to cope with the stress of a world of shadows or complete darkness?

The ophthalmologist should be familiar with how his patient has reacted to stressful situations in the past to have an indicator of how the present stress will affect him.

The cooperation of patients, in general, is necessary for an optimum result in the surgical or medical treatment of disease. The ophthalmic patient needs to cooperate, to an even greater extent, while being subjected to varying degrees of sensory deprivation. To permit healing to take place, the eye patient must often remain quiet for days. He must have the mental capacity to understand the reasons for restriction of his activities.

Often, the ophthalmic patient's general sensory acuity is diminishing due to advancing age. His contact with the

23

external world may have decreased gradually over a protracted period of time until all he has left is his TV or newspapers. If he is cut off from these by visual problems, he may begin to hallucinate. He may become depressed and be a suicide risk. In the event that these phenomena go unnoticed by the physician charged with the patient's care, the results could be disastrous.

A psychiatric evaluation of the ophthalmic patient would give the ophthalmologist a greater understanding of who his patient is, how he got to be this way and by inference, how he will respond emotionally to the contemplated course of action. Whether the patient will cooperate with his treatment or fight it can be ascertained with reasonable certainty along with what might be the best way to secure the cooperation of the patient.

Psychiatric evaluation may be indicated in the ophthalmic patient who (1) develops severe depression, becomes psychotic or who seems to be losing contact with reality during the course of treatment for an eye problem; (2) is already depressed or has a history of suicide attempts, is psychotic or has a history of psychotic decompensation under stress; (3) has numerous complaints for which no organic basis can be found after thorough physical examination; (4) has a history of complications and/or poor results in treatment of previous medical problems; (5) appears to have difficulty in understanding and/or following directions; (6) has a history of prior psychiatric disorders and whose present mental condition is not clear; (7) has a history or shows evidence of organic brain disease; (8) has a history of repeated trauma to the eye; (9) has a history of drug abuse; (10) has a history of self-mutilation.

These are just a few of the areas which suggest possible psychopathology and the need for further investigation.

The attending physician who has the interest and the time can do a quite adequate psychiatric evaluation of his patient. However, if he is uncomfortable with involving himself in this process or if he feels that he lacks sufficient time to do it, the patient should be referred to the psychiatrist in the same manner that the ophthalmologist prefers referral of patients to him. The patient should contact the psychiatrist himself to make an appointment. The ophthalmologist in referring the patient should state what specific problems he is concerned with and what his plans are for further treatment of the patient. He should also tell the patient that he is concerned about him and wants further information in order to get the best results for him.

Psychiatric evaluation can be brief (less than thirty minutes) or it can take several sessions lasting one to two hours each and may include psychological testing.

The evaluation may involve only the patient and the examiner. At times however the patient's spouse, children, parents, other family members and even friends, neighbors and the patient's employer may be involved. The examiner might want to check with other physicians who have treated the patient for further information.

FORMAT

Often it is helpful for the examiner initially to follow an outline until he is comfortable and familiar with the kind of information being sought. As much as possible, however, the patient should be permitted to express himself freely, being guided by an occasional inquiry about a specific point for enlarging upon or for clarification. The following outline is useful:

Chief Complaint
History of Present Illness
Past History
    Family History
    Personal History
Mental Examination
    General Appearance and Behavior
    Stream of Talk
    Affect
    Abnormal Mental Trends and Content of Thought
    Suicidal Thoughts
    Mental Grasp and Capacity
        Orientation
        Attention and Comprehension

Memory
General Intelligence
  Insight
  Judgement

Chief Complaint

The presenting problem, symptom or the reason the patient has come for the evaluation is termed the "chief complaint". It may not be obvious to the patient. That is, he may be unable to state outright what his problem is, thus requiring careful inquiry on the part of the examiner. Such questions as those that follow will often reveal the chief complaint. Why are you here? How may I help you? What is your problem? What brings you to me? What is troubling you?

History of Present Illness

Here, the concern is with securing as much as possible the chronological evolution of the patient's primary complaint from its inception. Learning how it began and under what conditions should supply data about the patient's life at that time. Questions such as "What led up to the development of the problem? What has happened since then?" are useful. They are specific yet general enough to allow the patient to tell his story as he remembers it which will yield the additional facts about what the patient considered the important aspects of his life.

The examiner should discover how the patient felt about his problem at the time he first noticed it and afterwards. What developments have taken place since then? Has the problem progressed, improved, changed or remained the same? How does the patient feel about that? In what way has the problem affected the patient's life in terms of himself, his family, employment, pleasures, etc.? How does he feel about these things?

What does the patient think will happen as a result of the problem in terms of the above factors (self, family, employment, pleasures) and what are his feelings about that? Has the patient known anyone else with this kind of problem, if so, who and how did they handle it? How does the patient plan on dealing with the problem?

Past History

Family History

The family history should include information on Mother and Father as the patient remembers them from childhood on — how he related to them, they to him, them to each other and how the patient felt about these relationships. If the patient has siblings, their names, ages and relationship to him, to the parents, and to each other should be learned in addition to their present life situations.

Grandparents (maternal and paternal), aunts, uncles, cousins and any other relatives who lived with the patient or were important in his life should be learned about in a similar way to see what part they played in the patient's life.

Family interrelationships with problem handling should be explored, in addition, to help understand how the family functioned. This information is of vast importance since it shows what the patient's early model for family behavior was and how he may interact in his family. If his parents viewed illness as a weakness then the patient may tend to deny or minimize his eye affliction and feel that intensive or prolonged treatment or convalescence is unnecessary, therefore making him uncooperative.

What was the degree of early gratification? Did the patient and his family have sufficient supply of food, clothing, shelter and love? Were the parents sacrificing for the children? Did they give freely or grudgingly? This information helps to reflect the degree of internal security the patient feels.

Social relations with the family, neighbors, friends, etc. were early examples of how the patient learned to deal with those around him. Did the family go out as a unit or was it fragmented? Were the parents outgoing or withdrawn, permissive or restricting in social situations in general and with the patient's activities in particular? Learning how the patient felt about these things may tell us how he is with his family and with himself. This information might also give a hint to how much cooperation might be expected from the patient's family during his illness.

Personal History

A chronological development of the patient's life is sought here beginning with Birth and Early Development. Was the patient a wanted child? Were there problems with the pregnancy, delivery or neonatal period? Did early development proceed at an average rate? If not, what problems were there and how were they handled?

Education: The next aspect of the patient's past history to be examined is his education. How far he went in school and the kinds of grades he received will disclose information about his intelligence, motivation and ability to learn. Additional data such as the courses he did best and worst in, those he liked and disliked, his other school activities such as clubs, teams, sports, music, etc., how he got along with peers and teachers will help to round out the picture of the patient as a student. Did he quit school before finishing or change courses? What caused him to make these moves and what he did then should be learned. From these answers may be learned something about how the patient deals with adversity and stress.

Work: A work history is to the adult what a school history is to the child and adolescent. From it we can learn much about the patient's life after he left school. It should be approached chronologically beginning with his first work experience. What was his first job and how did he fare on it? Was he promoted or transferred and why? When he left what was the reason? What did he do then? Continue this method of inquiry until his most recent employment is covered. Ask about the hours worked, relations with employers and co-workers and his attitude about his work. Did he take his work home to finish or leave it undone? Was he driven by feelings of inadequacy and guilt about not being able to do a satisfactory job or was he confident in his ability and results?

Military History: May be considered a part of the work history. The data collected should include the branch of service, highest rank achieved and rank on discharge, length of service, the jobs done, demeanor, any conflict, feelings about being in and about leaving. This information will give an idea about how the patient dealt with authority.

Religion: In this area also the early experiences are important. The religion of the parents, whether the patient accepted it, whether he is still active in it or in another are asked, plus reasons for any changes that were made. What part does his religion play in his life now? Answers to these questions will reflect on the degree of responsibility the patient accepts for his problems and his willingness to help in their resolution.

Habits: The next area to be covered is the history of the patient's habits. First come his sleeping habits. How many hours per twenty-four-hour period does he spend sleeping? Does he have difficulty getting to sleep or staying asleep? Does he feel rested on arising? Sleeping difficulty is one of the signs of depression. Another is appetite disturbance. Has there been an increase or decrease? Has the patient lost interest in food? Does he get a full feeling quickly or get nauseated at meals? Is he excessively bowel conscious? Does he complain of constipation or diarrhea and what is his understanding of these terms? The depressed patient tends to focus his attention more on himself and his bodily functions and less on the world around him. Thus what went unnoticed for years and may be normal for that person now becomes a matter of great concern, being considered abnormal by the patient. This concern may progress to an obsession whereby the patient devotes most of his time, energy and attention to his bowel function.

The patient's use of drugs should be investigated including both prescription and nonprescribed drugs. What drugs has the patient used in the past, how much, how often and for what duration? Why was he taking them? What does he take now and why? Prolonged use of certain drugs such as barbiturates and tranquilizers indicate the patient's attempt to block out certain unpleasant feelings and may reflect unrecognized psychopathology. These patients may also have difficulty adhering to the prescribed dosage of medications such as narcotic and nonnarcotic analgesics, possibly inducing side-reactions or unexpected complications such as overdose.

Alcohol intake is usually considered separately from drug intake. How much, how often and for how long are the questions regarding alcohol ingestion to be asked first. If there appears to be a problem regarding alcoholism in the patient then further information should be obtained such as time of first drink of the day, whether the patient eats when drinking, and what he drinks. Has he had delirium tremens? Has he had treatment for alcoholism? The patient with an alcoholic problem may be less reliable in cooperating with treatment which requires his enduring sensory deprivation. He may hallucinate, become acutely anxious or may decide he does not care about the consequences and refuse to remain under treatment.

How much and for how long the patient has been smoking and how he feels about his smoking will give further information about his ability to withstand stress and deprivation in connection with treatment of his eye problems.

The patient's past medical history should include major illnesses and treatment, surgeries with reason for them and outcome, accidents and injuries, particularly head injuries and any sequelae. Has the patient had any venereal disease, treated or untreated? In female patients a menstrual history including onset, cessation, pregnancies, deliveries and complications, if any, should be obtained. History of previous mental illness, including what, when, where and how treated for how long?

Sexual History: This part of the patient's past history may be quite difficult for him to relate. It is an area for many people that is heavily emotion laden. However, if it is approached in the same manner that the remainder of the history is gotten, there should be little difficulty. Asking a question such as, "How old were you the first time you learned about sex and where babies come from?" should lead the patient into the topic without embarrassment. His feelings about this knowledge should be explored. The same procedure should be followed for his first date, petting, first sexual intercourse and subsequent encounters including age, feelings and frequency. Did the patient change partners often or remain with the same one? Did he engage in any activity other than genital intercourse? Was there any thought of or actual homosexual activity?

If the patient married was there any change in his sexual activity? Was there any change after pregnancies? It is not unusual to find a marked change in sexual appetite in certain men with immature personalities after their wives have babies. They may feel jealous and rejected and may feel an increased sexual desire or almost none if they become depressed.

The patient's present sexual activities are rather easily expressed at this point. Ask about frequency and degree of satisfaction and how he feels about it. The patient's marital history has already been touched upon, but it should be amplified here. The first marriage date, length and type of relationship patient had with spouse is asked. If there have been divorces or multiple marriages learn the reasons for the dissolutions. What kind of relationship is present now? Has it been changing for better or worse? What are the problems and what are the possible solutions?

How has the patient's problem affected his marriage or will it? What can he do and what does he expect his spouse to do about it? How does he feel about it? These answers tell something about the patient's inner strength and how he gets along in intimate relationships. How he will accept help and the dependent position is also inferred.

Personality Makeup: The information sought here will give a picture of the kind of person this patient is. It is often productive to ask the patient what kind of person he would describe himself as. Inquire about his temperament also. What are his outside interests, hobbies, etc., and how much time does he devote to them? What kind of interpersonal relationships does he have? Does he have close friends? Is he socially active? How do people treat him and he them? How do his friends view him? Does he have any difficulty getting along with people? If so, ask who, why, over what, for how long, etc.

Has the patient ever been arrested or done anything for which he might be arrested? If so ask what, when, outcome, etc.

Mental Examination

In this part of the psychiatric evaluation the patient's psychic functioning is looked at. It helps to complete the picture of what kind of person this is as well as who he is.

General Appearance and Behavior

Here a general description of the patient as he appears at the present moment gives a picture that is helpful in visualizing him. His age, sex, height, weight and coloring should be included with the manner of dress and grooming. In addition, the description should include the patient's demeanor and motoric activity. Is he withdrawn, outgoing, effusive, quiet or depressed? Does there seem to be any degree of psychomotor retardation or increased motor activity? Are there any prominent features about this patient?

Stream of Talk

How does the patient speak? Does he present his story in an organized, structured, meaningful way or is it disorganized and confused? Does the patient speak freely or does he seem to have difficulty saying what he wants to say? Does he start a sentence and then stop, unable to continue that thought? Is there difficulty in following what the patient says as though his thoughts are consecutively unrelated? When asked a question does he respond without answering the question or does he continue talking about one thing even though he has been asked about something else? Is his speech free-flowing or hesitant? Is his response to questions prompt or delayed? Does he use strange words or strange combinations of words in his responses? Many of these questions would be answered affirmatively in persons with psychotic thought processes, most commonly schizophrenics.

Affect

This term refers to feeling tone and emotion. To evaluate affect one must observe how the patient looks and sounds. Does he seem happy or sad? Does he laugh about morbid or tragic events? Does his face mirror the emotion that would ordinarily be associated with what he is discussing or is his face unexpressive and flat? Is there a vacant blank staring expression on the face (flat affect)? Is there a change in facial expression consistent with a change of subject being discussed and to what degree?

Does the patient have any awareness of his feelings? Can he admit to feeling angry when that emotion is visible on his face?

These guides to the patient's feeling tone enable the psychiatrist to have a glimpse of the patient's internal world and help him to gauge the proximity of it to the world of reality.

Abnormal Mental Trends — Content of Thought

The patient with visual impairment may tend to become suspicious of others and quite fearful as his ability to visually test reality is diminished. He may see a plant as a threatening animal or perceive street or house noises as dangers to him. To examine the patient's mental trends it is necessary to learn something of how and what he thinks. In what way does he account for his present difficulties? Can he discuss them lucidly, concisely and spontaneously or is he reluctant to share his thoughts?

Does the patient seem distrustful? Is he concerned that his problems are disease related or does he feel that someone or something is causing them? Is there any expression from the patient that he is being punished for something he feels guilty about, or does he feel persecuted or singled out for some higher purpose (delusions)?

Has he heard voices when no one else was there? Has he seen things that he knew were not there? Does he recall having any other strange sensations involving the senses of taste, touch or smell? If he answers affirmatively, then further information should be obtained such as when and where it happened, duration of the experience and a description of it. Learn how the patient felt about it and what he thinks of it now.

In observing the patient during the interview, the examiner should determine if any such phenomena are occurring. Does the patient repeatedly look off to one spot in the room or move his eyes quickly to one side or turn his head similarly as if to catch sight of something there? Does he seem to be listening or responding verbally to some unseen stimulus (hallucinations)?

Suicidal Thoughts

In learning about the patient's life, we need to know something about how he views death. Is it a friend or enemy? Has he contemplated suicide or attempted it? When, how, and how many times? Has he thought about it lately? Does he have any plans about it at present?

The ophthalmic patient facing loss of vision may become a serious suicide risk. There are those patients who equate the loss of sight or the loss of an eye to the loss of life.

It is also helpful in gauging the depth of the patient in despair to ask about his plans for the future. If he has immediate and long range plans which are reasonable he may be considered less of a suicide risk than the person without such plans.

Mental Grasp and Capacity

This part of the mental examination deals with the abilities and level of mental functioning.

Orientation: Does the patient know where he is and how he got there? Can he give the date, day and time of day? Does he know who the examiner is and his function? Is he aware of who he is? Patients with organic brain syndromes and some of the psychotic disorders will often be unable to supply correct responses to the above questions.

Attention and Comprehension: Is the patient alert? Does he remain attentive to the business of the interview or is he easily distracted? Does he seem to understand what is happening and the purpose of the interview? Is he aware of his illness and its relationship to the interview? The patient whose mental functioning is impaired may not be able to understand or give his undivided attention to the interview situation.

His mental functioning may be further tested by checking his ability to retain and recall data. This is done by giving the patient a name or date to remember, then asking him to repeat it after five minutes and again near the end of the session. He is also asked to repeat a series of numbers forward and another series backward. He should be able to correctly recite seven forward and five backward.

Memory: Testing in this area differs from that preceding in that the patient is asked to recall information from his life and not that supplied by the examiner.

Recent memory may be tested by asking what the patient had for breakfast or lunch that day, who accompanied him to the interview and something of the news of the day. He should also be able to supply correctly his address, telephone number and the names of the people living in his household.

Remote memory may be checked by asking the patient's birthdate and birthplace, how far he went in school and the names of the schools he attended. He should be able to tell how long he has lived at his present address, his wife's maiden name and when they married and the dates and places that his children were born.

General Intelligence: This area is evaluated by checking the patient's general fund of knowledge and his ability to do abstract thinking. The general fund of knowledge is tested by asking a series of questions in keeping with the patient's schooling such as those that follow. Name the last three presidents, the mayor and the governor. Name the seasons of the year. What do plants need to grow? Where is the nation's capital? How are an orange and a tomato alike? Different? How are a dog and a cat alike? Different? How many feet in a mile? What is the speed of light? Who was Hamlet?

Abstract thinking is tested by asking the patient to interpret proverbs in his own words. Usually when asked the meaning of "People who live in glass houses shouldn't throw stones", the normal patient will talk about the hazards of pointing out problems in others when problems are present in oneself. The person with disordered thought processes may be unable to answer or may respond concretely in terms of stones breaking the glass. This person usually will have difficulty doing mental calculations such as subtracting serial seven's from one hundred. He will often have trouble doing other simple math problems such as combinations of multiplication and subtraction or addition and division. The difficulties may be in terms of inability to do the work, prolonged time intervals, errors, or declining ability with continued testing.

Insight: Refers to the patient's understanding of his problem and his part in its genesis. By this point in the examination the interviewer usually has enough data to determine if the patient knows what his situation is. The patient should also have some inkling as to why he has his problem and what he does to contribute to it. If such is not the case, asking the patient directly how he thinks his present difficulty developed should give some estimate of his insight.

Judgement: Refers to the patient's ability to function in his usual environment properly. If the patient has been making foolish and/or impulsive decisions or has been behaving in an inappropriate way at work or home, his judgement may be considered impaired.

A dynamic formulation should be developed to summarize the interview giving the interviewer's ideas of how the patient's difficulties began and reached the present state. It should include the patient's early background dynamics as well as the immediate ones and give one an understanding of the factors leading to why the patient is in his present state.

A psychiatric diagnosis should be made as well as a character or personality diagnosis. The psychiatric diagnosis involves labelling the particular neurotic or psychotic symptom complexes shown by the patient. The personality diagnosis refers to the life-long deeply ingrained maladaptive behavior patterns of the patient and differs qualitatively from the psychiatric findings. This information is easily obtained from the *Diagnostic and Statistical Manual of Mental Disorders* published by the American Psychiatric Association.

REFERENCES

1. Grinker and Robbins: *Psychosomatic Case Book*. Blakiston Co., New York, 1954.
2. Ripley, H. S.: *The Psychiatric Examination, Comprehensive Textbook of Psychiatry*. Williams and Wilkins, Baltimore, 1967.
3. Stinnett, J. L. and Hollender, M. H.: Compulsive Self-Mutilation. *J Nerv Ment Dis, 150*:5, May 1970.
4. Sullivan, H. S.: *The Psychiatric Interview*. Norton, New York, 1954.
5. American Psychiatric Association: *Diagnostic and Statistical Manual of Mental Disorders*, 2nd Edition, Washington, 1968.

Chapter 3

REACTION TO THE LOSS OF SIGHT

Paul J. Schulz

EMOTIONAL REACTIONS

THE physically normal individual has had a lifetime of experience in evaluating and testing his environment through his sense of sight. He has come to depend on and trust his sight for the performance of many of his daily tasks. He has learned to use this sense as a tool to satisfy his needs, to gratify his desires, and as a simple means of enjoying his environment. His use of sight has been such an integral part of his earliest experience that he may not even be consciously aware of the degree to which he depends on it for his daily functioning.

Once an individual has lost his sight, he becomes acutely aware of how much of his daily activity had previously been concerned with sight. He suddenly discovers that even simple tasks are now difficult to perform. As a sighted person he selected clothes with a glance to determine color, texture and design. He could sit at the table and see what food was being served. Again with a glance he could observe the location of his cup or glass. He could easily regulate the amount of food on his fork or his plate. When walking he could avoid objects with no undue effort.

As a blind individual, he now finds that he can no longer observe and control his environment with his former ease. He must now learn new techniques in order to perform these same simple tasks. In many cases, he is forced to depend on others to do things he can no longer do himself. He must ask someone else to help select his clothes; he must ask someone else to read the menu at a restaurant. He can no longer read his personal mail, but must share the information with another individual. He has lost his autonomy. In social situations he may feel ill at ease, because he is not sure when a comment is addressed to him. He may be uncomfortable during introductions, because he is not sure that he is facing the other individuals. He may not feel free to move around the room, because he is uncertain of the location of objects and people.

Nearly all areas of functioning are affected to some extent by the loss of independent movement or action. This is true whether the activity involves traveling to and from work, going shopping, visiting friends, or keeping track of children who are playing. Very frequently the onset of blindness makes it impossible for a person to retain his former job. He must retrain for a new occupation, and, during this time, he is often unable to earn a living or support his family. When the loss of sight comes to a wife or mother, she can no longer cook or clean the house with her former ease. She is burdened with the added anxiety of adequately caring for her family.

Initially, the difficulties or problems faced by a person who has recently lost his sight may seem insurmountable. Things that were once done without thought or effort now require concentration and attention.

Any physical change in the environment, or any change in the ability of an individual to cope with his environment, requires on his part a change or adjustment. When the change is as drastic as that resulting from the loss of sight, the person must mobilize all the resources at his disposal to make this adjustment. In turn, the effort required produces an emotional reaction which, in most cases, follows a predictable pattern.

Normally the emotional reaction to the onset of blindness proceeds through three stages. The initial stage is that of shock, followed by a period of depression, after which the phase of reorganization begins. These stages, however, are not always present. Their presence or absence may be affected by personality factors as well as the suddenness and severity of the onset of blindness. They may vary with regard to the intensity and duration of each stage. In some cases they may be present, although partially disguised.

Sudden and Drastic Loss. The sudden and total loss of sight is a severe blow, as is the loss of any physical organ. Shock is nearly always present as the initial reaction. The patient may remain in this state for a period of days or weeks. This is usually, but not always, followed by a period of depression, which later proceeds into the phase of reorganization or adjustment.

Nearly all reactions are more marked or acute with sudden and complete blinding. The patient is more helpless and is more aware of his limitations. Because his loss has been complete he cannot hide the extent of his loss from family or friends.

Drastic and Recurring Losses. When the condition involves a pattern of drastic loss and recurring losses, the emotional features include depression and anxiety. The degree to which these emotions appear is related to the degree of visual loss. The patient will react with depression to the severe loss that has already occurred. In addition, he will experience anxiety concerning the possibility of further losses. Because the trend is always in the direction of further loss, he will anticipate the eventual total loss of sight. He has already experienced the gradual restriction of his activity as his sight has diminished. In all likelihood he will not have become aware of his ability to make a physical adaptation to total blindness or to the further reduction of sight. Thus, his expectation will be that blindness means total helplessness.

During the time that he experiences these losses he will undoubtedly depend on strong hope. At best he will hope for recovery of sight. At the least he will hope to retain his remaining vision. However, as long as his condition is progressive, this hope will be in contradiction to the facts. It will not be based on reality.

If, however, the condition becomes stable so that a period of weeks or months elapses with no further loss, the anxiety will be dissipated, or at least diminished. At this point the patient can also begin to deal with the feelings of loss. Counseling or psychotherapy can benefit the individual even though the condition is still in a progressive state. He can begin to work through his feelings of loss. Furthermore, the anxiety can be relieved as the patient is helped to become aware of his adaptive ability.

Gradual and Steady Deterioration. When the pattern of visual loss is one of gradual but steady deterioration occurring over a period of many years, it is unlikely that there will be a marked reaction to the loss. This is particularly true in the earlier period of loss. During such a long but gradual change, the patient is often able to make the necessary adaptation in a gradual manner. He has the opportunity to adjust both physically and emotionally, because no sudden demands are made on his adjustive mechanisms. Such a person learns to use his sight as efficiently as possible. If certain portions of his visual field are blocked out, he will accommodate himself to this change by turning his head or body. He will usually be able to do this in such a way that even close associates are not aware of the change. For all practical purposes he is still a sighted person, even though he has lost considerable sight.

However, a depressive reaction may still occur, particularly when the loss of sight has reached a point where a major change in his life situation is unavoidable. This may occur when he is no longer able to drive an automobile, perform normal duties as an employee or housewife, or when it is no longer possible to read. Such persons will occasionally fail to recognize a friend in passing. These occurrences may evoke feelings of stress or embarrassment. One teenager who was losing his sight failed to recognize his mother as she passed him on the street. The experience was devastating to him, because it made him aware, for the first time, that he was going blind.

It is at such a point that the patient is brought into direct confrontation with the awareness that he is severely limited in his capacity to function. He may be forced to deal with the term "legal blindness" as it applies to him. Since the onset is not sudden, he does not experience shock. Because of the gradual nature of the loss, he may not experience the severe anxiety that results from rapid loss. However, he may become depressed, because he can no longer function as he once did. His self-concept and his relationship with others change. He must now resolve the feelings that attend such changes.

The following case history gives a fairly typical picture of a person who loses his sight gradually:

> Arnold V. is thirty-nine years old, married, and the father of three children. The diagnosis was retinitis pigmentosa. He had been gradually losing his sight over a period of ten years, but he still retained sufficient vision to assist him in traveling. He had never experienced any sudden or drastic loss of sight, and he had not experienced any severe emotional reaction to restricted vision. The time came, however, when his employer felt he could no longer perform his duties and terminated his employment. The loss of his job was a severe blow, which precipitated brief periods of depression. He verbalized feelings of lowered self-esteem. However, he had a stable, well-integrated personality, and quickly returned to his former feelings of self-worth. He compensated for his loss by remaining active, and, whenever possible, doing things for others. He developed new hobbies, such as bowling, and expressed a strong desire to retrain and obtain employment.

Fluctuating Vision. One of the most difficult conditions for any patient to cope with is one in which the remaining sight fluctuates noticeably. When the loss is sudden and complete the patient knows the full extent of his loss. When the condition is progressive he knows not only the present extent of his loss, but also the possible outcome. When, however, the condition fluctuates he is never sure from one day to the next whether his sight will improve or become worse.

The patient is well aware of the serious nature of his loss. However, at some point there is slight improvement. The improvement may last for a period of days, weeks or months, but inevitably there is again a deterioration of sight. If the fluctuations are great enough, the patient will be more likely to react strongly. However, the fluctuations need not be great. In fact, the patient will focus on the most minute changes in acuity. He will continually check his sight on environmental constants to determine if any change has taken place.

The patient may already be depressed because of the serious loss he has experienced. As his sight noticeably improves, he begins to hope that it will continue to do so. As his sight again decreases he feels despair, not only because of the loss of sight but also because of the frustration of his hopes. If the pattern repeats itself more than once, he also begins to feel anxiety.

What the patient needs at this point is to be kept in touch with reality. If fluctuation is a pattern in the specific condition, he needs to know this. When he has been informed that such is the nature of his condition he can keep his hopes in check. Thus his subsequent disappointment will not be as great.

> Judy M. is thirty-one years of age, married, and the mother of two children. Her diagnosis was retinal hemorrhage of unknown cause. Her sight had been gradually decreasing over two years. It began fluctuating after it had decreased to about 5 percent of normal vision. She became extremely depressed and verbalized acute feelings of anxiety. Whenever her sight improved, she expressed strong belief that she would see again. When her sight decreased she became pessimistic, expected to lose her sight completely, and expressed suicidal thoughts. At one time she felt she could associate only with blind people; at another she commented that the presence of other blind persons depressed her. Her sight stabilized about eight months after her initial contact with the rehabilitation agency. She was able to resolve many of her feelings associated with the loss of sight. For example, she was initially very self-conscious about carrying a cane. Although she retained enough vision to aid in traveling, she now was willing to carry a cane to insure safety when crossing streets. She began improving her skills in housekeeping. At one critical point in her adjustment, she commented that now she knew there were many things she could enjoy even without sight. Although she occasionally commented on the possibility of total blindness, she was no longer frightened by the prospect. In addition, her depression had lifted and she seemed to be making a good adjustment.

Hostility. Everyone has characteristic ways of reacting to stress. He may feel mild anxiety in ambiguous situations; or he may be irritated by frustrating situations. These reactions are an integral part of his normal pattern of behavior.

When a severe crisis occurs, or when the person is placed under extreme stress, he will react with his characteristic response but to an exaggerated degree. Thus, if he feels irritation in a mildly frustrating situation, under stress he will be furious in the same situation.

The person whose characteristic response is anger will certainly feel resentment and may express these feelings when he learns that he is losing his sight. If he is religious he may feel anger toward God for having allowed this to happen. He may feel resentment against some vague but unkind fate. Or he may feel and express resentment toward his doctor.

This anger may be unjustified. The doctor may have done everything that was medically possible. The family may have contributed its best efforts toward obtaining the best medical help. Nevertheless, he strikes out at whatever object is available. He is, in fact, reacting to his own feeling of impotence in the face of his loss.

Often the expression of hostility is prevented by the presence of some other emotion. If the angry person also feels strong anxiety because of his helpless condition, he will be in conflict. He feels anger but dares not express it because he might not receive the help he realistically needs.

If anxiety is the stronger emotion he will suppress his anger. He still feels the anger but cannot express it. He resolves the conflict by turning the anger inward. Thus, it adds to, and becomes a part of, whatever depression he is experiencing.

The unfortunate aspect of this inner directed anger is that it is increased in intensity because it is suppressed. The blind person is aware that if he were not dependent on others he would be free to express his anger. Because he has chosen not to express it, he feels self-devaluation. Ultimately he focuses these feelings on his blindness, which he feels has created this emotional impasse.

Anxiety. Anxiety is a common feature of the early stages of adjustment to blindness. This may vary from mild feelings of apprehension at the prospect of any unusual activity, to acute anxiety leading to withdrawal. In the latter case it is extremely difficult to persuade the newly blinded person to participate in almost any activity. He generally prefers to remain confined to his own home.

Anxiety may stem from the expectation of physical injury.

During the early stages of adjustment, the blind person may be poorly oriented even in his own home. He often bumps into furniture or walls. In some extreme cases the person becomes lost or confused about his location in his own home. He may become so unsure of his direction that he walks through a wrong door and into a closet.

During his early attempts to move about the house, the newly blinded person may actually receive minor but painful injuries. As these occur at unexpected moments, he becomes sensitive to the possibility of further injury. These experiences cause him to be fearful, and the fear then causes him to become tense. His movements are awkward and inhibited. His anxiety is so acute that he loses awareness of cues from his other senses. Because he is tense, he is particularly unaware of kinesthetic cues, which are indispensable for skillful movement without sight. In addition, his increased muscular tension actually increases the likelihood that he will fall if he encounters some object.

Where such anxiety exists, it can be dealt with in psychotherapy. However, anxiety can also be reduced after training in mobility and orientation. Such training teaches the blind person to walk defensively. He learns how to orient himself in walking through a room and avoiding objects. He develops the techniques that are essential for moving about his home and neighborhood. Ultimately, he may even develop the ability to travel about the city. Additionally, his family can learn the appropriate way to walk with a blind person. This training helps minimize the conflict that often centers around inept guiding and the anxiety of the blind person.

The blind or visually impaired person may also experience anxiety in anticipation of social encounters. He expects difficulty in his ability to function in unfamiliar surroundings. He has not yet adapted to his own surroundings and for this reason is sure he will not be able to adapt quickly to the home of a friend.

The prospect of social interaction may be even more anxiety arousing. He expects his friends and acquaintances to be awkward and ill at ease in his presence. Undoubtedly, some persons will behave in such a fashion. They will not know what to say or how to help. However, the salient fact is that he expects such reactions, but he is not sure how to cope with them. In addition, he is sure that his own behavior will be inept. If he retains some vision, he may be concerned that if he tries to hide his condition he will make some slip that will either give his condition away or make him seem clumsy.

Most newly blinded persons find it difficult to verbalize these fears. They tend to rationalize their withdrawn behavior. They will use excuses such as "I'm too tired to go out" or "I'd rather stay home and listen to music".

Until such persons achieve some measure of social competency, their anxiety will restrict their activities. Once they develop skill in moving about and in dealing with social situations, such anxiety should be reduced. Consequently, they become more active. They will not only feel more at ease themselves, but also will be able to put others at ease.

Dependency. Accompanying any major loss of sight is a degree of realistic dependency. If a person cannot read or drive an automobile, he will certainly need to receive help in these areas from someone who can see. The need for assistance will be even more pronounced during the early period that follows the loss of sight. During this time the blind person requires help with some tasks that he can eventually do for himself.

However, some individuals demand and expect more help than is actually necessary. They use friends and relatives to do things that they could actually do for themselves. They exaggerate their helpless condition in an attempt to evoke pity from the onlooker.

Other persons, however, react to their realistic dependency by refusing help even though they need it. They attempt to perform tasks for which they are not prepared by experience or training. At other times they endanger themselves or others by their behavior. A typical case would be one of a person who has not received mobility training and yet refuses help when crossing a street. One elderly man who was totally blind attempted several times to back his car out of the driveway by using his cane to follow the edge of the lawn. He could not possibly have known whether or not anyone was behind the car.

While normal attempts to acquire skill and independence are admirable, such behavior as driving a car is foolhardy. It is, in all probability, a reaction against the realistic dependency needs stemming from the loss of sight. As a blind person develops capability in many areas he finds less need to overreact to those situations in which he is clearly dependent.

Denial. The mechanism of denial is one means of dealing with threatening or anxiety arousing situations. In some cases the person denies the reality or severity of his condition. He attempts to function as though he had no visual problem. Thus, he frequently finds himself in impossible or embarrassing situations. The threatening or anxiety arousing aspect that elicits denial is the inferior status of his condition. He experiences a strong need to prove himself equal with sighted persons. He expects that those he meets will consider him to be inferior. As a result he prefers the alternative of possible embarrassment to one of being known as being blind. Denying the physical reality of blindness is, of course, more possible when the person retains some sight. What he does, in effect, is to deny the true nature of the loss.

The visually impaired person may also deny the affective content or emotional meaning of the loss. He expresses his denial with comments such as "Blindness is only a minor nuisance". The patient maintains this fiction by never admitting to himself the serious nature of his visual loss. Until he deals emotionally with the loss on a level of reality, he may never come to accept his loss and develop a new self-concept. Thus the denial actually interferes with the process of adjustment. It prevents the person from functioning in an effective manner.

> Stanley J. is twenty years old. He is an unmarried college student living with his parents. He is totally blind as the result of chemical burns received during a laboratory experiment. He underwent a period of shock lasting about a week while still recuperating in the hospital. Initially, he claimed he was not depressed. His denial was expressed by a comment "Blindness isn't so bad. I must be cut out for it." He became

involved in a rehabilitation program in which he took necessary courses, such as braille and mobility. Approximately six months after beginning training he was confronted with the realistic limitations of blindness. He had to be picked up by friends instead of driving himself; he went to parties and found many of the activities or games were designed for persons with sight. He felt strong resentment when friends talked about visual experiences, such as the way a car or girl looked. Finally, his fiancée was not sure she wanted to be married to a blind man. He became very depressed. However, he began to deal with real feelings about the loss of sight. He developed a new concept of himself as an adequate and capable blind person. He returned to college and eventually was married. These changes were possible only after he resolved his feelings of loss and began to deal realistically with the fact of blindness.

Self-Consciousness. One problem that many blind persons find difficult to resolve is the feeling of self-consciousness. If the individual was self-conscious prior to the loss of sight he will feel even more vulnerable to observation when he becomes blind. As a sighted person he could quickly determine if someone were observing his actions. As a blind person, however, he cannot know if he is being observed. He may feel uncomfortable or embarrassed, but he cannot glance around, see that no one is watching, and then continue with his task. This is particularly true when he first learns to travel with a cane. He is no longer just another person walking down the street. He is sure that everyone within watching distance is observing him. In fact, he may be the only person on the street, but he has no way of knowing this. As he acquires skill in tasks, such as traveling and eating, much of this self-consciousness diminishes.

Shock. When a person experiences a sudden and drastic loss of sight he will react with shock. The primary feature of this shock phase is a feeling of numbness and unreality. Sometimes a patient will talk about the nightmare quality of his experience. Such a reaction is, in a sense, an emotional withdrawal. It is a defense against an intolerable situation. As one patient described the situation, "I can't believe this is happening to me." He seemed to be talking about the experience in a detached manner. Cholden (1958) states that this reaction serves a useful function. He describes the reaction as being " ... a time to gather his strength for the coming ordeal".

Depression. The phase of reactive depression that follows shock may last for a period of weeks or months. The duration of the depression varies from one individual to another. It may not occur immediately but may be delayed until the patient is confronted by the limitations of his blindness. In the case of some individuals who do not receive adequate help, the depression may continue for years as an insipient condition in which an acute reaction can be precipitated by seemingly insignificant events.

During the phase of depression, the person is often quite inactive. He may feel helpless and undesirable; he is easily frustrated even when performing simple tasks, and often reacts with anger to these situations. He may have difficulty in sleeping; he often cries excessively; and he frequently expresses feelings of self-pity. Furthermore, he may feel different from the sighted and feel he can only associate with the blind. If the newly blinded person is a man, he may have feelings of insecurity about his manhood; if the person is a woman, she may feel that she is no longer attractive. There is usually a tendency to dwell on the limitation of blindness, and there is nearly always a lowering in self-esteem.

Cholden describes the period of depression as a time to mourn or grieve for something that is lost. This is, incidentally, not merely an interpretation of feelings. Occasionally, a patient who is unsophisticated regarding the adjustment process will make a comment such as, "I feel as though I'm mourning for something", or "I feel just like I did when my mother died."

Because blindness has this meaning for many patients, they should be allowed to express their grief, as in the case of a real death. Suppression of the feelings only delays the beginning of adjustment. In addition, when a patient is told not to cry or is told to cheer up, he feels an implicit condemnation of his feelings of grief. Thus, he is not only denied an opportunity to express his grief, but is also made to feel guilty for experiencing the feelings.

Reorganization. The process of reorganization or adjustment begins sometime during the period of depression. There is rarely a dramatic transition from depression to reorganization. Instead, the change is normally quite gradual.

As the person learns to perform simple tasks and develops limited skill in finding his way around his own home, he becomes aware that he is not totally helpless. His initial attempts may meet with failure, which results in feelings of frustration and anxiety. However, he soon discovers that he is capable of doing many things that he once thought were beyond his ability to perform. As his skill increases he may come to the realization that he is not inferior, only physically limited.

The transition from depression to reorganization, in addition to being gradual, may be quite erratic. The blind person may have setbacks in the learning of a skill. He may meet with a learning situation that is quite complex and become discouraged. Sometimes he feels that he can never master the skills necessary for adequate functioning. When this occurs, he may again be plunged into a period of depression. As reorganization progresses, these periods of depression will become shorter and less severe. They will also occur less frequently. As his skill increases, the blind person has less reason to be depressed. He also begins to rebuild his self-confidence. One man who had been very depressed over his social ineptness became quite exhilarated when he learned to cut his own steak. He asked a friend to watch and instruct him in his own apartment. Once he had improved this skill, he again was eager to eat in restaurants. Thus it is evident that even simple learning can have a positive effect on the process of adjustment.

It is during the phase of reorganization that the patient will be able to make the maximal use of rehabilitation services. He will more rapidly acquire the special skills associated with effective functioning. He will also be able to develop his social skills to greater advantage. It is, in short, the period during which he should be able to become a well-adjusted blind person.

Levels of Adjustment. There are many levels of adjustment. The ideal adjustment is represented by a person who has acquired skills necessary for adequate functioning as a blind person. Such a person is physically and socially active. He is involved in normal community life. Where the limitations of blindness prevent him from performing some activity in work or recreation, he will substitute an activity that is within his ability to perform. For example, he can no longer drive a car, but he can learn to travel to work on public transportation. He is not able to play baseball or volleyball, but he can bowl. The important fact is that he is still active.

The following case history is an example of good adjustment:

> Virginia J. lost her sight completely in an automobile accident. She was divorced and the mother of two children, whom she was supporting. She had been a secretary to an attorney for several years prior to her loss of sight. She underwent a period of shock and was depressed for a period of approximately two months after the accident. She was, however, highly motivated to return to work in order to again support her children. During the early period of adjustment, her mother assisted with housework and in caring for the children. After her recovery, Virginia enrolled at a rehabilitation center and took courses such as braille and home management. She took mobility training so she could travel independently. She was able to retrain and return to her former employers as a legal transcriber and receptionist.

There are, however, many blind persons who never achieve this level of adjustment. They are limited by personality factors that interfere with good adjustment. Perhaps overprotective family members prevent them from attempting or undertaking activities not traditional for a blind person. Furthermore, their inability to resolve their feelings about the loss of sight frustrates any attempts made to involve them in rehabilitation training.

> Sandra B. is a fifty-three-year-old married woman with no children. She had been a diabetic for twenty years. Her

condition was diagnosed as diabetic retinopathy. Her sight decreased gradually over a period of one year. Then she suddenly lost her remaining sight. This sudden loss of sight was a severe shock and she became deeply depressed. During the first few months of her blindness she would become disoriented in her own home. At times she could not find the door to get out of her bedroom. She made unsuccessful attempts to learn her way around the home and occasionally tried to cook. However, her husband discouraged these attempts. He was extremely concerned that she would burn herself while cooking. Mr. B. took over most of the household duties. Mrs. B. resented this, but was too fearful and too passive to insist on doing things for herself. She enrolled in rehabilitation courses, but soon dropped out of the program. The reaction of this woman was so severe she was referred for psychotherapy. Her anxiety was so acute that it interfered with any activity she attempted. She was extremely self-conscious and refused to carry a cane. Her severe depression continued and she frequently mentioned feelings of inadequacy and worthlessness.

Through counseling or psychotherapy it is possible to maximize the achievement or functioning ability of a newly blinded person. He can be helped to resolve his feelings about his loss. He can be helped to deal effectively with the interference of family or friends. As these changes take place within him, he can also make effective use of whatever training he receives.

FAMILY REACTIONS

Initially the news that a family member has lost, or is in the process of losing, his sight, is a shock. It may not be as severe as it is for the person who has suffered the physical loss, but it is, nevertheless, a shock. Any injury or loss to an individual is felt by all those who care for him.

Under normal conditions, the closer the relationship, the greater will be the emotional effect. Usually the feelings will be mixed. In addition to feelings of grief or compassion, there are often feelings of guilt, which may be centered around the manner in which the person lost his sight. If the condition was preventable, the family member might feel responsible for not having done something to prevent it. Another form in which guilt may be expressed is in the thought, "Why can I still see when he is blind?"

As adjustment progresses, the various family members may not know how to react to the unfamiliar behavior of the person who has lost his sight. They are not sure whether to comfort or encourage the person in his trouble — whether to accept his grief or discourage any display of emotion. They may be uncertain whether to help or try to force independent behavior. Some family members may feel that the newly blinded person is too demanding during the early period of his blindness. They may feel resentment for his demands, which in turn arouses feelings of guilt. Often counseling is the only means by which they can understand and resolve these feelings. Occasionally, however, the awareness that these feelings are present and quite natural under the circumstances makes it possible to keep them under control.

As the behavior of the individual changes during the adjustment process, the role of the family must change accordingly. Initially the blind person requires much help even in simple tasks. He is hesitant and often anxious as he has not yet learned what he can do. Over a period of time, however, he learns his capabilities, becomes more confident, and increases in skill.

Overprotection. The tendency to overprotect the newly blinded person is, perhaps, the most common reaction. Often the oversolicitous family member anticipates every possible need or wish of the blind person. He is permitted to do almost nothing for himself. He is led from one room to another and from one chair to another. If he says he is thirsty, someone quickly gets a glass of water. His food is cut for him. He is discouraged from attempting any activity unaided. In almost every way he is treated as a helpless invalid. The outcome, of course, is that the blind person never has an opportunity to learn or develop skills.

Harold M. is a congenitally blind nineteen-year-old. His blindness resulted from retrolental fibroplasia (RLF). He was an only child and was denied many of the normal activities and experiences of childhood, because of his mother's great fear for his safety. For example, she admitted that she could never allow him to play with neighborhood children because she was afraid he would wander into the street. On the other hand, she was extremely punitive when, in his exploration, he destroyed some household bric-a-brac. Her constant attendance on him during his early teens caused him considerable embarrassment in his peer relationships. As a result of his lack of opportunity for activity he was poorly coordinated. Although he had taken some mobility training, he was a poor traveler and presented an awkward appearance. He was socially inept and complained about his lack of friends. He felt that none of the young people he met really liked him. Although he was an adult and was enrolled in some college courses, his mother still persisted in her sheltering behavior. She drove him almost everywhere he went and even took a college course herself so she could be around to lead him to his classes.

The overprotective family reinforces dependence and discourages independence. Thus, the blind person is denied the one thing that is essential for good adjustment. He is prevented from practicing or performing various tasks and, therefore, can never become skilled in their performance.

If the blind person is reasonably objective about his needs and has sufficient ego strength, he may be able to resist these smothering tendencies. However, this gain may be at the cost of family equilibrium. If, on the other hand, he has strong dependency needs or anxiety about attempting activities, he will succumb to the pressure. Thus, when overprotectiveness and dependency needs form complimentary patterns within the same family group, the effects are detrimental to ideal adjustment.

The negative effects of overprotection are even more pronounced when they are present in the parent of a small child or in the adult children of an elderly blind person. The child is realistically dependent on his parents for the satisfaction of his physical and emotional needs. He cannot assert himself, and obviously does not know that he has an alternative. Similarly, many elderly blind persons are dependent on adult children for various services. It may be difficult for such persons to insist that they can perform a particular task for themselves. They may feel that if they insist on performing the task for themselves, they will offend the family and will thereafter not receive assistance with some task they cannot perform unaided.

Denial. Various family members may find it necessary to deny the reality of blindness in a close family member, because the presence of blindness is threatening or anxiety arousing to them. The threat infers the possibility that they might also lose their sight. Furthermore, the family may find it difficult to face the disappointment of normal expectations. The career that the family had planned for the child is no longer possible. The career of a husband is cut short because he can no longer perform his duties.

The family tries to minimize the full extent of the loss. As long as some vision remains, the family members can convince themselves that the loss is not as severe as they have been informed. In this way they can maintain their expectations. Thus, they force the blind person to function under considerable stress, because he finds it difficult to meet their unreasonable demands. For example, a teenage boy may be expected to participate in sports such as football when his restricted vision makes this almost impossible. As a result, the blind individual is forced to deal with feelings of anxiety and frustration as well as with his feelings of loss.

If the person is totally blind, it is more difficult for a family member or relative to accuse him of misrepresenting his condition. However, the family may attempt to minimize the emotional effect of the loss. They meet any display of emotion with comments such as, "Things could be worse" or "Don't feel so sorry for yourself". In effect, whether the denial is of the emotional meaning of the loss or of the physical limitations of the handicap, the visually impaired person is forced into an impossible situation. Either he is not permitted to express his feelings, or is expected to function at a level that is beyond his ability.

Rejection. In some cases one or more members of the family may react by rejecting the visually handicapped person. He is excluded from many family activities. A child may be left frequently with a babysitter while the family takes an outing. The excuse that education in a school for the blind is more effective is used as the basis for removing him from the family group. One sixteen-year-old congenitally blind girl verbalized feelings of rejection because of her childhood school experience. She was convinced that her parents had sent her to a residential school for the blind because they could not cope with her blindness. She felt that she could have been educated in a school nearer home. Her feelings of rejection focused on her blindness, which she considered to be the cause of her parents' attitude. Thus she felt that because she was blind she must deserve an inferior status.

A sighted husband or wife may deliberately choose activities in which the blind mate cannot participate during the early stages of adjustment. They may seek a divorce or separation because of an inability to deal with the reality of blindness. This is more frequently the case with younger couples who have not yet had an opportunity to build a stable relationship.

> David R. gradually began to lose his sight at the age of sixteen due to retinitis pigmentosa. Initially his only symptom was night blindness. He was still able to participate in sports and normal social activities in high school. He worked for several years as a shipping clerk in a freight company. He was married, but had no children. Approximately one year after their marriage Mr. R was forced to quit his job because of the drastic reduction in his sight. He stated that at this time the marital relationship became strained because of financial problems. He desperately looked for work but was unable to get another job because of his limited vision. His wife began to spend much of her time at the home of her parents. She admitted to him that her mother had advised her to get a divorce. He admitted that their communication had never been very good, but he felt they loved each other. When they had spent all their savings he offered to give her a divorce, but was shocked when she initiated proceedings. At this time he was extremely bitter and expressed great anger toward her family. He felt that the marriage would never have dissolved except for the interference of his wife's parents. In addition,

his bitterness, anger, and resentment were focused on his loss of sight, since he believed that his in-laws could never have influenced his wife if he had not been blind.

While such overt rejection is readily observable, the rejection may take a more subtle form. The blind family member might seem to be involved in normal activities. However, he is emotionally separated from one or more members of the family. The sighted person may withhold affection. On the other hand, he may simply ignore the blind individual. Thereupon, he becomes simply an undesirable appendage rather than an integral part of the family unit.

The effect is, of course, extremely destructive to the visually impaired person. He is usually very much aware of the rejection but is unable to cope with it because it is related to his blindness, which is a condition beyond his control.

Acceptance. The ideal and most desirable reaction is, of course, acceptance. The family accepts the blind person on the basis of what he is and always has been as a person. They realistically consider his blindness for what it is — a physical handicap that is beyond his control. They realize that he can adapt to the condition and still live a full and useful life. Furthermore, they do not magnify the effects of blindness, but treat it as a problem that can and must be solved. They consider the potential of the blind person to be of greater importance than they do the immediate, and possibly temporary, inability to function.

Marie J. is thirty-five, married, and the mother of three children. Her blindness was caused by diabetic retinopathy. She retained peripheral vision in one eye. The onset of blindness occurred gradually over a period of two years. Mrs. J. admitted that she had been depressed, although her reaction had not been a severe one. Her husband and children were helpful but never interfered when she wanted to do something herself. Mr. J. was very supportive and compassionate toward her, and expressed understanding of her feelings of loss. According to Mrs. J., they had even cried together over her loss. Similarly, she seemed able to understand what he was experiencing at this time. In addition, Mr. J. did as much as possible to help her get the training that would insure the greatest degree of independence for his wife. Although this experience was undoubtedly a very trying one for the entire family, it was apparent that their relationship was strengthened by this shared experience.

Family With Blind Child. All of the family reactions described earlier may be present in the families of blind children. When a child is born blind or when a young child loses his sight, the family will react with shock. Subsequently, they will experience grief and disappointment. They may, in addition, feel apprehension and guilt. They may feel overwhelmed by this new responsibility. They are certainly not prepared, by training or experience, to deal with the special problems of raising a blind child.

For these reasons it is imperative that these parents receive help as soon as possible. They need counseling to resolve their feelings concerning their child. They need guidance and information regarding ongoing problems and ways to meet the special needs of a blind child. Above all, they need referrals to agencies where such help is available, and they should be assisted, if necessary, in making the initial contact with an agency.

Appropriate Reactions. Reactions such as overprotection, denial, and rejection are detrimental to the adjustment of the blind person. They interfere with the acquisition of skills needed for adequate functioning. Furthermore, they contribute to the emotional maladjustment of the blind person. Thus, not only the blind person suffers, but the family also must continue to deal with the negative effects of such maladjustment.

A more appropriate approach is to encourage the blind or visually impaired person to enter a program of rehabilitation. This program would include both personal counseling and training in the various skills necessary for good adjustment. The family need not minimize the seriousness of the situation. However, emphasis can be placed on the potential for a full and useful life. In addition, it is essential that the family allow the person to mourn for his lost sight, without attempting to cut short the period of grief or discouraging the display of emotion.

The family can also help to obtain paid or volunteer readers and guides. In this way the assistance required during the initial, and relatively helpless, phase of blindness does not place an undue burden on the family. Such a burden often leads to feelings of resentment. Furthermore, it sometimes causes the blind person to feel that he is a burden.

The family should also be aware that when a person first loses his sight, he will often bump into objects around the house. In time the frequency of these incidents will diminish. It is appropriate to express sympathy but only in proportion to the degree of injury. Overreaction, however, on the part of a spectator will only increase the anxiety of the blind person. He may react to this anxiety by directing hostility toward anyone who happens to be present. In fact, however, he is angry with himself for his blunder.

During the early phase of adjustment, the family will need to offer more help than will be needed later. Over a period of time they will learn what the blind person is capable of doing. They may, however, find it difficult to relinquish their role as helpers as the blind person begins to acquire greater skill. They will be tempted to do things for him that he can actually do for himself. They can help in a more constructive way if they can devise means by which he can perform a task by himself. The former course encourages an attitude of dependence while the latter facilitates the development of relative independence. As he develops independence, the blind person discovers that he is not helpless and that he is still a useful member of his family group and of society.

In any case, one of the more important services the family can render is to be understanding and patient. It cannot be overemphasized that the person who has recently lost, or is in the process of losing, his sight is operating under considerable tension. If he is able to function at all, it is with great difficulty. Performance of even the simplest tasks of daily living produces emotional strain. Under these conditions it is not unreasonable that the individual is irritable, often angry, and easily upset.

If the various family members react to this emotional distress by becoming distressed themselves, they will only add to the tension under which the blind person is operating. If, however, they can indicate that they understand the reason for his unusual behavior and maintain some measure of patience toward him during this period of learning, they will greatly facilitate the adjustment process.

In time the blind person will become accustomed to his new way of life and will become more efficient in the techniques of daily living. Eventually, he will be able to function in a relaxed and skillful manner. When he has achieved this goal, the family can be confident that they have contributed to the efficient functioning and emotional well being of the blind person.

RESISTANCE TO REHABILITATION

One of the most important services that a doctor can render is to refer a newly blinded or visually impaired patient to a rehabilitation center, where he can receive adequate training. Most persons, when informed of their condition, will accept such a referral. They may feel conflict about taking such action, but they will do whatever is necessary to improve their situation. Occasionally, however, a patient will not accept a referral for rehabilitation. He may refuse openly or he may appear to comply, but will delay in taking action.

There are several factors that lead to such resistance. They are not always verbalized by the patient, but they are implicit in his resistance. Among these factors are hope for recovery, negative attitudes toward blindness, family interference, and anxiety.

Hope For Recovery. One of the most crucial factors affecting the person's willingness to enter a rehabilitation program is hope for recovery. As long as the patient believes that there is some possibility that his sight will improve, he will, in all likelihood, resist any attempt to begin rehabilitation training. He may or may not verbalize this hope to the doctor. However, underlying any apparent acceptance of his condition is the expectation that there is a possibility of recovery in the near future.

This expectation may be based on a religious belief that a miracle will occur; it may result from a misunderstanding of information received from the doctor; or it may persist in spite of anything the doctor can say to the contrary. In the latter case he will go from one doctor to another, hoping to find the one physician who will produce the medical miracle. A variation of this expectation may be the person who does not become involved in training because he depends on the possibility of a breakthrough in medical knowledge of his condition.

No matter what the underlying belief, the outcome is the same. The patient withdraws; he sits and waits. Ultimately, he discovers that he has exchanged years of useful and productive possibility for a hope that is never fulfilled.

Other persons may actually accept the referral. They may attend classes in a rehabilitation center, but they do not make full use of the training. They make only halfhearted attempts to acquire necessary skills. As in the case of the overtly resistant, the basis for the negativistic behavior is the belief that if they wait long enough they will never have to make use of the training.

It may be possible that some individuals are so mature or are so motivated by economic or personal pressures that they can undergo training effectively while still maintaining the hope for recovery. Such cases, however, are extremely rare and require greater objectivity and maturity than the average person possesses. In addition, it would be difficult, if not impossible, to determine in advance whether a particular individual has such qualities. Furthermore, such a person only postpones the time when he will have to deal with the emotional reality of his situation. Eventually he must face the fact that his sight has not improved and that he is a blind or visually impaired person.

Anxiety. Many people react with anxiety to any novel or unfamiliar situation. The unfamiliar situation may have some special meaning for the person or it may simply be a case of being confronted with the unknown. A child may be attending a summer camp for the first time and fears the mysterious new experience. A student may be apprehensive about his first semester in college. A young couple may feel "nervous" about the beginning of the marital relationship. Or an adult may have mild feelings of panic over the prospect of an interview for a new job. The precipitating factor is usually the newness or unfamiliarity of the experience.

The degree of anxiety may vary from one individual to another. The feelings may be mild and controlled or they may be so acute that they interfere with the person's ability to function. If the feelings are sufficiently acute he may withdraw from the situation or avoid it altogether.

When a newly blinded person is asked to attend a rehabilitation center, he is faced with such a novel experience. He is unfamiliar with the physical surroundings he will encounter. He has no knowledge of course material or how he will be taught. Nor is he sure how he will be able to function in the social interaction that is an inevitable aspect of any teaching situation. How will he meet people? How will he recognize them? How will he find his way from one room to another?

These are realistic considerations and they often lead to feelings of anxiety. The complicating factor for any newly blinded person is that he lacks the one tool that was once his most useful means of dealing with an unfamiliar situation. While he could still see, he was able to obtain visual cues that he needed to evaluate the new situation. He could recognize persons as he met them in passing. He could easily follow directions to find classrooms. He was also easily able to avoid obstacles and dangerous elements of the new situation, such as stairways. He must now function in similar situations without being able to see. He must rely on his other senses, which have not yet been trained to serve as substitutes for sight.

Because he has not yet received training, the blind person lacks confidence in these other senses. In addition, he may be unsure of his ability to learn without his sight. One woman commented that she lost her ability to spell several months after she lost her sight. She had always been a good speller, but now was unable to spell many formerly simple words. She realized that the reason for this change was her inability to refresh her memory while reading. This realization shook her self-confidence, since she believed it would affect her total learning ability.

While many persons experience some anxiety when considering the possibility of entering rehabilitation training, they are usually able to function in spite of it. However, occasionally an individual experiences such acute anxiety that he cannot face the prospect of the new experience. He reacts by resisting attempts to refer him for training. These people may not verbalize their anxiety. In fact, they will usually present many "reasons" why they cannot, or need not, attend. They cannot express their feelings of anxiety because this admission would further lower their already poor self-esteem. Therefore, they prefer the alternative of rationalizing their resistant behavior.

Negative Attitudes Toward Blindness. In addition to hope for recovery and anxiety, the blind person's negative attitudes toward blindness may contribute to his resistance to referral. Many stereotyped attitudes concerning the image of a blind person exist in our culture. Sighted people generally think of the blind as inferior. They view him as a helpless and inadequate individual, and believe him to be in a low socioeconomic class. Finally, they think of the blind as being unattractive to look at — someone who sways from side to side, shuffles when he walks, is stoop-shouldered, gropes awkwardly, and dresses sloppily. In other words, the image of a blind person is usually one that would evoke pity not envy.

The newly blinded person will probably have inculcated many of these attitudes. It is unlikely that he has ever had a primary relationship with a well-functioning blind person. He has no reason to doubt the validity of the cultural attitudes. Thus, he finds it difficult to assimilate the new concept of himself as a blind person.

Not only is it difficult for him to accept this self-image, but now he is being asked to become identified with a group of blind people at an agency. To many newly blinded persons this seems like a confirmation of their new inferior status. They feel that they are being separated from normal contacts and are being segregated with other members of the inferior group.

For such individuals it is important to point out that the

association is only temporary. They can be assured that they need stay only for a period of training. It is even more important to indicate that this training can help them function more efficiently, and that they need maintain no contacts with other blind persons beyond their training period.

Frequently, once a person with such reservations realizes that he can control his relationships, he is more willing to accept a referral. Undoubtedly he will develop some friendships as a result of his contact with the agency. However, he does know that he has the option to live his own life and continue his old relationships.

> John B. is a totally blind, twenty-two-year-old diabetic. He has been blind about one year and lost his sight gradually over a period of approximately five months. At the time he lost his sight he had been in college for two years. Mr. B.'s mother telephoned to ask for help in getting her son involved in some rehabilitation program. She stated that he was quite resistant to any suggestion that he attend an agency for retraining. During the initial telephone contact with the client he commented that adjustment to blindness was not as difficult as he had expected. This was, perhaps, because he lived at home and had severed most of his social connections. He spent most of his time in sedentary activities and was dependent on his family for most of his daily functioning. His resistance to involvement in any rehabilitation program seemed to stem from two sources. While sighted he had observed some blind people. They had apparently not been able to function very well, and he did not wish to be identified with such persons. In addition, he felt considerable anxiety about the prospect of returning to school and doubted his ability to function in a school setting. Furthermore, he dreaded the social contacts he would be forced to make since he was not sure how he would be accepted as a blind person. During the course of counseling he was able to resolve many of his feelings about the loss of sight. He also made tentative efforts to renew his former social relationships. When we terminated counseling, he had applied for admission to a residential training center for intensive rehabilitation training.

Family Interference. In many ways the attitudes of the family mirror and reinforce the attitudes of the patient. The family, as well as the individual, may believe that a blind person can never be retrained. They may visualize the traditional image of the man with dark glasses and a tin cup standing on a street corner, or its modern equivalent, which is that all blind people live on welfare. Since they cannot reconcile this negative image with the person they know, they prefer to believe that he will never really be a blind person. Thus, they encourage him to believe that he will regain his sight or that his condition is not as serious as he has been led to believe. For this reason they feel that he will never need rehabilitation training.

The blind person may wish to receive training, but he finds that the family resists his efforts in this direction. In some cases they passively resist his efforts to obtain information. They simply do not help him in getting telephone numbers or in writing for information. They may find excuses for not providing him transportation to a rehabilitation center.

On the other hand, the family may actively discourage the blind person from entering rehabilitation training. They point out that if he attends an agency, learns to use a cane, or learns braille, he is "giving up".

This resistance to referral can be extremely destructive to the newly blinded person's potential. It undermines the efforts of the physician who is trying to refer the patient for rehabilitation training. This prevents the patient from making immediate and full use of these services. In this way the negative attitudes of the family prevent the blind person from receiving the training and counseling he needs in order to function independently and efficiently.

All the preceding factors in some way influence resistance to referral. They may not all be present in each person who refuses to explore the services offered. In some cases one factor alone suffices to produce a negative attitude. In others a combination of these factors are present in the same individual. However, it is important to be aware that these factors exist and may be the basis for the resistance of the patient.

It may be possible for the physician to deal with their effect without referring to them directly. If, however, the patient persists in his refusal to accept services that can be extremely valuable to his effective functioning he may have to be referred for counseling or psychotherapy, where the problems can be dealt with directly.

Rationale for Rehabilitation Training. In the previous discussion we have considered a number of factors affecting the adjustment of a newly blinded person. He must resolve his own feelings of loss. He must cope with the reactions of his family. Eventually he must meet with friends and strangers in the community and deal with their reactions. Finally, he must adapt physically to life with little or no sight.

Inevitably the question will arise, "Can he accomplish these objectives unaided?" Certainly, it is true that in the past many blind persons have done so. They have taught themselves to travel and have developed techniques for their daily functioning. However, they have had to learn by their own experience or, occasionally, with help from some other blind person. Such trial and error learning is obviously ineffective. In addition, it is time-consuming. Many of these blind persons have spent years in this learning process — years that could have been spent in more productive activity if help had been available. Above all, they have expended much unnecessary emotional energy to gain this knowledge. In addition, the person who trains himself will never have complete knowledge of techniques and devices that facilitate effective functioning, for example writing guides, special tools, cooking aids, and braille thermometers. So, although a blind person can, by trial and error, teach himself to travel, eat, and keep house, he can learn more with greater ease and efficiency with the help of qualified professionals.

Although physical retraining is important, it is even more essential that the person receive help with his feelings about blindness. Whether a patient is reacting with depression, anxiety, or mood swings, it is important to be aware that he can benefit from intervention by a counselor or psychotherapist. Through such intervention, he can be helped to resolve his feelings about his loss, understand his reaction, and learn to deal with the reactions of family and friends. He can, thus, make more effective use of whatever rehabilitation services are available.

The time for intervention is, of course, critical. If he receives professional help early in his period of adjustment, the patient should react more favorably. At this time his defenses are down, because of the crisis he is experiencing. If he is permitted to attempt his adjustment without professional intervention he may develop attitudes, behavior, and a self-concept that are far from ideal. Once he has passed through the initial crisis phase, these attitudes may crystallize. They are then less amenable to psychotherapeutic intervention.

Whether a blind person is attempting to deal with his own feelings or adapt physically to his condition, he can accomplish more and do this more quickly when he receives professional help. He will have the benefit of their training and knowledge. Above all, he will have the benefit of their experience in working with other blind persons. With physical retraining and emotional counseling, he has an opportunity to be assimilated into the community as a self-supporting and useful individual, who can live comfortably with his blindness.

REFERENCES

1. Carroll, Rev T. J.: *Blindness — What It Is, What It Does and How to Live With It*, Little, Boston, 1961.
2. Chevigny, H. and Braverman, S.: *Adjustment of the Blind*, Yale U Pr, New Haven, 1950.
3. Cholden, L. S.: *A Psychiatrist Works with Blindness*, American Foundation for the Blind, Inc., New York, 1958.
4. Finestone, S.: *Social Casework and Blindness*, American Foundation for the Blind, Inc., New York, 1960.
5. Schulz, P. J.: A group approach to working with families of the blind, *The New Outlook for the Blind, 62*:3, 82-86, March 1968.

Suggested Reading

Blank, H. R., Psychoanalysis and blindness, *Psychoanal Q, Volume XXVI*, No. 1, 1-24, 1957.

Chapter 4

PATIENTS WITH EYE SYMPTOMS AND NO ORGANIC ILLNESS: AN INTERDISCIPLINARY STUDY*

MICHAEL P. GROSS, M.D. AND SHERWIN H. SLOAN, M.D.

ABSTRACT — The eyes and the visual functions receive great emotional investment. Ophthalmologists often overlook the emotional aspects of eye disease and overdiagnose hysteria in their patients. This project was a combined psychiatric and ophthalmologic study of patients without organic eye disease who presented with symptoms at an outpatient ophthalmology clinic. These patients differed from ordinary eye patients by age (younger), duration of symptoms (longer), and type of chief complaint (nonvisual). A large number of these patients were felt to have significant psychiatric illness, although the presence of organic eye illness did not protect against psychiatric difficulty. Tubular visual fields, like any conversion symptoms, are not diagnostic of hysteria. Greater use of the psychiatric consultant is urged.

INTRODUCTION

THE human eye is a more highly developed organ than those of smell, touch or hearing. Due to its extraordinary long range of perception, the eye serves as an early warning system for detection of danger. In addition, it is indispensable in the fight or flight mechanism in providing orientation for all voluntary motor activity. The activity of looking is very much involved in sexual behaviors. It is no wonder that there exist strong emotional ties to the eye and the process of vision.

Excellent review articles by Greenacre (1) and Hart (2) deal with the individual and cultural psychologies of the visual process. They emphasize that magical powers are uncon-

*Originally published in *The International Journal of Psychiatry in Medicine*, 2:298-307, 1971.

sciously attributed to the eye, and all forms of sexual and aggressive significance are attached to the organ itself. This appears in folklore and mythology, where the eye is widely seen as a talisman, frequently a symbol of divine power (the sun) or great evil (evil eye). Blinding was a frequent punishment especially for culturally forbidden lustful looking but also for the expression of aggressive impulses. Also, in psychoanalytic studies of individuals, the eye and its sight are present in many fantasy forms. The eye is sometimes equated with either the male or female genital. Delusional patients experience consciously the convictions that the eye transmits influences, and undergoes changes in appearance. Flight from the stresses of reality can be expressed via the visual mechanism (blepharospasm, functional myopia, amblyopia, and changes in the visual field).

Teachers of ophthalmology such as Drews (3) and Schlaegel (4) repeatedly remind their students of the importance of the psychology of vision. They note that emotional considerations seem to be ignored too often as technology explodes with new "hard data" and treatment methods for organic eye problems. We have noted that even when emotional problems are recognized by the ophthalmologist, his response is pessimistic, apathetic, or worse, rejecting of the patient. Hysteria is defined by Schlaegel (4), an otherwise sophisticated psychosomatic ophthalmologist, as "malingering on an unconscious level," a misleading contradiction in terms. The ophthalmologist tends to see all functional eye symptoms as diagnostic of hysteria, a condition that means to him something curiously linked to malingering. This is an error that must surely account for some of his feelings of anger and helplessness with these patients.

The first clinic for psychosomatic ophthalmology at the Jules Stein Eye Institute opened in the fall of 1970. This study is a survey of a sample of the patients referred to that clinic between September 1970 and March 1971. The focus of this study was on those patients who complained of symptoms related to the eye, but who had no significant ophthalmic pathology. The purpose of the study was to determine the number of such patients at this clinic and to determine if they might have significant psychiatric illness.

METHODOLOGY

Selection of Patients

Patients selected for this study were those who presented at the general ophthalmology clinic for diagnosis and treatment and who, after complete eye examination, were thought to have no significant disease to explain their ophthalmologic symptoms. Patients who were thought to have *both* significant eye disease and psychopathology were not included in this study.

Patients selected for treatment at Jules Stein Eye Institute are not a random population of ophthalmology patients. Telephone screening in the outpatient department usually eliminates those with requests for refraction only. The remaining patients are seen at the outpatient department of Jules Stein Eye Institute.

Referral to the psychosomatic ophthalmology clinic was made only from the general ophthalmology clinic. This was usually after a single visit, although some patients referred to the psychosomatic clinic had been general eye clinic patients for a number of years. After referral, the patients were reexamined by one of the authors (S.H.S.) and his ophthalmology staff. After all the necessary studies were completed, those patients showing no evidence of organic illness to account for their symptoms were asked if they would agree to be interviewed by a psychiatrist.

Control patients were adult outpatients at Jules Stein Eye Institute with documented eye disease. They were randomly selected from the general eye clinic, and were given a questionnaire by the clinic social worker. In addition, their medical charts were reviewed by one of the authors (M.P.G.), to obtain demographic data, 'data related to their eye illness, and screening for psychiatric history.

QUESTIONNAIRE FOR CONTROL PATIENTS

I. Asking patients to participate
  A. You are fortunate to have problems that the doctors can observe and treat.
  B. Others, less fortunate, have eye problems which cannot be treated by the

ophthalmologist.
  C. We need information from you to compare treatable with untreatable patients. We hope to become able then to treat more people.
  D. Your name will not be used. No one reading our records will be able to recognize specific patients.
 II. Prior to taking psychological history section of questionnaire
     Many of the untreatable patients have emotional problems.
     We will ask you about your psychological background as a means of comparison. We realize that people with treatable eye problems can also have emotional problems. Comparing these emotional problems with those of untreatable patients will enable us to take better care of all of our patients.
III. Items on the questionnaire (obtained from patient or his chart)
  A. Identification and demographic data:
     Age, marital status, sex, etc.
  B. Ophthalmologic data:
     Chief complaints, duration, ophthalmologic diagnosis, visual field data
  C. Psychiatric data:
     Ever had nervous breakdown or been in psychiatric hospital?
     Ever seriously thought about or attempted suicide?
     Ever felt you needed psychiatric treatment?
     Has a doctor ever suggested that you see a psychiatrist?
     Ever been under care of any mental health professional?
     History if any of above answered "yes."

Conversion Reaction of the Visual Fields (Tubular Visual Fields)

Tubular visual fields are those in which the arc subtended by the patient's gaze becomes smaller as the test objects are moved away. The visual field pattern reported by the patient remains the same size at both the near and distant positions, a physiologically impossible phenomenon. In nontubular fields, the arc remains unchanged as the objects are moved near or far. The visual field pattern will then be of similar shape, but larger when the testing board is moved away from the patient. This is the case whether the visual fields are normal or "restricted" by organic illness.

Psychiatric Examination — It was explained to the patients that the interview was for the purpose of research, that therapy would not be done, and that their participation was valuable to us. Psychiatric examination consisted of a single sixty-to ninety-minute interview. An attempt was made to obtain a history, mental status examination, and psychiatric diagnosis if significant psychopathology was present. Referral for psychiatric treatment was offered when it was felt to be appropriate. Data are summarized in Figure 4-1. One patient who did not follow through to permit complete psychiatric evaluation is included in the data with diagnosis deferred.

Patients Refusing Psychiatric Interview — A significant number of patients (six) refused to be interviewed by a psychiatrist. To determine whether these patients differed in any other way from the patients agreeing to have psychiatric evaluation, the charts of these patients were reviewed to obtain demographic and clinical data. Whenever possible, a retrospective presumptive psychiatric diagnosis was applied. This was done in cases where there had been previous psychiatric consultations on the chart and sufficient feedback from the examining ophthalmologist to support a diagnosis of mental illness. These "diagnoses" were educated guesses at best. Results are included in Figure 4-1.

Psychiatric Diagnostic Criteria — The criteria of Cassidy et al. (5) were used to establish the diagnosis of manic-depressive disease. Schizophrenia was diagnosed by the criteria of Langfeldt (6), anxiety neurosis by the criteria of Wheeler et al. (7), and obsessional state by the criteria of Pollitt (8).

Because of the tendency of the ophthalmologist to label as "hysterics" many patients who do not actually have the disease, we took a special interest in this area. Strict criteria for the diagnosis of hysteria have been established by Perley and Guze (9), and Woodruff et al. (10). The diagnosis by these criteria rests upon finding a dramatic complicated medical history beginning before age thirty-five, with the patient showing no fewer than twenty-five specific physical symptoms in nine of ten specified symptom-groups, and having no other diagnosis by clinical impression. According to Perley and Guze (9) and to Woodruff et al. (10), these requirements were necessary in order to predict hysteria as they defined it: a chronic disorder which remains essentially unchanged over a follow-up period of six to eight years.

Pt.	Age	Sex	Mar.	C.C. Yrs.	Primary C.C.	Secondary C.C.	Ophth. Diagnosis	Visual Fields	History Psych. Care	Psychiatric Diag. (Interview)	Retrospective Psych. Impression	Other
V.A.	56	F	D	34	Pain		None	Not Done	No	Hysteria: Conversion Reaction		
N.B.	32	M	S	15	White secretion		None	Not Done	No	Depressive Neurosis		
E.D.	60	F	D	32	↓Vis	Dizzy	None	Not Done	Yes	Deferred		
H.H.	45	F	M	3	Pain		None	Tubular	Unk	Conversion Reaction; Undiagnosed Psych. Illness		
V.H.	60	F	W	5	F.B. Sens.		None	Not Done	No	Depression; Conversion Reaction		
F.L.	58	F	M	3	Pain	↓Vis	None	Tubular	Yes	Mental Retard; Depression; Conversion Reaction		Incipient Psychosis. Suicide Risk
P.P.	35	F	M	2	Pain		None	Not Done	Yes	Hysteria; Conversion Reaction		Suicide Risk
S.P.	63	F	W	6	F.B. Sens.	↓Vis	None	Tubular	No	Depression: Hysteria; Conversion Reaction		Suicide Risk
M.W.	65	F	W	1	Eyes close		None	Not Done	No	Depression; Conversion Reaction		
A.A.	76	F	M	6	Sens. Light		None	Not Done	Unk			Refused Interview
R.F.	43	F	M	10	Pain	Sens. Light	None	Tubular	Yes		Hysteria	Refused Interview
A.B.	28	F	D	7	↓Vis		None	Tubular	Unk			Refused Interview
G.H.	53	F	D	2	F.B. Sens.	Pain	None	Not Done	Unk			Refused Interview
M.A.	27	F	M	8	Night blind	↓Vis	None	Not Done	Yes		Schizophrenia; Pass. Depend. Personality	Refused Interview
S.G.	32	F	D	Unk	↓Vis		None	Normal	Yes		Hysteria; Alcoholism Manic Depressive	Not Asked
B.S.	38	F	M	7	Pain	Sens. Light	None	Not Done	Yes		Depression; Hysteria	Not Asked
H.H.	57	M	D	1	↓Vis	Pain	None	Tubular	Unk		Organic Psychosis; Alcoholism	Refused Interview Abnormal Liver Function

Figure 4-1. Experimental Group; Interviewed and Uninterviewed Patients; No Organic Eye Disease; C.C.-Chief Complaint; Vis-Decreased Vision; F.B. Sens-Foreign Body Sensation.

In general, the ophthalmologist tends to overdiagnose hysteria, using very few and incorrect criteria, such as the presence of conversion reactions. This study employed modified criteria for the diagnosis of hysteria in order to be as liberal as possible and to include in this category some patients who did not meet all of the criteria of previous researchers. (In fact, only one patient, P.P., would have met the strict criteria for diagnosis of hysteria. The liberalized criteria permitted inclusion of two more patients as hysteric in the group that received psychiatric interview.) For this study, the diagnosis of hysteria was based on criteria including multiple physical symptoms with or without medical explanation, multiple hospitalizations and surgical procedures, sexual difficulties such as dyspareunia, frigidity and undue stress with menstrual functions, histrionic personality type, and relative indifference to or overconcern with symptoms. Clinical impression of hysteria was given higher priority than the strict fulfillment of symptom categories.

Patients were frequently felt to have significant psychiatric illness without meeting any of the complete criteria stated by the authors cited above. The categories of anxiety state and depression (depressive reaction) were applied when such conditions existed with evidence not sufficient for inclusion in categories of manic-depressive disease as described by Cassidy (5) or anxiety neurosis as described by Wheeler (7).

RESULTS

The results are presented in descriptive form. Because of the low numbers of patients, the data has not been subjected to statistical analysis.

Seventeen patients without organic eye disease comprise the "Experimental Group" of patients. Nine of these patients received psychiatric interview and are included in the data as "Experimental Group: Interviewed." Six patients refused to be seen by a psychiatrist. For administrative reasons, two other patients without organic eye illness were not asked to have psychiatric examination. These eight patients are included in the data as "Experimental Group: Not Interviewed." These data are summarized in Figure 4-1.

Eight patients with documented organic eye disease received questionnaires as described in the Methods section. These data are included in this study as "Control Group," and are summarized in Table 4-1.

Table 4-I. Control Group: Patients with Documented Eye Disease

Pt.	Age	Sex	Mar.	C.C. Yrs.	Pri- mary C.C.	Sec- ond- ary C.C.	Ophthal- mologic Diagnosis	Visual Fields	History of Psych. Care	Suicide Thoughts
V.C.	62	F	M	12	↓Vis.	Float- ers	Retinitis Glaucoma Susp.	One meter only O.S. Only Restricted	NO	NO
A.S.	63	F	M	3	↓Vis.		Surg. Aphakia Cataract Glaucoma Susp.	One meter only O.D. Only Restricted	NO	NO
A.M.	49	M	M	10	↓Vis.		Cataracts Ret. De- tachmt.	Not done	YES	YES
E.H.	57	F	W	1	↓Vis.		Cataracts Ret. Hemor- rhage	Not done	NO	NO
D.S.	68	F	W	9	↓Vis.		Cataracts Corneal Dyst. Glaucoma Susp.	One meter only Restricted	NO*	NO
M.H.	70	F	S	6	↓Vis.		Surg. Aphakia complic.	Not done	NO	NO
M.M.	54	M	M	2	Pain		Iritis 2ary. Glaucoma	One meter only Restricted	NO**	NO
C.B.	69	F	W	3	↓Vis.		Cataracts	Not done	NO***	NO

*Possible conversion blindness. See text.
**History of reactive depression, significant. See text.
***History of untreated syphilis, multiple somatic complaints. See text.

Comparison of General Data from Control and Experimental Groups

Patients with functional eye problems were younger (48.3 as compared to 62.3 years), but had suffered for a longer period of time with their eye symptoms (7.6 as compared with 5.5 years) than the patients with organic illness. Experimental group patients who agreed to participate in psychiatric interviews seemed to be older (53.9 versus 41.8 years) and to have much longer duration of chief complaint (9.4 versus 6.0 years) than those patients who were not interviewed. Small numbers of patients in each group make speculation on this phenomenon of limited value now. One of the eight Control patients gave a history of psychiatric care, while seven of sixteen Experimental group patients had received psychiatric treatment or evaluation. The number of women predominates over the number of men in all groups of patients in this study. This reflects the general sex distribution of patients at the ophthalmology clinics. Sex of the patient was not a distinguishing factor between Experimental and Control groups. These comparisons are summarized in Table 4-II.

Table 4-II. Experimental and Control Group Comparison of Results

	Control	Experimental Group		
		Interviewed	Not Interviewed	All (Total)
Number	8	9	8	17
Age	62.3*	53.9*	41.8*	48.3
Male/Female..............	2/6	1/8	1/7	2/15
Duration Chief Complaint (Yrs.)	5.5*	9.4*	6.0*	7.6

*The items marked with asterisks are averages which were calculated excluding the highest and lowest value in the series.

Ophthalmic Chief Complaint

The ophthalmic chief complaint of "pain" or "foreign body

sensation" significantly discriminated the Experimental (functional) group from the Control (organic) group of patients. While pain and foreign body sensation were primary or secondary chief complaints in eleven of seventeen patients felt to have functional problems, these complaints were almost never seen in the organically impaired Control group (one patient). Decreased vision was the primary or secondary chief complaint in only seven of seventeen Experimental group patients (41%), while this was the chief complaint in seven of eight of our sample of patients with organic disease (88%). The category of "pain" included all forms of head and eye pain which the patient presented to the eye clinic physicians as primary or secondary chief complaint. Decreased vision, "↓vis.," includes not only blurring and distortion of visual image, but also decrease in total light perception (excluding "night blindness").

Table 4-III. Ophthalmic Chief Complaint

	Control	Experimental		
		Interviewed	Not Interviewed	All Experimental
Primary Chief Complaint				
Pain	1	4	2	6
Decreased Vision	7	1	3	4
Foreign Body Sensation		2	1	3
Sensitivity to Light			1	1
Eyes Close (Involuntary)		1		1
White Secretion		1		1
Night Blindness			1	
Primary and Secondary Chief Complaint (Sum)				
Pain	1	4	4	8
Decreased Vision	7	3	4	7
Foreign Body Sensation		2	1	3
Sensitivity to Light			3	3
Eyes Close (Involuntary)		1		1
White Secretion		1		1
Night Blindness			1	1
Dizzy		1		1
Floaters	1			

Patients with functional illness showed a much greater variety of nonvisual complaints than those in the Control group. (See Table 4-III.)

Psychiatric Findings in Experimental Group: Interviewed Patients

Significant psychopathology was felt to be present in all nine of the patients who received psychiatric interview. Data were sufficient to make specific psychiatric diagnosis (or diagnoses) in seven of these patients. Often, several diagnoses were applied to patients. Conversion reaction was present in seven of the nine interviewed patients in the form of tubular visual fields, foreign body sensation, pain, or photophobia. Significant depression was present in five, and hysteria was diagnosed in three. One patient was felt to have mental retardation. Three patients were felt to be abnormally high suicide risks. Three patients gave past histories of psychiatric treatment or evaluation.

Psychiatric Findings in Experimental Group: Not Interviewed

After review of the charts of the eight patients who refused or were not asked to have psychiatric interview, it was possible to make presumptive psychiatric diagnoses in five. Four of the five received more than one diagnosis. Hysteria was presumptively diagnosed in four patients, alcoholism in two, depressive syndrome in one, manic-depressive disease in one, schizophrenia in one, personality disorder in one, and organic brain syndrome with psychosis in one. Four of these eight patients had documented histories of psychiatric treatment or evaluation. There were no data regarding the presence of suicide risk.

Psychiatric Findings in Control Group Patients

Only one of the eight Control Group patients gave a positive psychiatric history on the questionnaire, having received treatment for depression with suicidal ideas. Review of the charts of these patients, however, showed that patient D.S., while having her contact lenses fitted, complained of intermittent total blindness. This is almost surely a conversion reaction phenomenon, but it was not possible to specify which diagnostic category applied to this patient. Patient M.M. reported to the examining physician that since the onset of his eye problems he had suffered from weakness, constipation, headache, nervousness and depression, a picture consistent with reactive depression. Patient C.B. had a medical chart which indicated many undiagnosed physical complaints as well as a history of syphilis inadequately treated in 1928. Organic brain disease had not been investigated.

Relationship Between the Finding of Tubular Visual Fields and the Diagnosis of Hysteria

Tubular visual fields were found in six of the Experimental Group patients. Normal visual fields were found in one Experimental patient. Visual field testing was not done in the remaining ten Experimental patients. Two patients diagnosed with hysteria showed tubular fields when tested. One patient diagnosed with hysteria showed normal visual fields. Significant psychiatric illness other than hysteria was thought to be present in three patients with tubular visual fields. One patient with tubular visual fields was not diagnosable by chart review for psychiatric illness.

Visual fields were tested and were abnormally restricted in four of the eight Control patients. In these patients the fields were examined at the standard object distance (one meter) only. It was therefore impossible to determine if these abnormal fields were also tubular. (See Table 4-IV)

DISCUSSION

Significant psychiatric illness was felt to be present in all nine of the patients without organic eye disease who agreed to

Table 4-IV. Relation of Tubular Visual Fields to Diagnosis of Hysteria

	Experimental Group		
	Interviewed	Not Interviewed	All Experimental
Visual Fields Measured	3	4	7
Tubular (Conversion)	3	3	6
Nontubular (Normal)		1	1
Hysteria Diagnosed	3	3*	6
Hysteria/Tubular Fields	1	1*	2
Hysteria/Nontubular Fields		1*	1
Hysteria/Not Tested	2	1*	3
Other Illness/Tubular Fields	2	1*	3
No Diagnosis Possible/ Tubular Fields		1*	1

*Patient not interviewed: Diagnosis of hysteria made via evidence from review of chart.

psychiatric interview. Chart review indicated at least five of the remaining eight Experimental Group patients also suffered from presumptive emotional illness. Three of the nine interviewed patients were thought to be above average suicide risks at the time of interview. Seven of the seventeen Experimental Group patients had a history of psychiatric evaluation or care. Only one of the Control patients gave a history of psychiatric illness, but three others in this group may have had significant emotional difficulty as suggested by chart review. The finding of strictly functional eye complaints in patients requesting only ophthalmologic evaluation indicates that the presence of significant psychiatric illness is also very likely.

The presence of organic eye disease certainly does not rule out the presence of psychiatric illness, and in these cases, too, the patient may present for eye examination only. This is dramatized by the fact that during the course of this investigation, one of the authors (S.H.S.) referred two patients from the ophthalmology clinic directly to the psychiatric emergency service for immediate evaluation. These patients both had organic eye disease and were ineligible for our study but were felt to be in emotional crisis despite the fact that they were seeking care only at the ophthalmology clinic. Special psychiatric problems of patients with impaired vision are reviewed by Adams et al. (11).

Our findings indicate that patients with functional eye problems present a different picture to the examining physician than those with organic eye disease. They are younger but have had their symptoms for a longer period of time than patients with organic illness. The chief complaints of patients with functional illness are less likely to include decrease in visual functions *per se,* and are more likely to include problems with pain, foreign body sensation, photophobia, periorbital muscle difficulty, and dizziness.

Engel (12), Ziegler and Imboden (13), Krill and Newell (14) and Perley and Guze (9), all researchers in both psychiatry and ophthalmology, warn of the error of diagnosing hysteria on the basis of conversion reaction alone. They emphasize that conversion symptoms accompany many psychiatric syndromes. Despite this, the finding of tubular visual fields is often assumed to be diagnostic of hysteria. In fact, the term used by the ophthalmologists in the records to describe this finding is usually "hysterical visual fields." This study suggests that the finding of conversion reaction in the form of tubular visual fields does not establish such a diagnosis, nor does the finding of normal visual fields rule out hysteria. It is recommended that the term "hysterical visual fields" be discarded and replaced by one more appropriate, such as "tubular visual fields." Wider use of psychiatric consultation might assist the ophthalmologist when severe disturbance is suspected.

Further study is necessary in order to delineate the incidence of conversion reaction related to the visual fields. Patients with documented organic eye disease have not been tested in this study for the presence of tubular visual fields.

Of the patients presenting for eye examination, but without organic eye disease, about one-third may be expected to refuse referral for any form of psychiatric evaluation or help. These are the patients who will especially challenge the physician's commitment to treat the "whole patient." They will frustrate him by presenting urgent symptoms, by demonstrating no organ pathology, and by being unable to give up the symptoms when told that there is no physical disease. Although they never state it, they often need the support of contact with physicians to maintain their tenuous adjustment. The option of the ophthalmologist is then either to send the patient away, or to maintain this contact and support often with no more treatment than artificial tears and a few minutes of his time. This is not an easy alternative for a physician who is accustomed to sophisticated scientific and often dramatically successful treatment of organic illness, and who feels untrained in the treatment of psychological pain.

REFERENCES

1. Greenacre, P.: The eye motif in delusion and fantasy, *Am J Psychiatry*, *5*:553-79, 1926.
2. Hart, H. H.: The eye in symbol and symptom, *Psychoanal Rev*, *36*:1-21, 1949.
3. Drews, R. C.: Organic versus functional ocular problems, *Int Ophthalmol Clin*, *7*:665-96, 1967.
4. Schlaegel, T. F., Jr.: Psychosomatics: the second face of ophthalmology, *Int Ophthalmol Clin*, *8*:409-85, 1968.
5. Cassidy, W. L., Flanagan, N. B., Spellman, B. A. and Cohen, M. E.: Clinical observations in manic depressive disease, *JAMA*, *164*:1535-46, 1957.
6. Langfeldt, G.: The prognosis in schizophrenia, *Acta Psychiat et Neurol Scand Supple*, *110*:7-66, 1956.
7. Wheeler, E. O., White, P. D., Reed, E. W. and Cohen, M. E.: Neurocirculatory asthenia (anxiety neurosis, effort syndrome, neurasthenia), *JAMA, 142*:878-89, 1950.
8. Pollitt, J.: Natural history of obsessional states, *Br Med J*, *1*:194-98, 1957.
9. Perley, M. J. and Guze, S. B.: Hysteria: the stability and usefulness of clinical criteria. *N Engl J Med*, *266*:421-26, 1962.
10. Woodruff, R. A., Clayton, P. H. and Guze, S. B.: Hysteria: an evaluation of specific diagnostic criteria by the study of randomly selected psychiatric clinic patients, *Br J Psychiatry*, *115*:1243-48, 1969.
11. Adams, G. L., Pearlman, J. T. and Sloan, S. H.: Guidelines for the psychiatric referral of visually handicapped patients. *Ann Ophthalmol*, *3*:72, 1971.
12. Engel, G. L.: Conversion symptoms, in MacBryde, C. M. (Ed.), *Signs and Symptoms: Applied Physiology and Clinical Interpretation*, 5th ed., 650-68, Lippincott, Philadelphia, 1970.
13. Ziegler, F. J., Imboden, J. B. and Meyer, E.: Contemporary conversion

reactions: a clinical study, *Am J Psychiatry, 116*:901-10, 1960.

14. Krill, A. E. and Newell, F. W.: The diagnosis of ocular conversion reaction involving visual function, *Arch Ophthalmol, 79*:254-61, 1968.

Chapter 5

STRESS AND STRABISMUS*

Morris C. Beckwitt, M.D.

*"For the ego perception plays the part
which in the id falls to instinct."*
(Freud, 1923)

ABSTRACT — With the aid of clinical examples, an attempt
was made to indicate the circumstances and the nature of the
psychologic stresses that predispose, precipitate, or perpetuate
strabismus and amblyopia.

The view emphasized here is that strabismus and amblyopia may be understood as a regressive, maladaptive, defensive visual response of certain predisposed infants to the
threat of object loss and separation.

Recent evidence from studies on the development of visual
perception and early mother-child relations were cited, especially, that of Spitz and Robeson. They have shown that the
infant's face-to-face, eye-to-eye contact with a loving mother
is essential for his emotional attachment to her, and for the
development of his object relations and communication. Insufficient or improper stimulation and support from the
mother in the eye to eye encounter may interfere with the
infant's innately determined maturation and development of
the visual apparatus and visual perception. Such insufficiency of contact and communication between infant and
mother in the symbiotic phase of development, also, predisposes the infant to excessive vulnerability to object loss
and separation anxiety.

The highest incidence of onset of strabismus occurs between two and one-half and three years, or during the infant's
greatest struggle with separation and individuation. It is at
that time that the vulnerable infant may have trouble with
severe ambivalence towards his mother, and find it hard to

*This article reprinted with permission from the *Israel Annals of Psychiatry, Vol. 9*, #1,
April 1971.

hold on to the idealized, good mother image, while he tries to reject the bad one.

The infant's immature ego and visual apparatus may act as an oculo-prehensory organ, and participate magically in the visual effort to cling to the good object, while trying not to see or to reject the bad object. A conflictual situation then develops which may be defensively and maladaptively expressed by the symptom of strabismus.

In convergent strabismus, which occurs in two-thirds of all cases, the defensive emphasis is on the visual clinging or convergence spasm. In divergent strabismus the emphasis is on the rejection, or visual thrusting away of the frightening object into the distance.

Surgical treatment of strabismus is usually performed on children between the ages of three and six years, when the traumatic impact of hospitalization, separation from home, and the fear of eye surgery inevitably aggravates their age specific castration anxiety and guilt. This makes the problem of strabismus and its psychologic etiology and treatment all the more important for us to consider.

BINOCULAR vision and the capacity to orient, locate, and follow objects, to judge their size, speed and direction of movement, is one of the greatest biologic adaptive achievements for survival and reflects millions of years of selective evolution.

In the human infant because of his slow maturation and development, and his prolonged dependence on the maternal environment, the development of the visual perceptual system is susceptible to all the vicissitudes of the early mother-infant relations. The quality of the early mother-infant stimulation and support, especially the quality of the early eye-to-eye contact and affectomotor communication, have a direct influence on the developing visual apparatus; not only on the binocular reflexes, but their integration with the perceptual, libidinal, and cognitive processes. According to recent researches, based on the work of R. Spitz (1965) and his followers, the mother's face, especially her eyes, along with the breast, are the first objects of the infant's interest and regard. First the eyes, and gradually the rest of the face, become the "focus and locus vitae," for attachment behavior and the establishment of social contact and communication. (This important theme will be developed later in greater detail.)

Nonparalytic concommitant strabismus, commonly known as squint or cross-eyes, is a condition which makes its appearance in infancy between the ages of one to six. Nonparalytic strabismus affects about 2 to 3 percent of the population at large, has been reported as high as 7 percent in crowded city areas, and is especially high in institutions for abandoned and neglected children. Rarely, an infant is born with one eye out of alignment which fails to straighten out during the first few months. It may remain thus, unless corrected. Strabismus develops very seldom during latency or in older people, and when it does it usually is reversible and of obvious psychogenic origin (Lyle 1959). Among infants who develop strabismus the highest frequency of incidence tends to correspond to the natural phases and crises of development. The frequency of onset is specially high during the separation individuation phase of development at the age of three. Usually, up to the age of three, the stress is basically severe separation anxiety or the panic of a threatened personality dissolution.

What makes strabismus different from other psychosomatic infantile conditions is that it may not only lead to an irreversible conspicuous facial deformity, but produces an amblyopic impairment of vision in the deviant eye, and if uncorrected, serious personality difficulties.

The precipitating stress that provokes the strabismic response may come from a variety of sources depending upon the age of the child, the nature of the conflict, his maturity, and the circumstances in his social environment. The most common sources of stress derive from oedipal conflicts, sibling rivalry, envy, jealousy over a new baby, or parental cruelty and rejection. The susceptibility to strabismus probably develops in the infant's disturbed symbiotic relation to his mother from inadequate face-to-face stimulation and support. When regression takes place it includes this symbiotic phase, as well as the phase of separation individuation.

During these early phases of development, visual perception of objects and their representations are still easily distorted by the pressure of strong pregenital drives and their corresponding primitive ego defenses of denial, splitting, isolation, projection and introjection (Jacobson, 1957, Schilder, 1950, Sperling, 1959).

According to Gesell (1959) and his group, all infants have the potentiality to squint. Transient intermittent strabismus is not at all uncommon in the first few months of infancy. He quotes the observation, "Infants squint with flatulence, older children with rage." The more satisfactory the visual interaction between infant and mother had been during the symbiotic phase, the more pleasurable and skillful the visual activity, the more strongly and effectively would the ego function involved become developed and remain intact under stress of separation and individuation. Mahler (1960) has frequently remarked on the regularity with which the autonomous ego functions develop in infancy provided there is a sufficiency of "matching communications" between infant and mother.

Strabismic reaction in the older child will generally occur after a series of provocations that rendered the child vulnerable by their cumulative effect. Sometimes an earlier trauma that produced an intermittent strabismus from which the infant had recovered, is reactivated by the symbolic or real similarity of the new trauma.

The predisposition to the regressive primitive strabismic response must be looked for not only in heredity but in the pathology of the early mother-child relations when the binocular reflexes are undergoing maturation and integration with the progressive ego development of the child.

There is justification, therefore, to consider the strabismus syndrome as a *developmental, maladaptive, psycho-physiologic distortion, part hereditary and part environmental* like other well-known psychosomatic conditions that originate in infancy. As such, it is suggested that strabismus be considered merely one of a variety of maladaptive infantile (ego-id) responses to emotional stress in the mother-child relation.

Under the stress of severe separation anxiety, or the panic of threatened intrapsychic object loss and ego dissolution, the vulnerable, regressed visual apparatus may act like an "oculo-prehensory" organ. It then mobilizes an excessive "convergence-accommodation" response in the effort to bring the object close to the mouth for oral mastery or incorporation. As Freud (1910), Spitz (1965), and Fenichel (1945) have frequently pointed out, "taking into the mouth or spitting out is the basis for all perception, and in conditions of regression one can observe that in the unconscious all sense organs are conceived as mouth-like." Just as in convergent strabismus the primitive defensive emphasis is on bringing the desired object to the mouth, so in divergent strabismus the defensive emphasis is on denying, rejecting, or thrusting away of the object. This, in essence, is our psychologic hypothesis of the etiology of strabismus.

The etiology of nonparalytic strabismus has puzzled ophthalmologists for a long time. The concensus of current ophthalmologic opinion still puts heavy emphasis on heredity and constitutional predisposition and considers refractive errors, toxicity and fatigue as the chief precipitating factors. When the stress of psychologic or emotional factors are considered, they are put last on the list. It is therefore all the more interesting to note that Lyle and Bridgeman (1959) in their recent edition of the authoritative textbook on Squint, state: "For the future investigators there remain two problems unsolved. One is the precise etiology of strabismus in children, and the other is the nature of the faculty of binocular fusion," (i.e., the fusion of the separate images from each eye into a stereoscopic image).

Among psychoanalysts, Freud (1910), Abraham (1927), Ferenci (1928), Fenichel (1945), Greenacre (1952), and others, have written on psychogenic visual disturbances, but little, if anything, has been written on the etiology of strabismus.

In his essay on psychogenic visual disturbances according to psychoanalytical conception Freud (1910) said, "When an organ which serves two purposes overplays its erotogenic part, it is in general to be expected that this will not occur without alterations in its response to stimulation and in innervation, which will be manifested as a disturbance of the organ in its function as a servant of the ego." This formulation is still valid today, even if psychosomatic theory has undergone numerous elaborations by Alexander (1950), Deutch (1953), Spitz (1951), and recently, in the writing of Schur (1955) on the metapsychology of somatization.

It may be of historic interest to note that the very first case reported by Breuer and Freud (1893) in their studies of hysteria, the case of Anna O., had developed strabismus suddenly, according to the authors, while nursing her dying father. Clearly this is also a case of separation anxiety and threatened object loss, as well as fatigue.

Inman (1921), a British ophthalmologist and psychologist, after studying 150 cases of children who had strabismus, stated: "There are authentic instances of a squint having dated from some fright or from occasion of jealousy such as the birth of a baby sister or brother ...". "Anxiety," he said, "can be a definite factor in its development. Unfortunately the connection is not always recognized, because surgeons and parents have still to learn the lesson psychologists have been teaching for decades — that what a very young child sees and hears may sometimes induce not only emotional distress but even actual illness — even if the subtlety of the circumstances escape notice." He arrived at the conclusion that "the appearance of strabismus in a young child was an indication of difficulties in the mother-child relation that interfered with the child's normal development."

An excellent critical review of the theories and the mechanisms underlying the etiology of convergent and divergent strabismus was written (in 1957) by Ernest Rappoport, a Chicago psychoanalyst. It was published in the *Eye, Ear, Nose and Throat Journal,* under the title, "Anger, Apathy and Strabismus." (Working independently, it seems we both arrived at rather similar conclusions.) My own clinical observations, which I shall report to you, and some of the current research in the field of infant visual perception, support these views.

In the summary of his paper, Rappoport says: "If we interpret convergent strabismus as a tightening of the ego defenses, then divergent strabismus represents a giving up of the defenses in a reality situation which appears hopeless. Then we may say that the child has relinquished the struggle for contact with a mother who is unapproachable, and has turned out its eyes in despair, or for search in an unknown vacuum."

Rappoport further says:

> "Strabismus, heterotropia, seems to result from a hostile over-stimulation, or from a lack of stimulation of the child by the parent. There is evidence that internal (convergent) strabismus, estropia, derives from a chronic state of anger and spite, and is a spastic cataleptic fixation of the convergence mechanism combined with persistent accommodation for the purpose of bringing the object closer to control and master it ... External strabismus, esotropia, in which the medial rectus has lost its physiological predominance, comes from an attitude of resignation or apathy leading to convergence insufficiency and abandonment of accommodation ... It represents a regression to a very primitive ego state comparable to the quadruped sniffing the ground and turning the eyes up and out by using an archaic type of doubling binocular vision, or to even earlier aquatic ancestors who did not yet practice accommodation."

Before turning to a consideration of some clinical examples of strabismus, a brief review of a few idiomatic expressions and attitudes, based on everyday empirical observations, might be of interest.

Rappoport (1959) pointed out that not only do people believe that their eyes cross when they get angry; i.e., get "cock-eyed mad," but that animals such as cats, dogs and even chickens show convergence reactions when in a "devouring" rage. In Spanish, the word for anger, "enojo," translates literally "eyes turned in." The German word for squint is "schielen," and to look at somebody with "schielen augen" means to look with hostile envious eyes. This corresponds to the American expression "cross-eyed with envy," and the English equivalent to look asquint or askance. In Far Eastern, especially Japanese, art enraged warriors are generally depicted with eyes in a convergent strabismus. Similarly, their pantomine actors (Kabuki dancers) sometimes converge their eyes to indicate extreme anger.

CLINICAL CASE MATERIAL

When a child of three whose eyes have been straight all his life suddenly becomes cross-eyed in response to a traumatic emotional experience, even the most casual observer is forced to take notice of the fact. The observed phenomenon becomes like an experiment in nature that arouses interest and demands a *psychologic* explanation.

Let me illustrate. Jamie, whose sudden onset of strabismus I had an opportunity to study, developed her eye condition under the following circumstances. The mother left Jamie before she was a year old in the care of a variety of neighbours and baby-sitters in order that she might go to work. Then for about a year-and-a-half thereafter, Jamie remained with one maternal elderly woman to whom she became strongly attached. During this time Jamie seemed to develop normally. When the parents moved to another city, Jamie lost her devoted nurse and suffered great distress for several months while the mother tried unsuccessfully to find a new one for Jamie. Three months after, Jamie finally formed an attachment to one of the women in the nursery. This woman also left abruptly, and did not return. In this atmosphere of insecurity, following repeated abandonment, Jamie became more irritable and more difficult to manage. One day the mother was notified at work by the head of the nursery that Jamie suddenly became cross-eyed with a convergent strabismus. Jamie, aged three, had now become exceedingly distrustful of strangers, including doctors. The examining ophthalmologist noted that the degree of her strabismus became worse as he approached to examine her or when he tried to get her to cooperate. Her eye condition became irreversible and failed to respond to any form of medical treatment. When she entered school, she also developed a peptic ulcer.

* * *

Tom was almost five years old when he developed a convergent strabismus. He developed it when he learned from his mother that he had been adopted in infancy. The onset of his strabismus was also sudden and dramatic. Tom had been raised in a well-kept nursery during the first year of his life before his adoption. His adopting mother who recalled vividly the circumstances of the onset of his strabismus gave the following details about his early history. At age one, when she first saw Tom in the nursery, he seemed to have caught her eye in a fascinating manner. While standing in his crib, he followed her movements wherever she went, and seemed to her to look with such pleading and accusing eyes at her whenever she tried to pick up another infant, that she felt compelled to return to him. (Sally Prevence (1961), who has studied abandoned children in nursery homes, has also remarked on the lonely, object hungry looks of these infants). Tom seemed to have developed normally to all outward appearances, and had no evidence of visual difficulties before or at the time when his mother frightened him so with the disclosure about his adoption. Some weakness in Tom's early object relations and consequent fragility of his ego's capacity for object constancy must be assumed, however, as a result of the original maternal abandonment to a nursery. There were other conditions and circumstances that made Tom particularly vulnerable. He had been left in the care of the family laundress for over a month while his mother went to nurse the father at their summer cottage where he was recuperating from pneumonia. The laundress, who then functioned as housekeeper and caretaker for Tom, had moved into the home with her seven-year-old daughter. This girl became Tom's playmate, and soon introduced him to mutual sexual explorations. Tom was quite stimulated and frightened by these sexual games. Feeling abandoned and being in the oedipal phase of his development, he reacted with severe guilt and castration anxiety. He had barely been reunited with his parents when the mother, on the advice of a neighbor, decided to inform Tom about his adoption. When Tom understood what was meant by adoption, he turned pale, began to vomit, and his eyes crossed. The mother quickly realized that she had frightened him with her information, and wanting to reassure him, kept repeating that she had chosen him from all the other children in the nursery because she loved him best and that he was her beautiful little boy. His eyes remained crossed however in a convergent (alternating) strabismus until corrected surgically at age fifteen and one-half.

In later adolescence, following the corrective eye surgery, he became a voyeur with a special interest in five-year-old little boys. Whenever he developed severe anxiety, he was impelled to find and seduce a beautiful five-year-old boy, a representative of his good former self, and to reassure himself by looking lovingly and admiringly at the little boy's penis. During psychoanalytic therapy it became clear that this compulsive voyeuristic behavior not only was needed to reassure himself against castration anxiety, but also severe separation anxiety, and the panic of identity loss (as well as object and reality loss.) He was thus repeating in the voyeuristic act his mother's unsuccessful attempt at reassurance to her "beautiful little boy."

In a recurrent childhood nightmare, related to his attempt at mastering his severe castration anxiety and identity diffusion, he would peer intently at the genital area of a child trying to ascertain whether it was the genital of a boy or a girl. He would then wake up with a severe headache and pain between his eyes. (This was the first case of strabismus that I studied and reported in 1954.)

* * *

One three-year-old little girl began to squint when her mother gave birth to a baby brother whom the father, whose name was John, named after himself. In addition to the obvious jealousy conflict which precipitated the strabismic reaction, there were several other contributing factors which rendered this girl vulnerable. The little girl had, with good reason, considered herself to be her father's favorite and was quite unprepared for the father's sudden shift of interest to his newborn son. Furthermore, while the mother had gone to the hospital to give birth to the new baby, the little girl had mistakenly assumed that a house across the street, to which the family had considered moving, was the place where the mother and the new baby were staying. When this house across the street caught fire and burned down, the little girl became frantic, believing her fantasy that mother and baby had perished in the flames. The memories of this experience were recalled in therapy when reactivated in the transference. The patient remembered watching the fire across the street, soiling herself, pulling the curtain down on herself in panic, and lying on the floor screaming unconsolably. This may have been the real precipitating trauma that mobilized the strabismic convergence spasm. However, the patient's family date the onset of her convergent strabismus to the arrival of her baby brother a few days after the fire incident. This girl's eyes remained crossed until corrected surgically at the age of fifteen. Although she had a good cosmetic result, one eye remained amblyopic, and she never developed stereoscopic vision.

* * *

John, a two-year-old boy, who was left-handed like his mother, was forced by his father to eat with his right hand. Once when the child forgot and began to eat soup with the left hand, the father struck the boy's hand and spilled the soup in his face. The child left the table crying, and when next seen he had developed a convergent strabismus. The condition proved unresponsive to orthoptic treatment and was surgically corrected at age fourteen-and-one-half. A more detailed history revealed that when the boy was about nine months old, his father had also tried to make the infant hold his bottle in the right hand. In the struggle that ensued, the bottle dropped and broke on the floor. The baby then refused any bottle, became dehydrated and had to be hospitalized. While in the hospital he developed pyelitis and suffered from painful urination. It is not known whether John reacted with a transient strabismus in response to the traumatic loss of his nursing bottle and separation from his mother. This little boy reacted with extreme castration anxiety later when he saw a little girl's genitals at the age of two-and-one-half. He made the discovery when his mother went to the hospital to give birth to another baby, and the father put him in the bathtub together with a visiting little girl. Pointing to the girl's genital and crying, "Tushy, baby, tushy, baby," he ran from the bath in panic, clutching his own penis. When he calmed down he was able to explain that "Tushy, baby" meant that the little girl had no penis but a tushy-like cleft in the front as well as in the back. It is not clear why the child developed the strabismus at the time that he did, at the dinner table, and not in response to the earlier threats, unless we assume that it was the cumulative effect of the repeated traumata that finally produced this regressive spastic convergence response.

Usually the onset of strabismus is less sudden. It has a tendency at first to be transitory and intermittent, with appearance and disappearance under psychic stress or fatigue. Sometimes the interpersonal and intrapsychic conflicts are not obvious. However, a careful history will usually bring to light some of these psychogenic factors.

* * *

Two little sisters, aged three-and-one-half and two-and-one-half, developed divergent strabismus under the following circumstances. The older child, who was born two months premature, continued to be physically delicate and susceptible to frequent colds, gastrointestinal upsets and asthma. The mother, as might have been expected, was overanxious, immature, and insecure. The baby began to manifest transitory strabismus at about eight months. The strabismus became constant at three years and she was operated on at three-and-one-half. A few weeks later, the two-and-one-half-year-old sister developed a similar divergent strabismus. Since the younger sister was very competitive and obviously jealous of the older, an imitative identification was suspected and soon confirmed. In her eagerness to reassure the older child about the impending hospitalization for the eye surgery, the mother tried to make the event into an interesting and enjoyable adventure with promises of daily gifts, frequent visits, and numerous references to the wonderful time "big sister" would have with that nice doctor in the hospital. She succeeded only too well in arousing the younger sister's desire to share in the great adventure. How identification with a member of the family who has strabismus interacts with a hereditary predisposition remains a moot question.

The interplay of the hereditary and environmental factors was not clarified when it was learned that the father's left eye also turned outward in a divergent strabismus whenever he became emotionally excited. This anxious mother, who had difficulty disciplining the little girls, had generally exhausted her patience by the time the father returned home from work and would then demand that he discipline them. This he did, even if reluctantly and resentfully. At such time his left eye would turn out and his facial expression would reflect his anger. One must wonder how the father's facial appearance during the spanking experience affected the sensitive little girls in the pre-oedipal and oedipal phases of their development, and led to an identification with the aggressive father. Perhaps much that we had attributed to heredity may really have been of environmental origin.

* * *

The case of four-year-old Randy points up several interesting issues connected with strabismus and its treatment. Randy and his mother were referred for psychotherapy by the ophthalmologist who had successfully operated on the child's eyes when he surmised that the mother's attitude contributed to the child's eye difficulties. One day when Randy went for a post-operative checkup, the mother brought along his older brother. To the surprise of the doctor and mother, the good surgical result with Randy's eyes was suddenly undone when the older brother was brought into the examining room. This experience forced the ophthalmologist to consider the role of psychogenic factors in the etiology of strabismus. Randy's eyes became free from strabismus again as soon as the positive transference was re-established and the mother's favorite, Randy's hated rival, was kept out of the treatment room. When the mother came for psychotherapy it was possible to learn more about the psychogenic factor that contributed to the onset of Randy's strabismus. The mother, an attractive and energetic woman of thirty, had made Randy unconsciously the target for her childhood rivalry with her brother. When she learned that her brother was planning to move to the West Coast to be near to their parents, she was overcome with an uncontrollable urge to move to the same city. She then launched a relentless and successful campaign to convince her husband to liquidate his prosperous business as well as his established social position in a midwest community, and to move to the West Coast. Randy reacted to the strain of moving and the mother's excessive irritability towards him by chronic whining. This made his mother all the more impatient and angry with him. At this time the mother blamed Randy's unhappy whining on the fact that the boy had a small urinary meatus, and succeeded in convincing a local pediatrician to enlarge it surgically. The surgical procedure was performed without anaesthesia while the mother held the shrieking child in her lap. By the time the family moved West, Randy had a definite convergent strabismus and the above-mentioned corrective surgery soon followed. During the brief period of analytic psychotherapy it was also learned that Randy's mother had suffered in childhood from intense envy of her brother who seemed to her more successful, as well as the mother's favorite. Not until she became an adolescent and developed into a beautiful girl did she feel she had partly displaced her brother in the parent's affection.

* * *

Another typical example of psychogenic childhood strabismus that I had an opportunity to study over a period of years is that of Annie. Annie was adopted immediately after she was born through arrangements with the biologic mother who was known to be an attractive, healthy woman. The adopting parents had three boys and the mother wanted very much to have a daughter but was afraid to risk another difficult pregnancy. Annie had the best physical care that money could provide and a great deal of attention. She seemed to develop normally and grew into an exceptionally beautiful child at age three when she developed strabismus. Annie's mother, who is a rather narcissistic woman, loved her little girl accordingly. She was very proud of her beautiful baby girl, called her "living doll," and enjoyed dressing and exhibiting her like a living doll. However, much of the every day nursing care was entrusted to an aging menopausal housekeeper who had been with the family many years and was planning to retire. The mother, who was eager to go on a vacation holiday before she lost the housekeeper, left the three boys, aged twelve, eleven, and seven, and the three-year-old little girl in the care of the now irritable and resentful housekeeper. As soon as the parents left on their vacation, the housekeeper had difficulty controlling the boys. They fought among themselves and refused to obey her. The little girl suffered most during this period. She was, psychologically speaking, abandoned by her parents to an emotionally unstable menopausal woman, and a hostile brother of seven who had always been very jealous of her. The seven-year-old brother told her that she did not really belong to the family like the other siblings, and threatened that unless she submitted to his sexual manipulations, she would be gotten rid of and sent back where she came from. The little girl's insecurity was still further undermined when the housekeeper in desperation threatened to quit and leave them all, unless they behaved better.

Because I had the opportunity to observe the little girl during this period, I saw the development of the strabismus from the very beginning. When the above-mentioned threats to the little girl's safety were discovered and partly relieved, the strabismus receded. It was possible to observe how the strabismus increased and decreased according to the level of the child's security or anxiety, as these problems were dealt with. For a while it looked as if we had succeeded in preventing the development of a strabismus. However, when the parents returned and the mother noticed the child's intermittent strabismic eye difficulty, she could not avoid making an issue of it, and anxiously drawing the child's attention to the visual defect. No amount of persuasion, discussion and explanation could keep the mother from focusing on the child's periodic strabismus. Attempts to get the mother into psychotherapy to protect the mother-child relation were also unsuccessful. Soon the strabismus became constant, and the mother insisted on surgical correction. The surgery was only partly successful, and after years of orthoptic treatments, the eyes became almost cosmetically straight. By the time this child reached latency, she was fat, sullen, had difficulty in school, and was very unhappy.

* * *

Let us now consider a one-year-old infant. Kay, who showed signs of a developing convergent strabismus before she was one year old, was a ten months' pregnancy. Her anxious mother could not give birth to her until the tenth month of pregnancy without the help of her former psychotherapist. Although Kay was born robust and well-developed, looked and behaved like a month-old infant, the mother tended to project her hypochondrical fears onto her infant and had difficulty at times in looking directly at her baby. Kay's mother was encouraged to address herself directly to her baby and to carry the baby facing her, but she preferred to carry the baby facing away from her. The father liked to carry the baby under his arm like a sack of potatoes. These details are mentioned because of their relevance to the current researches that are being carried out on the role of *eye-to-eye contact* in the establishment of infant-mother attachment and communication.

* * *

It was Spitz (1965) who drew attention to the fact that the newborn infant has a *selective and preferential* interest in the mother's eyes. Biologists and ethnologists have found the same to be true in animals (Lorenz 1950). Greenman (1963) and

Wolf (1963) have found that the infant's smile has a profound effect in arousing and directing her maternal interest to her infant. They also found that direct eye-to-eye contact is the most effective stimulus to evoke the infant's smile. Even mothers who had felt anxious or indifferent before, soon became more interested in their infants when the infants began to smile. The mothers actually began to enjoy taking care of their infants and playing with them. The smile, they found, made the mothers feel as if the infant not only saw them, but recognized them and appreciated them. These mothers, when questioned, also felt that when the infant began to smile at them, he became a person, and that this was the beginning of their social relation. Some mothers have found that once visual contact has been established, it may dominate the feeding situation and evoke more excitement than the breast.

Spitz (1965) said, "The smile is the first human, active, directed intentional behavioral manifestation, and the first transition from complete passivity to inception of active social behavior."

According to Greenman (1963), "Vision exceeds the essential role it plays in perception of the outside world and in differentiating the self from the nonself ... in that ... one of the primary ways in which human beings (like animals) communicate at a nonverbal level is by looking at each other ... and when visual communication does not exist between humans, something deviant and pathological often existed in the relationship." This empirical fact is reflected in the idiomatic expression about the importance of "seeing eye-to-eye."

Schaeffer and Emerson (1964a), in their observations, have found that "after eye contact is established, infants actively seek their mother's eye and that situations in which visually maintained contact is interrupted are the most provocative of separation anxiety."

Robeson (1967), in his related studies, reported on the frustration of a mother who made vigorous but unsuccessful attempts to catch the eyes of her infant while he persistently avoided her gaze. At one point, she could not control herself and shouted angrily, "Look at me!" (It is not clear whether such an infant gaze aversion is an expression of a primary autistic attitude, or is secondary to maternal rejection. Only continued research will help to clarify this issue).

In the case of the infant, Kay, whose mother could not give birth to her until the tenth month of pregnancy and needed the help of her (former) psychotherapist, that same psychotherapist made the observation that the infant had no difficulty looking straight at her when held, but the infant tended to avert her gaze from her anxious mother. Sometimes, when facing her mother, instead of turning away her head or averting her gaze, Kay squinted. Kay's squint became gradually more pronounced, and when she was eleven months old she developed intestinal intussusception which needed surgical correction.

While Robeson (1967) did not study the effect of conflict in the early visual encounters between infants and their mothers in relation to strabismus, his observations and those of his colleagues are nevertheless considered relevant to this topic of our interest.

Of course not all infants withdraw equally in response to inadequate or hostile visual contact with their mothers, nor do they develop strabismus, but the case of a three-week-old infant described by Robeson (1967) who tried unsuccessfully to capture his mother's gaze because his mother felt "he looked daggers" at her, is reminiscent of Kay who developed strabismus and (later) intestinal intussusception under the insecure care of her hypochondriacal mother. (Incidentally, intussusception which develops in "healthy" infants has no known etiology. Is it perhaps also psychogenic in origin?)

Rappoport (1957) had an opportunity to analyze a rejecting mother whose daughter had divergent strabismus from earliest infancy. He found that the mother's unconscious attitude, as it had appeared in recurrent dreams, had expressed the wish not to give birth to the child but to push the child back where it came from. She also wanted in her dreams to prevent the milk from flowing by putting hair pins through her nipples. The mother later suffered from agoraphobia and attacks of blepharospasm — both of which symptoms Rappoport found to be defensive attempts to deny that the baby was her child. "To this mother," he said, "the child did not represent a separate person but an organ of her body, an eye. It was by means of a blepharospasm that she had tried to hold onto the eye tightly, or to refuse seeing that the child was born."

From the studies of Schilder (1950), Werner (1957), Weckowitz (1957), and others, we know that perception in the young infant is very susceptible to distortion by strong emotions. When frightened or very angry, perceived objects and object representations may appear to approach and get bigger or recede and get smaller according to the mental state and desire of the infant. The phenomenon of *macropsia* and *micropsia* which may accompany the onset of strabismus are in part explainable by regressions to these infantile states of perception. (Anna O., [Breuer-Freud (1893), Sperling (1959)] the first case reported by Breuer and Freud also developed macropsia shortly before the onset of her convergent strabismus.)

Gesell's (1967) studies of the development of vision in infant and child have demonstrated how the eye bridges the space interval between it and the object of regard by motor attitudes or *prehension* and *locomotion* which embrace the entire skeletal musculature including the mouth, hands and the oculo-motor muscles. The eyes of the young child from one to three act like an *oculo-prehensory* organ that grasps, pulls and pushes objects in space. The participation of the infant's eyes in the real and magical manipulation of objects is in keeping with the "primary process" or magical thinking of this age group. The rapid fluctuations in the convergence and accommodation are in keeping with the above intentions and manipulations and can be observed and described with the aid of an ophthalmoscope or retinoscope.

Gesell and his group have noted and recorded the convergence and the refractive changes of accommodation that the infant's eyes undergo as he reaches, grasps, pulls or pushes toys or other objects of regard.

For example, taking or grasping of a toy produces a characteristic accommodative change in the lens of the eye which causes a reflected beam of light to have an "against motion," while giving or thrusting away a toy produces the opposite motion in the same beam of light. By this method it is possible to observe how closely the accommodation changes of the eye parallel the grasping, pulling, pushing or rejecting of objects.

Whether in strabismus the main visual pathologic defensive effort against object loss is to ignore and reject the object or to grasp and cling to it, may depend on innate as well as learned factors; on constitutional predisposition to autism or symbiotic clinging.

Benjamin (1959), who studied individual variability of responses in infants, noted how some infants have greater preference for grasping, while others for thrusting or throwing away objects as a defense against object loss. How these tendencies are correlated in detail with the development of convergent and divergent strabismus would also make an interesting study.

Tennes and Lample (1969), who worked with Benjamin, have found in their experimental studies that separation anxiety of infants which begins at seven to eight months usually reaches its peak at eighteen months and is intensified by the level of aggression between the mother and infant. It is of interest to note eighteen months is also one of the nodal points for the development of strabismus.

However, the greatest number of cases of strabismus give a history of onset between two-and-one-half to three when the infant is becoming aware of anatomic sexual differences and is struggling to master the developmental tasks of separation and individuation, as described by Mahler (1960) and Ekstein (1966).

This is also a period when the child has to master such differences as between self and object, inside and outside, good and bad, right and wrong, as well as right and left. The primitive defenses of denial, splitting, isolation, projection and introjection are employed to deal with good and bad self and objects and their endopsychic representations. In the struggle to cling to the good object and to avoid the bad, the visual perceptual apparatus is involved in a parallel effort to see the good and to avoid seeing the bad (i.e., the bad object and object representation.) Caught in the conflict between the need to see and the fear to see, the desire to cling and the desire to reject, the delicate binocular relfexes become disrupted by a convergent or divergent strabismus depending on the predominant defensive attitude and constitutional predisposition.

The very young child can solve the conflict between *the need to see and fear to see disturbing reality,* by seeing with one eye and a part of his ego, while denying reality or suppressing it in the other eye which becomes amblyopic. The fetishist does something similar with the defensive split in his ego. One part adheres to reality, while the other distorts it according to his needs and wishes. However, he does this without impairing his vision. When the visual apparatus of the child is directly involved, the same type of conflict may produce strabismus, amblyopia, and other visual disturbances. The amblyopia, if severe enough, may also help the child avoid the discomfort of diplopia and the disfigurement of strabismus. But this leaves him without the capacity to develop binocular fusion and stereoscopic vision. Lacking a developed fusion capacity to mediate between the claims of convergence and accommodation, the child remains vulnerable to strabismus at a later date if and when exposed to sufficient stress.

Normally, when not overburdened by stress, the reflexes of accommodations and convergence are integrated so that one dioptre of accommodation produces one dioptre angle of convergence. The fusion vergence reflex if established after age three, mediates between the accommodation and vergence reflexes. It assures that the image of the object of regard falls exactly on the macula of each retina and the two images formed can be fused or synthesized by the cortical ego, to produce one stereoscopic image (Lyle, 1969).

Age three is not only the age when an intermittent strabismus may become more pronounced and permanent (Gesell, 1959). Not infrequently a successful resolution of the separation-individuation crisis leads to the disappearance of the intermittent strabismus. Good understanding and good relations between infant and mother will do most to facilitate the integration of the fusion reflex, which once established tends to prevent strabismus. The fusion reflex is believed by ophthalmologists to be fully established by the sixth or seventh year, at which time the visual apparatus is also considered to have fully matured. That is why nonparalytic strabismus and amblyopia seldom develop after the child goes into latency (Lyle 1959).

When strabismus has developed, the best treatment is to look for and to eliminate the conflicts in the child's human environment and to restore the child's security. Only a friendly and understanding orthoptic therapist can be helpful, because what conflict and interpersonal stress has torn asunder, only a benign and understanding orthoptic therapist can help bring together.

Most orthoptic therapists, like speech therapists, are good technicians who are insufficiently aware of the role of conflict in the etiology of these disturbances, and their effectiveness is limited accordingly.

Because surgery is now performed as early as possible to correct the strabismus and to avoid the development of amblyopia in the deviant eye, the traumatic impact of the surgery itself can also add to the difficulty. Hospitalization, separation from home, and the castrative threat from the surgery when the child is naturally susceptible to separation and castration anxiety, may sometimes harm as well as help. All these considerations make the problem of strabismus, its etiology and treatment all the more important for us to consider.

SUMMARY

It is the purpose of this presentation to call attention to the role that psychosocial stress in the mother-child relation and later intrapsychic conflict play in the complex etiology of strabismus and amblyopia. Most ophthalmologists, insufficiently aware of the psychologic interplay between mother and infant and its effect on maturation, tend to put the psychologic factor last on their list of causes.

With the aid of clinical examples, an attempt was made to indicate the circumstances and the nature of the psychologic stresses that predispose, precipitate, or perpetuate strabismus and amblyopia.

The view emphasized here is that strabismus and amblyopia

may be understood as a regressive, maladaptive, defensive visual response of certain predisposed infants to the threat of object loss and separation.

Recent evidence from studies on the development of visual perception and early mother-child relations were cited, especially that of Spitz and Robeson. They have shown that the infant's face-to-face, eye-to-eye contact with a loving mother is essential for his emotional attachment to her, and for the development of his object relations and communication. Insufficient or improper stimulation and support from the mother in the eye-to-eye encounter may interfere with the infant's innately determined maturation and development of the visual apparatus and visual perception. Such inadequate visual contact and communication between infant and mother in the symbiotic phase of development also predisposes the infant to excessive vulnerability to object loss and separation anxiety.

The highest incidence of onset of strabismus occurs between two-and-one-half and three years, or during the infant's greatest struggle with separation and individuation. It is then that the more vulnerable infant may have trouble with severe ambivalence towards his mother, and find it hard to hold on to the idealized good mother image, while he tries to reject the bad one.

The infant's immature ego and visual apparatus may act like an oculo-prehensory organ, and participate magically in the visual effort to cling to the good object while trying not to see or to reject the bad object. A conflictual situation then develops which may be defensively and maladaptively expressed by the symptom of strabismus.

In convergent strabismus, which occurs in two-thirds of all cases, the defensive emphasis is on the visual clinging or convergence spasm. In divergent strabismus the emphasis is on the rejection, or visual thrusting away of the frightening object into the distance.

Surgical treatment of strabismus is usually performed on children between the ages of 3 and 6 years, when the traumatic impact of hospitalization, separation from home, and the fear of eye surgery inevitably aggravates their age specific castration anxiety and guilt. This makes the problem of strabismus and its psychologic etiology and treatment all the more important for us to consider.

REFERENCES

1. Abraham (1913): *Restrictions and Transformations of Scoptophilia in Psychoneurotics.* Selected Papers on Psychoanalysis, Chapter IX, Hogarth, London, 1927.
2. Alexander, F.: *Psychosomatic Medicine,* Norton, New York, 1950.
3. Benjamin, J. D.: *Dynamic Psychopathology in Childhood.* Grune, New York, 1959.
4. Breuer-Freud (1893): *Case Histories,* Standard Edition, *II,* 21-48, Hogarth, London, 1955.
5. Deutch, F.: *The Psychosomatic Concept in Psychoanalysis,* Intl Univs Pr, New York, 1953.
6. Ekstein, R.: *Child of Time and Space of Action and Impulse,* Appleton Cent, New York, 1966.
7. Fenichel: The scoptophilic instinct and identification, *Jo, 18*:6-24, 1937.
8. Ferenczi: Gulliver phantasies, Jo, 9:283-300, 1928.
9. Freud, S. (1910): *Psychogenic Visual Disturbances According to Psychoanalytic Conceptions,* Standard Edition, *11*:209-218, Hogarth, London, 1957.
10. Freud, S.: *The Ego and the Id,* Standard Edition, 19, 1923.
11. Gesell: *Vision: It's Development in Infant and Child,* Paul: Hoebner, New York, 1959.
12. Greenacre: *Penis Awe and Penis Envy: Drives, Affects, Behavior,* Intl Univs Pr, New York, 1953.
13. Greenman, G. W.: *Visual Behavior of Newborn Infants — Modern Perspective of Child Development,* Edited by A. Solnit and S. Provence, 1963.
14. Hart, H. H.: The eye in symbol and symptom, *Psychanal Review, 36*:1-21, 1949.
15. Inman: Emotions and eye symptoms, *Br J Med Psychol,* 2:46-67, 1921.
16. Jacobson, E.: Denial and repression, *J Am Psychoanal Assoc,* 5:61-92, 1957.
17. Lample and Tennes: Some aspects of mother-child relationship pertaining to infantile separation anxiety, *J Nerv Ment Dis, 143*:426-437, 1966.
18. Lorenz, K.: The comparative method for studying innate behaviour patterns, *Symp Soc Exp Biol,* Cambridge U Pr, London, 1950.
19. Lyle, T. K. and Bridgeman, G. J.: *Squint,* Bailliere, Tindall and Cox, London, 1959.
20. Mahler, M. S.: Thoughts about development and individuation,

Psychoanal Study Child, 15:104-127, 1960

21. Rappoport, E. A.: Anger, apathy and strabismus, *Eye Ear Nose Throat Mon, 38*:473-482, 1959.

22. Robeson, K. S.: The role of eye to eye contact in maternal infant attachment, *J Child Psychol Psychiatry, 8*:13-25, 1967.

23. Schaefer, H. R. and Emerson, P. E. (1964a): The development of social attachments in infancy, *Monogr Soc Child Dev, 29*:94, 1964.

24. Schilder, P.: *The Image and Appearance of the Human Body,* Intl Univs Pr, New York, 1950.

25. Schur: Comments on the metapsychology of somatization, *The Psychoanal Study Child, 10*:119-164, 1955.

26. Sperling, M.: Some regressive phenomena involving the preceptual sphere, *Int J Psychoanal, 40*:304-308, 1959.

27. Spitz, R. A.: The psychogenic diseases of infancy, *Psychoanal Study Child, 6*:255-275, 2951.

28. Spitz, R. A.: *The First Year of Life,* Intl Univs Pr, New York, 1965.

29. Weckowitz, T. E.: Size constancy in schizophrenic patients, *J Ment Sc, 103*:432-436, 1957.

30. Wener, H.: *Comparative Psychology of Mental Development,* Intl Univs Pr, New York, 1957.

Chapter 6

STATUS MEDICAMENTOSUS OPHTHALMOLOGICA

Sherwin H. Sloan, M.D.

> Washed spodium mixed with grease, and
> not of a thinner consistence than dough, is
> to be carefully triturated, and moistened
> with the juice of unripe raisins; and
> having dried in the sun, moisten until it is
> the consistence of an ointment. When it
> becomes again dry, let it be finely levi-
> gated, anoint the eyes with it, and dust it
> upon the angles of the eyes.
> ......from the Works of Hippocrates

EACH day vast numbers of our patients anoint their
globes with a wide assortment of medicaments. I am not
speaking of the thousands of patients who daily take topical
ophthalmic medication for glaucoma, conjunctivitis, or iritis
but of the equally numerous population that make their weekly
trip to the local drug store and fill their shopping carts with
vials of fluid and salves that will cure their itching and burning
eyes, headaches, tired eyes, lazy eye, painful eye, anxieties, and
depression. To many of these patients the ritualistic applica-
tion of fluids becomes a form of topical ambrosia.

With the perpetuation of the above process, the entity described by Wahl (1967) as "Status Medicamentosus" has become
increasingly prevalent, and in ophthalmic practice, it is frequently missed. In the process of self-medicating with available
preparations, containing such ingredients as phenylephrine
and ephedrine, which promise to soothe and heal sore eyes,
patients may produce a chronic irritative syndrome that may be
further exacerbated when the ophthalmologist offers yet
another "cure" in the form of an additional drop, albeit this

one by prescription only. It is all too easy for the ophthalmologist, in his harried practice, to supplant the patient's self-medication with an equally irritative drug and continue the circular route of frequent changes of medication in order to eradicate the persisting symptoms.

The obvious necessity for a thorough ophthalmic examination of these patients needs no further elaboration. The usual complaint is of nonspecific irritation, eye fatigue, or itching and burning of the eyes. The examination may reveal mild conjunctival infection, mild papillary hypertrophy or show no significant physical abnormalities. A careful elucidation of medications the patient is using is of utmost importance. As Wahl states, it is helpful during the examination to return to the question of present and past medication — without appearing critical — in order to elicit any omissions. One may find an incredibly long list of drugs, which the patient has diligently tried over a period of time to relieve his symptoms. On questioning the patient, it is frequently found that none of the drugs alleviated the symptoms, thus necessitating the substitution of one drug for another or the use of several at once.

When the drug store items are exhausted, the patient may begin the rounds of the ophthalmologists in the community seeking some relief from his affliction. The list of medicaments has by no means been limited exclusively to prescription drugs and to accepted proprietary items. In our clinic, the liquids reportedly used to bathe eyes have varied from lemon and cactus juice to Lavoris® mouthwash! Home and folklore remedies, even with the supposed sophistication of medical knowledge of the general public, have not vanished from our culture. Once the exclusion of specific organic disease is accomplished, the ophthalmologist must not succumb to the easy pitfall of supplying the "magic drop" instead of trying to elucidate, with an additional small amount of time, other aspects of the patient's complaints.

The symptoms of which these patients complaint constitute one of the most common problems seen in the ophthalmologist's office. Typically, when we see a patient with these nonspecific symptoms and cannot attach an organic cause, we tend to label the patient neurotic; and indeed this may be true. But all too frequently, the physician will not pursue questioning the patient in order to develop sufficient rapport to establish additional factors paramount to the patient's complaint. Many patients will be found with underlying fears regarding vision and having the most rudimentary and bizarre conceptions of visual function. On closer examination, these patients will commonly express the fear of going blind which they feel the constant itching and burning portends. They cease all nonessential visual function such as reading, watching television or movies in order to allay and delay deterioration of their vision and eventual blindness. They spend the day bathing, washing and soothing their eyes with their various medications and compresses. One of my patients begins each day by laboriously mixing a solution of weak boric acid, meticulously boiled on the stove and placed in a sterile jar for bathing her eyes as the day — and her anxieties — moves on. The day of the eye cup is still with us! In this day of devotees to health food fads and astrological cures for disease and stress, it is no great surprise to find ophthalmic remedies prevalent within this section of the population. From the very common practice of ingesting vast quantities of vitamin A to prevent blindness has come the practice, in at least one of my patients, of happily applying carrot juice to her eyes to keep them safe from disease.

Indeed, the eye may become the neurotic organ of a patient, and all the manifestations of his anxieties may be concentrated in his eyes. "Irritations" can then be washed away by the use of some magical drop, and when one potion doesn't work, why not try another — and another? If the directions for the medication say use three times a day, why wouldn't twelve or twenty times a day hasten the healing?

Status medicamentosus, I believe, is a common entity in ophthalmology. As Dr. Wahl suggests, this diagnosis can be made with increasing frequency by keeping the possibility in mind of its existence. Not only may the patient arrive at your office, fresh with the self-induced disease, but all too often, the process is continued by the busy ophthalmologist. Frequently, it is too easy to substitute another medication for support, reassurance, and education of the patient. The patient also accepts this means of treatment; cure, of course, comes from the bottle or the tube rather than from the physician. Frequently, the patient may have myriad other psychiatric complaints and may be taking other medications in addition to the topical ophthalmic drugs.

What then can be done to treat this syndrome once the diagnosis is made? An understanding explanation of the problem to the patient, with reassurance and education regarding the fallacy of many beliefs pertaining to vision, is essential. Frequently, merely reassuring the patient of the normal healthy status of his eyes and of the frequency of these nonspecific complaints in our hectic smog-filled society is enough to produce a grateful patient. Removing the offending drops or salves and instituting a program of essential medication only is next in order. Some patients insist on taking a medication and, if so, an "innocuous" drop may be used sparingly and, when used judiciously with the physician's approval, may add a placebo effect. Beware of the tempting alternative which, unfortunately, occurs on too many occasions, that of dismissing the symptoms and iatrogenically continuing the problem by quickly clearing the office of the patient with several more prescriptions in hand.

Status Medicamentosus Ophthalmologica is common enough. Let not the ophthalmologist be a perpetrator of the syndrome.

REFERENCES

1. Wahl, C. W.: Diagnosis and treatment of status medicamentosus, *Dis Nerv Syst, 28*:318-322, 1967.

Chapter 7

EMOTIONAL ASPECTS OF HOSPITALIZATION OF A CHILD FOR STRABISMUS SURGERY*

LEONARD APT, M.D., MORRIS C. BECKWITT, M.D.
AND SHERWIN ISENBERG, M.D.

SIR WILLIAM OSLER, a brilliant clinician and teacher in the early part of this century, used to stress the importance of understanding the patient as a human being as well as establishing the correct diagnosis of his disease. This clinical maxim is especially important if the patient is a young child, because the young child can be easily frightened and traumatized.

Eye muscle surgery is performed frequently on children between the ages of two and six years. The trend is to correct an eye muscle imbalance early in life to help vision and binocular reflexes develop properly. To establish or reeducate binocular reflexes after the age of six or seven years is difficult, or unlikely, because maturation of the visual pathways and fusion capabilities probably have been completed. In the young child strabismus surgery may also be done for cosmetic reasons to avoid the cruel teasing of hostile peers once he enters school. The suffering experienced by these children and its effect on the development of their personalities have been observed and reported (1, 2, 3, 4). Correction of an obvious misalignment of the eyes for cosmetic reasons is also helpful to the mother, as she is usually sensitive to her infant's unattractive appearance. In other words, early corrective surgery when indicated removes a psychologic burden from both mother and child.

Although it is important to correct the child's strabismus early in life, for functional, cosmetic, and psychologic reasons,

*This article is reprinted with the permission from the *Annals of Ophthalmology*, *Volume* 6, No. 1, January 1974.

the ophthalmic surgeon must be aware that the young patient is sensitive and emotionally vulnerable to the effects of hospitalization and surgery, particularly of eye surgery. More specifically, there is considerable evidence that in some vulnerable children emotional stress from fear of injury and abandonment can precipitate or aggravate the strabismus. How to minimize for the child the inevitable emotional stress of hospitalization and how to protect him from undesirable consequences of the eye operation, becomes a challenging and delicate task for the ophthalmologist and the child psychiatrist.

EFFECTS OF HOSPITALIZATION AND SURGERY IN GENERAL

Many publications in the past few decades have reflected the rising interest in the psychologic responses of children to hospitalization and surgery. A critical review by Vernon and co-workers (5) of the literature dealing with the problem of the hospitalized child lists over 225 published and unpublished references, representing the collaborative efforts of pediatricians, psychiatrists, and psychologists. These authors attempted to assess the various causes of disturbances in hospitalized children and suggested procedures to minimize or prevent them. The following basic ideas are repeatedly stressed in their studies: (1) The young child who is dependent on his mother for security is vulnerable and easily upset when separated from her, especially when he is exposed to painful, frightening experiences in the strange environment of the hospital. (2) The younger the child, the more vulnerable he is to separation from home and mother and the less capable he is of adapting to the stress of hospitalization and surgery. (3) The child's security and his ability to endure the stress of hospitalization and surgery depends upon confidence and trust in both his mother and his doctor. (4) The doctor must establish and maintain such a relationship with the child and with the child's parents, especially the mother, in order to sustain a sense of security in her that she can transmit to her child. (5) A truthful, age-appropriate explanation to an older child of what he may expect in the hospital, an opportunity for him to ask questions, a friendly hospital atmosphere and, above all, frequent or continuous pre- and postoperative contact with the mother, can reduce the child's anxiety and speed his recovery.

Not until about six months of age does the infant begin to develop cathexis specifically toward the mother. From six months of age onward the child's main anxiety is "separation anxiety" because of its great dependence on its mother. In addition, the problems of the four- and five-year-old child are dominated by the sexual and aggressive fantasies of the oedipal phase of maturation and development. Hospitalization and surgery during the child's oedipal phase development is likely to arouse the age-specific fears of sexual mutilation (castration anxiety), sexual transmutation, and — in girls — impregnation. The fantasy world of children four to six years of age is populated by cruel giants, wicked witches, suffering Cinderellas, and frightened giant killers. If the surgeon is to avoid becoming the punitive giant or dangerous rapist of the oedipal child's fantasy life he must learn how to deal with a child of this age.

In a book *The Hospitalized Child and His Family* by a group of physicians at Children's Medical and Surgical Center of The Johns Hopkins Hospital, the authors repeated some of the previously mentioned themes (6). They also stressed the need for physicians and hospital personnel to regard the hospitalized child as a sensitive person and not merely as a subject of diagnosis, surgery, or other treatment. They emphasized the need to see each child in terms of his past history, social environment, and as a product of a home to which he will have to return after he leaves the hospital. Because they believed so strongly that family centered pediatric care was a valid medical concept of proven effectiveness, they attempted to utilize the hospitalized child's mother, whenever possible, in the nursing care of her child, by providing "living-in" facilities.

Robertson and Robertson (7) showed the stresses a "live-in" mother would prevent, when they studied the reactions of children between the ages of 1.5 and 2.5 years of age to separation from their mother. They found some of the stress factors to be the strange environment, inadequate substitute caretaker, strange caretaker, multiple caretakers, lack of understanding of cues and language, unfamiliar food and routines, and unusual demands on discipline.

Dombro (8) reported that in 1966 only 28 of 5550 general hospitals surveyed in the United States provided facilities for parents to spend the night with their sick children. Although a "live-in" mother helps bring a home environment to shelter the child, the hospital still acts as a foreign environment to stress the child. Dombro suggested a new professional person to work as an ombudsman to coordinate activities of the child's hospital stay, when the stay is not brief. This person would keep contact with parents and familiarize the child with the hospital while being responsible for his developmental and psychological needs.

Of the many studies reviewed and summarized in the literature, the one by Jessner and co-workers (9) of 143 children hospitalized for tonsillectomies is perhaps the most relevant to our present interests concerning the pediatric eye patient. Their study is relevant because of the similarity in the ages of the children and the brief period of hospitalization involved, even though the surgery is different. In general, they found a tonsillectomy to be a stressful experience for each child. It activated the deepest universal childhood fears of abandonment, mutilation, and death. Fear of abandonment was particularly acute in children of two to four years of age, while the hospitalized four- to six-year-old children were dominated by fears of mutilation, sexual transformation, or impregnation. The latter fear was prevalent especially in the girls whose mothers had recently given birth to babies in the hospital.

Without some awareness and understanding of these age-specific psychodynamic fantasies which are typical for the oedipal phase of the child development, some of the bizarre symptoms referable to the "tummy" or genitalia, which may appear during the time when the throat is still sore from the tonsillectomy, are quite incomprehensible.

Jessner and co-workers found that 20 percent of the children reacted severely to the surgery. These children, in addition to crying excessively, suffered disturbances in eating and sleeping and developed regressive symptoms of bed-wetting and bed-soiling, which lasted many months. The children who reacted so severely were easily recognized preoperatively as insecure and emotionally unstable, as were their mothers.

The importance of minimizing the hospitalized child's anxiety has recently aroused new and heightened interest in physicians who do open-heart surgery on children. Reinhart (10) found that children with low or average anxiety have half the mortality rate of the very anxious. He suggested the "employment of people who would pay attention especially to the psychological adaptation of the child" in order to reduce mortality and morbidity.

REACTION OF CHILDREN TO HOSPITALIZATION FOR STRABISMUS SURGERY

A few systematic studies deal specifically with the emotional aspects of the strabismic child hospitalized for eye muscle surgery.

Lipton (4) pointed out that once a child has a heterotropia, additional psychological factors enter into the child's development. The mother is concerned not only about the child's vision and well-being but also about the reactions of others. She worries that others may think her child different and perhaps stupid and damaged. The eye examinations remind her of the defect and revive negative feelings, guilt, and anxieties. Frequently, a young child becomes aware that others think of him as defective and repulsive; eventually he believes this himself and adopts as his own an opinion of low self-esteem. As a result he develops a distorted view of the world. These factors are additions to the emotional state felt by any child who is hospitalized and about to undergo surgery.

Pinkerton (11) wrote about the prevention of emotional sequelae in young British children following operation for squint and found that children from one to four years of age were fearful and insecure if both eyes were bandaged. Occasionally they suffered from nocturnal enuresis, frequent nightmares, aggressive conduct, or perhaps excessive nervousness. The onset of these reactions was traced to the hospitalization.

Vaughan (12), a British psychiatrist, reported on his observations of forty strabismic children from two to nine years of age, as part of a larger study of the effects of surgery in children. He divided the forty children into two evenly matched groups. The control group was treated in the usual manner, while the experimental group had the benefit of more frequent parental visits and three friendly ten- to fifteen-minute interviews with the psychiatrist. The first visit by the psychiatrist to establish contact was unhurried and unobtrusive and took place soon after admission. The children were encouraged to talk freely and to ask questions, which were answered briefly and truthfully. They were told what to expect in the hospital, when their parents would visit them, and when they would leave the hospital. On the third hospital day and on the fifth (their last) they were again visited by the unobtrusively friendly psychiatrist.

Vaughan found that in the control group of forty children, eight were disturbed while on the ward, thirteen at the end of the week and eleven at the end of six months. In the experimental group that received extra attention from the parents and psychiatrist, eleven were disturbed on the ward, six (i.e. seven less) were disturbed after one week, and only three (i.e. nine less) were disturbed at the end of six months. Four-year-olds and older benefitted most from the discussions and explanations.

Vaughan was impressed by the high rate of overanxious children in the strabismic group as well as by the high number of emotionally unstable parents, especially mothers. Nine of the forty parents — mostly mothers — who brought the children to the hospital gave them no explanation or advice. Four told deliberate lies to avoid upsetting them. Some of the children expressed fearful expectations of mutilation and eye enucleation. Vaughan concluded that one should "talk to the child in terms he can understand and allow him adequate opportunity to express his feelings. Ideally, this person should almost certainly be one of the parents."

A series of articles by British authors (13, 14, 15) dealing with emotional aspects of the strabismus patient during hospitalization, have prompted changes in British hospital routine. Mothers of children under five years old have been encouraged to "live in" with them in the hospital to prevent the severe distress and serious consequences of separation anxiety. The hospital stay of children undergoing strabismus surgery has been reduced from fourteen to five days or less. Because the British ophthalmic surgeon often has had insufficient opportunity to establish a close personal relationship with the child and his parents, the orthoptist, who is welcomed by the child as a known and trusted friend from outpatient visits, has continued as a stabilizing influence while the child is hospitalized. Some large private houses have been converted into small hospitals and equipped fully for eye surgery. The appearance of the building and the friendly informal atmosphere of a playroom, garden, family-like dining room and sitting room help put the apprehensive child at ease. Patients' eyes generally have not been bandaged postoperatively and never bilaterally.

Roper-Hall (16) sent out questionnaires to 178 parents to assess the effect of the above mentioned changes in British hospital management of the surgical strabismic children and found that nearly all parents wrote encouraging comments in support of the changed methods.

A pilot study by Steele and Apt (17) at the Jules Stein Eye Institute of the UCLA Medical Center to study anxiety in children undergoing eye muscle surgery, emphasized the importance of the mother-child relationship as the most essential variable and the one most difficult to control. Psychologic preparation of mother and child, instruction on what to expect in the hospital, and maintenance of a friendly hospital atmosphere were found to be helpful but of secondary importance compared to the basic parent-child relationship. They suggested that "further search be directed towards finding the most effective way of assisting mothers and children to deal with their anxiety-laden fantasies regarding eye surgery."

PRACTICAL RECOMMENDATIONS FOR MINIMIZING EMOTIONAL STRESS OF HOSPITALIZATION AND SURGERY

An understanding of the emotional difficulties and psychological risks involved in pediatric eye muscle surgery helps us to avoid them.

Since the foundation of the child's security is his parents, especially the mother, the foremost task of the surgeon contemplating surgery is to establish and to maintain trustworthy relations with the child's parents. Primarily this preparation consists of quelling the parents' anxieties. The ophthalmologist should take time to answer questions posed by parents and older children. Following are typical questions and our representative answers:

Question: Is this a serious operation?

Answer: Any operation is serious, particularly when a general anesthetic is used. Eye muscle operations are common procedures and usually are successful. Since we are dealing with humans and not mechanical factors more than one operation may be needed to ultimately bring the eye into good position. The risk with a general anesthetic in eye muscle operations at present is extremely low.

Q. Will there be much pain?

A. No, very little pain is involved. Drugs to relieve pain will be given after the operation if needed.

Q. Will my child be awake when he goes to the operating room?

A. Sedation will be given to reduce fear and anxiety, if necessary, on the day before surgery, but definitely, on the morning of surgery when he leaves the room for the operating theater.

Q. Will the eyes be bandaged after the operation?

A. Since bandaging both eyes simultaneously often increases fear, anger, and guilt, as well as a child's belief that he is being punished, one or both eyes will be unbandaged so that he can see.

Q. Will his vision be affected by the operation?

A. No, because eye muscle surgery is performed on the surface of the eyeball. The inside of the eye is not disturbed, so vision is not affected.

Q. Do you have to remove the eyes to perform the muscle operation?

A. No, the eye itself is not removed since the muscles are on the surface of the eyeball and are easily accessible to the surgeon.

Q. Will the sutures have to be removed?

A. The sutures are absorbable, and won't have to be removed.

Q. Will there be a scar?

A. There is usually little or no scar on the "white part" of the eye overlying the muscle location. No incision in the skin of the eyelids is needed to expose these muscles.

Q. Will there be many "needles" (injections)?

A. Most of the medications will be given by mouth or by rectum. Only one injection (e.g. Demerol® and atropine or scopolamine) is given one to two hours before operation because the stomach must be empty.

Q. How soon will our child be able to return to school?

A. The hospitalization is short (usually two days) and so is the convalescence (one to two weeks). The child usually is back to school in seven to ten days with full activity permitted in two weeks.

Q. Can I sleep in the hospital with my child?

A. Yes, we encourage one parent to "live in" with the preschool-age child in the hospital room. For the older child who may not wish the parent to "live in", unlimited visiting privileges are extended to the parent.

AGE-SPECIFIC RECOMMENDATIONS FOR THE HOSPITALIZED STRABISMUS PATIENT

From a few psychological aspects it is advantageous to operate on a child before six months of age. First, the aforementioned undesirable emotions of the parents and the child are not given time to develop. Second, since this period occurs before the child is able to recognize the mother as an individual, the cathexis is still transferable to a nurse or other hospital figure, and "separation anxiety" is avoided. Third, to help vision and binocular reflexes develop properly, the earlier the well-considered surgery, the better.

In dealing with the preschool child a cardinal principle is that the parents feelings will be mirrored in the child. Separation anxiety can be reduced by a close doctor-parent-patient relationship. The parent should be instructed to talk to the child in a pleasant, casual and positive manner a week before the operation, avoid details and explicitness, and say in effect, "The good doctor will fix your eyes next week and Mommy will be with you. There will be toys and other nice things there."

To prepare the child for the strange environment of the hospital, the mother can tell him a story about a little boy who went to the hospital. This story could be repeated several times adding different details to the adventurous trip, while repeating others for emphasis. The story should tell about his sleeping in a new bed, having his temperature taken by a nurse, and having doctors come to see him and to give him special medicine for his eyes. Depending on the skill and resourcefulness of the mother, the subject of going to the hospital also can be made into a game in which the child takes turns playing the roles of patient, doctor, or nurse doing physical examinations or in giving or taking medicine. He can help his mother pack and unpack his pajamas, his favorite toy, and his suit for going to the hospital, as well as for returning home from the hospital. He can be told that when he returns home he'll be welcomed by relatives and friends, who will be glad to see him, to love him, and to bring him presents.

The four- to six-year-old child in the oedipal phase of development needs more care in preparation for eye surgery. If possible, his ideas, attitudes, and fantasies should be ascertained, and taken into consideration. It is most important therefore for the doctor to gain and to maintain the child's trust and confidence. Does he believe his eye problem is due to his misbehavior? Is it a punishment for sexual curiosity? Will the doctor take out his eye? Children are often anxious about their condition but hesitate to ask about it. Fantasies and fears can be dissipated if a child is encouraged to talk, to ask questions, and to verbalize his fears. Brief, truthful explanations should be given in a positive and friendly manner. Again, the most important source of the child's security or anxiety is his parents, as well as those who function as his parents in their absence.

The parents' attitudes and fantasies about their child's eye condition and eye surgery also play a significant role before, during, and after the surgery. Their attitudes may also need clarification and reassurance.

A good approach for the physician to use in discussing hospitalization and operation with the patient is to talk directly to the parent while the child sits in the room. In this way, the child tangentially receives the needed information, but the parents receive whatever emotional trauma is involved. The ophthalmologist speaks directly to the child only when the child asks questions. By the end of the discussion, however, the child should be given the opportunity to ask questions.

If the level of anxiety in the child and the parents is high and not easily relieved, surgery might be postponed till the child is older and the family situation calmer. This is especially true if there has been hospitalization for serious illness, or a recent death in the family. Psychotherapy, if available, may be helpful for the parent and the child. The child of seven years of age and older has probably had strabismus for a number of years. He may have a history of several previous eye operations which has left him fearful and skeptical about further surgery. Since there is little likelihood of significant further visual maturation and development and no medical urgency, the surgery should be made more optional and more of the child's voluntary participation sought. It is all the more important, therefore, to establish good relations with the child and to win his cooperation and confidence on the basis of open and honest discussion of the advantages, risks, and emotional problems involved.

SUMMARY

While any hospitalization and operation is traumatic to child and parent, strabismus surgery, in particular, increases the stress. It is of prime importance to recognize that the level of anxiety in the child is proportional to the level of anxiety in the parent. The physician, therefore, should make a conscious effort to reduce the anxiety of the parents during the treatment of the child. To minimize the separation anxiety prevalent in preschool children, the mother should be encouraged to "live in" with the child during hospitalization and the stay should be kept as brief as possible. In the older patient, anxiety is reduced by an open discussion with parents and child of the impending hospitalization and surgery. In addition, intelligent use of sedation and analgesia, avoidance of simultaneously bandaging both eyes, minimization of injections, and the use of absorbable sutures have all been proven in recent years to reduce stress and anxiety in both parent and child.

REFERENCES

1. Gailey, W.: The cross-eyed child: A social as well as a medical problem, *New Orleans Med Surg J, 101*:398, 1949.
2. Hartman, E.: The effect of strabismus on the psychology of the child, *Ann Ocul, 189*:65, 1956.
3. Stromberg, A. E.: The psychology of the squinter, *Am J Ophthalmol, 30*:601, 1947.
4. Lipton, E. L.: Remarks on the psychological aspects of strabismus, *Sight Sav Rev, 41*:3, 1971.
5. Vernon, D. T., Foley, J. M., Sidowicz, R. R., and Schulman, J. L.: *The Psychological Responses of Children to Hospitalization and Illness,* Thomas, Springfield, 1965.
6. Haller, J. A., Talbert, J. L., and Dombro, R. H.: *The Hospitalized Child and His Family.* Johns Hopkins, Baltimore, 1967.
7. Robertson, J. and Robertson, J.: Young children in brief separation: A fresh look, *Psychoanal Study Child, 21*:264, 1971.
8. Dombro, R. H.: The surgically ill child and his family, *Surg Clin North Am, 50*:759, 1970.
9. Jessner, L., Blone, G. E., and Waltfogel, S.: Emotional implications of tonsillectomy and adenoidectomy on children, *Psychoanal Study Child, 7*:126, 1952.
10. Reinhart, J. B.: Measurement and management of anxiety of children undergoing open heart surgery, *Pediatrics (Aud Dig) 16*:22, 1970.
11. Pinkerton, P.: Prevention of emotional sequelae in young children during operation for strabismus, *Br Orthopt J, 13*:18, 1956.
12. Vaughan, G. F.: Children in hospital, *Lancet, 1*:117, 1957.
13. Billinghurst, L.: Observations on the psychological aspect of early surgery for squint, *Br Orthopt J, 12*:89, 1955.
14. Illingsworth, R. S.: Reaction of young children to admission to the hospital, *Br Orthopt J, 13*:14, 1956.
15. Ditcham, H., and Finch, S.: Further observations on the hospitalization of children with strabismus, *Br Orthopt J, 14*:97, 1957.
16. Roper-Hall, G.: Reaction of children to hospitalization for strabismus

surgery, *Br Orthopt J, 27*:100, 1970.
17. Steele, A., and Apt, L.: A methodological approach to measuring anxiety in children requiring eye surgery. Unpublished. University of California, Los Angeles, 1966. Research project.

Chapter 8

PSYCHIATRIC EXPERIENCES ASSOCIATED WITH EYE SURGERY AND TRAUMA REQUIRING PATCHING

JARVIN HEIMAN, M.D.

INTRODUCTION

THIS chapter deals with and explores a variety of disturbances (emotional, cognitive, and behavioral) which accompany ophthalmic conditions in which patching and immobilization occur. These disturbances are manifested most commonly after cataract extraction and during the treatment of retinal detachment, but have also been reported with trauma and other rare conditions. The focus is on clinical manifestations, etiological considerations, and treatment implications (both preventive and corrective).

HISTORICAL PERSPECTIVE

It is now well-documented that surgery or injury to the eye gives rise to a higher incidence of behavioral or emotional disorders than does surgery in other areas. Psychotic behavior, often referred to as delirium, has been described as occurring with cataract extraction, retinal detachment, and other forms of eye surgery and trauma, and has been reported in literature dating back to the late nineteenth century. The symptoms discussed covered a wide range. Restlessness, irritability, and insomnia were the milder manifestations. Frequently cases progressed to more flagrant psychotic behavior, often described as delirium, but including disorientation, extreme hyperactivity, auditory and visual hallucinations, persecutory delusions, uncontrollable behavior, and panic.

In the early literature of case reports and surveys, the frequency of symptoms was usually small, often 3 percent or less. The earlier reports usually described the most flagrant and obvious psychotic symptomatology. The tendency, as the syndrome has become better established, has been to include the more subtle and milder forms of symptoms. Also, in recent reports and studies, methods of detection have been refined. Because of these latter considerations, the studies done in recent years have reported a much higher incidence — 100 percent in some cases of retinal detachment.

The literature of the past two decades has attempted to go beyond case reports and to investigate these phenomena as to the etiology, prevention, and treatment. In addition to case reports and analyses of case studies, information and ideas evolving from other branches of medicine and psychiatry are pertinent to an understanding of these phenomena. Of major importance has been the growing body of knowledge accumulated in recent years concerning sensory deprivation and associated psychiatric sequelae. Reference is made to those areas in the section on etiology.

CLINICAL SYMPTOMS

The bulk of the studies and reports deal with cataract patients, with detached retina patients comprising a relatively small group. The average age of the cataract patient is about sixty. Detached retina can occur at any age, but the average patient tends to be younger, about fifty. Cataracts develop insidiously, and the patient usually undergoes treatment after a long period of a gradual reduced sensorium. Retinal detachment is an acute condition, and treatment requires a longer period of hospitalization. Although the cataract patient may be bilaterally patched, usually just the involved eye is covered, and this is done postsurgically. The patient with a retinal detachment is immobilized immediately and bilaterally patched for a period of time both pre- and postoperatively. As a result his movements are much more restricted than those of the cataract patient.

The initial psychiatric symptoms usually consist of anxiety and restlessness, manifested in varying degrees. Although these may be present upon admission to the hospital, most often the symptoms begin a few hours postsurgically. In some instances, however, their onset may be delayed for several days, and on rare occasions may not appear until after the patient's discharge from the hospital. The symptoms may persist for only a few minutes, or they may continue for several hours, days, or even months, necessitating extensive and prolonged psychiatric care.

The usual psychiatric course may progress from varying degrees of anxiety and restlessness to a state of irritability, agitation, suspiciousness, hyperactivity and disorientation. Some patients may go to great lengths to conceal their experiences, and offer instead a variety of hypochondriacal and somatic complaints. In some cases, more severe symptoms such as panic, illusions, delusions, and hallucinations (visual or auditory) may be present. Behavioral manifestations range from mild restlessness to hyperactivity and extreme agitations. The patient may leave his bed, may try to remove the patches from his eyes, and even attempt suicide by leaping from the hospital window.

In order to demonstrate the variety and kind of cases in which these experiences occur, the following clinical examples are presented.

Case 1

The patient, a seventy-two-year-old Caucasian woman, was admitted for surgery of a cataract in the right eye. There was a mild cataract in the left eye, but no immediate treatment was contemplated for this condition. The patient's background, both personal and medical, previous to her hospitalization was unremarkable. She was the mother of six children, several of whom lived in the immediate area and were professionally quite successful. Her husband, seventy-five years old, was retired and the couple was financially comfortable. The patient, from all evidence, was both emotionally and physically healthy.

There was no history of mental illness, alcoholism, or drug abuse.

At the time of admission the patient denied any anxiety about the surgery, and expressed "absolute trust in the doctor". There is evidence that she did not comprehend adequately the explanation regarding the anesthesia, which was done by local block. The first attempt was unsuccessful and had to be repeated; at this time the patient did exhibit some anxiety. Otherwise, the operative routine was uneventful. The patient was patched bilaterally immediately following surgery.

During the first twelve hours of the postoperative period, the patient's recovery was unremarkable. During the next twelve hours, she was observed "mumbling" to herself. Twenty-four hours postoperatively she was found walking about in her room, obviously disoriented. It was at this time that a psychiatric consultation was requested.

When seen by the psychiatrist, the patient was having auditory hallucinations. She stated that she was talking to her son (who lived several hundred miles away), and that she had spoken with God. Her thought processes exhibited loose associations, and she tended to "babble". The first step taken by the psychiatrist was to remove the patch from the left eye for a brief period (about fifteen minutes), so that the patient could observe him as they talked. At the end of his visit, the eye was re-patched. His subsequent visits numbered three to four a day, and were each of a duration of about fifteen minutes. During their conversations the psychiatrist employed increased tactile stimulation through touching her hand and arm. The patient also was placed on Stelazine® 2 mg daily.

Recommendations were made to increase sensory stimulation through channels other than sight. The husband visited frequently and brought flowers to the patient for olfactory stimulation. Visits by other family members and by the nursing staff provided additional auditory and tactile stimulation. Within twenty-four hours the patient had stopped hallucinating, and within thirty-six hours her trend of thought was coherent. There was no further looseness of associations. Five days following surgery, the patches on both eyes were removed. At that time she was free of any evidence of emotional distress, and there has been no recurrence of her psychosis.

Case 2

The following is a case in which trauma to both eyes necessitated emergency hospitalization, patching bilaterally, and surgery.

The patient was a forty-four-year-old man, employed as the business manager of a thriving law firm. He had been in good health all of his life, and although his wife described him as "temperamental", he had no discernible emotional problems previous to hospitalization. There was a history of mild to moderate drinking, primarily with business contacts.

The patient was injured in an automobile accident following dinner at a restaurant with his wife and a client. He hit his head across the steering column of the car which he was driving and suffered severe intraocular and intraorbital bleeding with clotting. The optic nerve was injured bilaterally. He was taken to a local emergency room where he was told that he needed surgery, but that his sight was unimpaired. Shortly after, the patient lapsed into unconsciousness and was transferred to a large medical center. At surgery bilateral orbital decompression was performed in an attempt to save his vision, and a repair of bilaterally ruptured globes was made. It was found that he had fractures of the nasal bones and both zygomatic arches. Although he exhibited severe trauma to the whole upper face, there was no evidence of any other neurological or intracranial involvement. Postsurgically, packs were placed in both nostrils and both eyes were patched.

When the patient awakened from the anesthesia, he was told that he was permanently blind. He became alarmed and agitated, and subsequently confused and disoriented. He became hyperactive, wandered around the room and demanded that someone be present in the room with him.

He began hallucinating (auditory and olfactory), and he became rapidly paranoid, with delusions that the doctors had blinded him and that his wife was going out with another man.

Twenty-four hours after surgery a psychiatric consultation was requested.

The psychiatrist found him crouching in one corner of the room, rocking, incoherent, and shredding the sheets from his bed. The patient was immediately placed on Stelazine 15 mg bid, and Thorazine® 50 mg tid and 100 mg at bedtime. He calmed quickly with the medication and the Thorazine was discontinued the following day, except at bedtime. Three days after the initial consultation he no longer was hallucinating, and after another two days he was no longer paranoid or delusional. He remained moderately depressed and expressed concerns that he might lose his wife and children because of his blindness.

Treatment consisted essentially of chemotherapy as described, and of reality-oriented psychotherapy, with the psychiatrist visiting the patient three or four times a day for brief periods of time. The patient's wife remained with him as much as possible, and there were frequent visits from business associates. He was assured that his position with the law firm remained secure, and that the firm would "hire eyes" for him when he returned to work. A representative of the Braille Institute began work with the patient while he was still hospitalized, and the hospital staff encouraged him to do as much for himself as possible. He was urged to listen to the radio to provide additional stimulation and to help him with his loss of time sense. As the depression abated, medication was gradually discontinued, and at the time of his discharge (three weeks from time of admission) he was receiving no drugs. Psychiatric follow-up on an outpatient basis was recommended for the moderate depression which remained. One month following his hospital discharge, he was working successfully once more, and adjusting to his loss of vision, both on the job and at home.

Case 3

A rather unusual case is that of a twenty-nine-year-old married man who suffered a left retinal detachment. He was immobilized, bilaterally patched, and hospitalized for approximately six weeks. At the end of his second week of hospitalization, he underwent surgery with excellent results. Patching was continued until three weeks postsurgery, at which time he was changed to pinhole glasses. He continued to wear pinhole glasses for approximately six weeks subsequent to his discharge from the hospital.

Previous to his injury the patient was described as distant, aloof, and passive, with a tendency toward moodiness and withdrawal. He had a long history of multiple physical complaints, such as epigastric discomfort, irritable colon, and anxiety symptoms. He was bright intellectually, and at the time of his injury was a graduate student in English.

During his hospitalization the patient was compliant and cooperative. Other than complaints relative to some epigastric distress and constipation, nothing unusual was noted. However, following his discharge from the hospital his wife described "strange behavior" on his part. He was irritable, described his home as changed, and became increasingly distant from his family. He became depressed and anxious, lost his appetite, developed severe insomnia, began having nightmares, confusion, and feelings of unreality. His depression intensified to the point of his considering suicide, at which time he was hospitalized on a psychiatric unit.

The patient was hospitalized for a period of thirty days. He responded well to the ward milieu, reality-oriented psychotherapy, and Phenothiazines (Chlorpromazine 25 mg qid). The use of the pinhole glasses was gradually discontinued. By the time of discharge from the hospital the patient had emotionally reconstituted to his premorbid personality state prior to his injury. His wife was also seen in psychotherapy, and both of them continued in psychiatric treatment after his discharge from the hospital.

This case is unique in terms of the long delay in the onset of the psychosis. The patient was clinically psychotic following his discharge from the medical unit until his admission to the psychiatric ward. He was a man with a great need to be taken care of, and this need was gratified while in the medical unit

when he had a rather intense involvement with a very nur-
turing young woman nurse's aide who spent a great deal of
time with him. In addition, he had a remarkable capacity to
conceal his pathology by his remoteness and general compulsive control which he was able to exercise over his feelings.

Although this case demonstrates a delayed onset psychosis, it
is important to stress and realize that it is not unusual for
patients to be able to mask or hide their symptoms. Patients
often are frightened by their experiences, may feel ashamed,
and may go to great lengths to mask or conceal what is happening. Obviously, the behavioral manifestations are those that
would be most obvious to observers.

ETIOLOGICAL CONSIDERATIONS

Causative or contributing factors to the syndrome under consideration have been multiple. Case reports often include the
author's speculations regarding etiology. Many of the case reports concerned cataract patients. Inasmuch as cataract tends to
be a disease of the older age group, it was felt that old age was a
highly significant factor. The psychotic episode was considered
as primarily related to underlying physical disease, senility, or
arteriosclerotic cerebrovascular disease. Some authors actually
referred to the syndrome as a senile psychosis. Alcoholism in
the background of the patient was considered highly significant, as well as other disease predisposing to organic brain
syndrome. The role of drugs (pre- and postoperatively) has
been felt to be of significance as a contributing factor. It is well
known that many of the hypnotics and sedatives can trigger a
delirious state or organic brain syndrome. This is particularly
so in patients with underlying physical disease, such as impaired liver and renal function, and in the older age group with
arteriosclerotic cerebrovascular changes.

The fact that these same experiences occur in younger patients patched for retinal detachment is a factor against age and
senile psychosis. It is thus evident that there are other factors
which must be taken into consideration. The premorbid personality and previous psychopathology of the patient, in which

there is a predisposition to regression under stress, has been felt to be of some significance. The stresses involved in these cases consist of the nature of the injury, loss of familiar surroundings, entry into the hospital with its associated anxieties, and fantasies concerning the outcome of the surgical procedure, with the possibility of loss of vision.

Perhaps the most significant and important factor to be taken into consideration, and one that has been increasingly appreciated in recent years, is the impact of the sensory deprivation. Perhaps in no other medical or surgical condition does the phenomenon of sensory deprivation occur to the degree that exists in the cases under discussion. First and foremost, by virtue of the disease process as well as the patching, these patients are deprived of one of the most important sensory modalities: their vision. They are also deprived proprioceptively by virtue of the immobilization involved. In older patients there may be a concomitant hearing loss which, in and of itself, contributes to a reduced sensory input. Other, perhaps less significant, forms of sensory deprivation include removal from familiar surroundings and people, and the potential for social isolation of the patient. This occurs with placement in single rooms, failure to provide the patient with adequate social stimuli, such as the presence of other patients, adequate staff contact, and in particular the establishment of a strong doctor-patient rapport.

A growing body of literature, particularly in the recent decade, has studied intensively the whole phenomenon of sensory deprivation and demonstrated beyond any doubt the occurrence of psychiatric sequelae and psychotic experiences after a period of total sensory deprivation. Of particular interest is a recent report which shows that many of the sensory deprivation phenomenon and experiences can be produced by visual deprivation alone (16). The other sensory modalities may not play as significant a role in the production of the symptoms. This has obvious special significance in the kind of patients under consideration inasmuch as the primary deprivation is visual. In recent years the case reports and studies on the syndrome under consideration in this chapter have tended to fall into two groups. There are those who feel that sensory deprivation plays a minor role; but the bulk of the studies and researchers feel that this is of the utmost and perhaps predominant significance.

PREVENTION AND TREATMENT

Prevention

Aside from the disturbing nature to both patient and staff, as well as the potential for more serious psychiatric sequelae (including suicide and prolonged psychiatric morbidity), the occurrence of the syndrome under consideration is associated with a higher incidence of postoperative complications. Obviously, the most important approach is to take whatever steps are indicated and necessary to prevent the onset of this condition. Once the decision is made to hospitalize the patient, it is most important to help alleviate anxiety about entry into the hospital and the anticipation of the upcoming procedures. A rapid introduction of the patient to a variety of contacts with the hospital staff and an adequate preparation of the patient for the procedures to follow should be an integral part of the admission procedure.

Weisman and Hackett (14) stress in their particular approach that this syndrome occurs most frequently in patients who are particularly predisposed to impaired ego functions and reality testing. Ego functions describe those facets of personality that are involved in perception, concept formation, judgment, decisions, and specifically the capacity to test inner and outer reality. Reality testing as an ego function describes the patient's capacity to evaluate the context of various levels of experience. They see the condition as a faulty adaptation to the psychic stress of visual deprivation and loss of familiar perceptual cues.

The possibility of obtaining early clues and perhaps screening procedures in order to anticipiate what patients may be prone to the development of this syndrome is somewhat hypothetical at this point. The state of the patient's physical health, both past and present, will give some information as to certain patients who might more likely run into difficulty. Such factors as age, arteriosclerotic cerebrovascular disease, impaired liver and renal function, and a history of alcoholism are specific examples. We know that older patients and patients who have had a history of previous delirium or other psychopathology are likely to have a higher propensity for regression under stress, and should definitely be considered as candidates for this syndrome.

Weisman and Hackett stress that a specific type of staff-patient relationship may be used to compensate for the deficit in reality testing, and thus relieve or prevent "delirium". The assignment of not only the doctor, but also consistent nursing personnel to work with the patient throughout his hospitalization, is a most desirable factor in aiding these patients in maintaining consistent reality testing. Careful preparation of the patient would include not only the presence and frequent contact of consistent personnel, but frequent reassurance, providing and encouraging free and open communication of fears and anxieties, careful explanation of procedures, what to expect, including the possibility of unusual experiences.

Ellis et al. (4) have described from a nursing point of view some of the techniques in approaching these patients. An awareness of the tendency of many patients to conceal unusual inner experiences should alert doctors and nurses to the possibility of their occurrence when the patient too freely volunteers "how well" things are going. In their study they showed that self-disclosure was significantly facilitated when the patients were told that other patients had had such experiences and wondered about them. The opportunity to talk about his experiences, to be reassured that they are not unusual under these circumstances, that they are usually transitory, is often a great relief to these patients. It is best to acknowledge that persons under the circumstances of eye surgery and patching may have unusual sensory experiences and that these experiences are not abnormal.

All steps that are taken to reduce the sensory deprivation variables should be a part of the prevention of this syndrome.

Certainly the rapid establishment of a nurse-patient and doctor-patient consistent rapport will help obviate this factor. All steps directed toward reducing the social isolation of the patient, such as the placement of the patients in wards rather than single rooms, frequent staff contacts, and the allowing and encouragement of family members to be present, as well as the encouragement of the patient bringing familiar belongings to the hospital, will help reorient, and provide perceptual cues that enhance reality testing.

The patients under consideration are those who are patched pre- and postsurgically, and some discussion of the patching process is in order. The origin and rationale of patching has been buried in the literature and tradition of ophthalmology dating back to the Middle Ages. Over the years it has become part of a standard procedure used to protect the eyes and "immobilize" eye movements in order to reduce complications. Patching has become commonplace and its continued use has been unquestioned. The implications of patching are manifold. First and foremost, it is an instrument of sensory deprivation, and inasmuch as a growing body of evidence indicates that it plays a significant role in the precipitation of the syndrome under consideration, the question arises as to the validity and necessity of the use of patches. This is a point made by Adams and Pearlman (1) and with which the author concurs. In other words, is the patching necessary, and in fact does the use of patching defeat the purpose for which it is used, namely, increase rather than decrease the incidence of postoperative complications.

This author is of the opinion that sensory deprivation factors are the primary elements in precipitating the syndrome in patients with a propensity for impaired reality testing, and that the whole rationale for patching needs to be seriously questioned and more thoroughly researched.

Another factor of unknown but suspected significance that pertains to the rationale of patching will now be mentioned. This is the occurrence of REM (Rapid-Eye-Movement) sleep that has become established knowledge arising out of research over the past two decades. It has been proven that during sleep there is a cyclic recurrence of rapid eye movements, approximately every ninety minutes, for varying durations of time, usually up to twenty to thirty minutes. This area is unresearched as regards ophthalmology patients, and particularly patched patients. The question arises, do patched patients have any higher incidence of REM sleep? REM sleep occurs independent of patching, and the eye movements involved can be quite vigorous. Another area of consideration, aside from the patching but involving the REM process, is the possibility of decreasing the REM periods as part of the process of immobilizing the eyes. Certain hypnotics, sedatives, and tranquilizers are effective REM suppressants, and may be of definite value in reducing eye motility, an advantage in reducing postoperative complications. This is an area that will have to await further research.

The discriminate use of drugs is another factor involved in prevention of the syndrome. It is well known that many of the hypnotics and sedatives in use are quite capable of precipitating a toxic psychosis or organic brain syndrome, particularly in predisposed patients such as those with arteriosclerotic cerebrovascular disease. This is partially related to the tendency of these drugs to reduce the patient's capacity to test reality, to receive perceptual cues necessary for orientation in reality testing. Weisman and Hackett (14) feel that their use or omission neither prevented nor relieved the "delirium". The drugs may calm the hyperactive patient, but because reality testing is not corrected, and possibly may be impaired, the course of the "delirium" is unchanged, or perhaps intensified. The most appropriate choice of drugs. if indicated, would appear to be the phenothiazines, which have the capacity to calm patients, with minimal reduction and possible enhancement of the patient's capacity to perceive and test reality. This was described in the case reports, and will be further discussed under the section on treatment.

TREATMENT

We are now dealing with a patient who has a known and

determined set of symptoms, either minimal or florid, and need to consider the necessary steps to bring the experiences (syndrome) under control. All preventative measures described in the previous section are an integral part of the treatment approach, and bear reiteration at this point.

The approach of Weisman and Hackett has been particularly elucidating. They stress that their goals were not the relief of psychiatric symptoms by the usual systematic investigation of conflict, but prevention and treatment by correcting faulty reality testing. Emphasizing the use of a specific type of doctor-patient relationship, mastery of the stress of the operation and patching is facilitated. In the initial stages of contact with the patient the doctor makes repeated efforts to identify himself as a distinct personality, describing procedures, and providing frequent descriptions of the physical surroundings. Areas of mutual interest that the doctor could share with the patient are quickly ascertained. Periods of effective functioning in the patient's life are emphasized. By a deliberate recollection of past achievements, the patient is assisted in appraising the threatening confusion of the present in terms of a happy and successful past. Their therapy is based on the hypothesis that if the doctor becomes an active collaborator in recapturing a period when reality evaluation was an optimum, the patient might also be able to reorient himself with respect to the damaged perceptions, misinterpretations, uncertainty and fear associated with the current illness.

Assuming that the primary etiological factor is the sensory deprivation involved, the first steps are directed toward this variable. Often merely the removal of the eye patches may help reverse the deprivation of an important source of reality testing and reestablish the patient to a more reality-oriented level. Should this not effectively relieve the symptoms or restore reality testing, it is important to emphasize that reality testing depends on the integrity of several levels of mental functioning. Additional methods of fortifying the patient's reality testing by providing supplemental perceptual cues to other sensory channels may be provided. Ascertaining those areas through which altered channels of stimulation can be provided is an important aspect of the initial evaluation of these patients. For example, patients who have obtained significant gratification in a particular sensory modality may be approached through this channel. A man who is a lover of a particular type of music may be provided with recordings or tapes; a patient who is a gourmet and savors particular types of food may be approached and stimulated through gustatory and olfactory channels; patients who do not speak English may be aided by staff or family who can converse in the patient's language; olfactory stimulation may be enhanced with flowers. Talking, touching, and a variety of other techniques are all examples of increasing sensory stimulation.

The actions described so far are often, in a high precentage of cases, sufficient to reverse and bring the syndrome under control. Should further treatment be necessary, the next step would be the use of appropriate chemotherapy, particularly the phenothiazines. The choice of the antipsychotic agent would depend upon the manifestations of the patient's psychosis. For example, paranoid patients often respond dramatically to low doses of Trifluoperazine (Stelazine), perhaps at levels of 2 to 4 mg per day. Hyperactive and agitated symptomatology is often brought under control by drugs such as Chlorpromazine (Thorazine) in doses of 25 to 50 mg qid. It is important to emphasize that older patients are often quite sensitive and experience a higher incidence of side effects with the phenothiazines. Because of this they should be used with caution and in lower doses.

Some patients, even with the institution of all of the measures previously described, will still remain psychotic. They may require psychiatric consultation, and need extensive follow-up, possibly psychiatric hospitalization, following the clearing of their basic eye problem.

REFERENCES

1. Adams, G. W. and Pearlman, J. T.: Personal communication, 1970.
2. Bruner, A. B.: The post-operative treatment of cataract. *Ohio State Med J, 91*:501-504, 1935.

3. Dayton, G. O. Jr., Traber, W. J., Kaufmann, M. A., and Gunter, L. M.: Overt behavior manifested in bilaterally patched patients. *Am J Ophthalmol*, *59*:864-870, 1965.

4. Ellis, R., Jackson, C. W. Jr., Rich, R., Hughey, G. A., and Schlotfeldt, R. M.: Suggestions for the care of eye surgery patients who experience reduced sensory input. *The Proceedings of the American Nurses Association Regional Clinical Conference — 1967.* New York, Appleton, 1968.

5. Flynn, W. R.: Visual hallucinations in sensory deprivation. *Psychiatr Q*, *36*:55-65, 1962.

6. Greenwood, A.: Mental disturbances following operations for cataract. *JAMA*, *91*:1713-1716, 1928.

7. Jackson, C. W. Jr.: Clinical sensory deprivation: A review of hospitalized eye-surgery patients. In Zubek, J. P. (Ed.): *Sensory Deprivation: Fifteen Years of Research.* New York, Appleton, 1969.

8. Jackson, C. W. Jr. and Pollard, J. C.: Sensory deprivation and suggestion: A theoretical approach. *Behav Sci*, *7*:332-342, 1962.

9. Kales, A., Adams, G. L., and Pearlman, J. T.: Rapid eye movement (REM) sleep in ophthalmic patients. *Am J Ophthalmol*, *4*:615-622, 1970.

10. McRae, R. I.: Psychiatric reactions to eye surgery. *JAOA*, *63*:1049-1052, 1964.

11. Pearlman, J. T.: Personal communication, 1970.

12. Solomon, P.: Sensory deprivation. In Freedman, A. M. and Kaplan, H. I. (Eds.): *Comprehensive Textbook of Psychiatry.* Baltimore, Williams & Wilkins, 1967.

13. Stonecypher, D. D. Jr.: The cause and prevention of postoperative psychoses in the elderly. *Am J Ophthalmol*, *55*:605-610, 1963.

14. Weisman, A. D. and Hackett, T. P.: Psychosis after eye surgery. *N Engl J Med*, *258*:1284-1289, 1958.

15. Ziskind, E., Jones, H., Filante, W., and Goldberg, J.: Observations on mental symptoms in eye patched patients: Hypnogogic symptoms in sensory deprivation. *Am J Psychiatr*, *116*:893-900, 1960.

16. Zubek, J. P.: *Sensory Deprivation: Fifteen Years of Research.* New York, Appleton, 1969.

Chapter 9

GUIDELINES FOR THE PSYCHIATRIC REFERRAL OF VISUALLY HANDICAPPED PATIENTS*

GEORGE L. ADAMS, M.D., JEROME T. PEARLMAN, M.D.
AND SHERWIN H. SLOAN, M.D.

Emotional stress is known to accompany visual problems. This fact is apparent in patients with real or threatened acute loss of vision. Patients usually respond to a loss of vision in one of three ways: by acceptance, by denial, or by depression — with or without concomitant anxiety. A progression through these three patterns of response, which varies in its pace and qualitative characteristics, is not always seen by the physician. The response of any given patient can almost be predicted by his previous response pattern to emotional stress. Acceptance and denial are the two most frequently encountered and healthiest patterns of response. They require the least attention, usually by only the ophthalmologist and his ancillary personnel. Depression, although the least common response, can be lethal. A patient who responds to visual loss with depression requires at least a psychiatric consultation to aid the ophthalmologist in his management. In severe depression, the patient will probably require short- or long-term psychotherapy, chemotherapy, or some combination thereof. Psychiatric consultation can be requested from a psychiatrist in private practice or a local community mental health center.

O PHTHALMIC disorders are usually accompanied by emotional stress. A review of the literature of the past ten years revealed approximately 1,000 articles on topics related to psychosomatic ophthalmology. Very few of these articles, however, are geared to aiding the practicing ophthalmologist. Most

*This article has been reprinted with permission from the *Annals of Ophthalmology*, *Vol. III*, page 72, 1971.

ophthalmologists have difficulty in knowing when to refer a patient to a psychiatrist. Usually, there is no hesitation in referring patients with obvious emotional disturbance, such as a frankly psychotic episode, agitation secondary to sensory deprivation (black patch psychosis), or reaction to loss of vision without recognizable organic disease. The ophthalmologist, however, may have difficulty in knowing when to make a psychiatric referral of the patient who has suffered an acute partial or total loss of vision or who is threatened by such a loss in the future.

Most patients will react to partial visual loss in much the same way as they have to other crises in their life. Although there are no easy "rules of thumb" for the physican to follow, there are some practical guidelines which can be helpful to the ophthalmologist in dealing with the emotional stress precipitated by visual loss. The majority of patients respond in one of three ways: by acceptance, by denial, or by depression with or without severe anxiety. These three mechanisms are discussed and illustrated by typical case histories. The role of the ophthalmologist in the evaluation and management of the problem, as well as the possible need for psychiatric consultation, is stressed.

Acceptance

The first type of patient to be considered accepts his visual handicap in a realistic manner. He has been successful in coping with life's problems and has been able to resolve successfully the emotional conflicts of childhood and adolescence. He has sufficient ego strength to face adversity with confidence and determination. The patient does not panic and employs healthy defense mechanisms to deal with his visual problem. He typically avails himself of vocational rehabilitation and other methods of adjusting to a new life pattern, including the study of Braille. In short, the patient will usually accept the available alternatives and then act.

Case 1. The patient is a thirty-year-old man who was referred to the Jules Stein Eye Institute with the diagnosis of developmental glaucoma. He had an enucleation of the left eye in 1960 after several unsuccessful surgical procedures to alleviate elevated intraocular pressure. When first seen in the clinic, the patient's pressure in the right eye measured 28 mm Hg, and field loss had occurred despite maximum medical therapy. Vision in the right eye was 20/70. A filtering iridectomy was performed. His vision deteriorated postoperatively, and Diamox® (Lederle) and pilocarpine were required to keep the pressure within normal limits.

Following surgery, the patient suffered a two-day period of acute anxiety. His vision had not returned to the degree he expected, and he became fearful that he would never recover the preoperative visual acuity. He was obsessed by the thought that his right eye would hemorrhage and become completely blind as had his left eye several years before. He was immediately relieved when his physician assured him that the decrease in vision was temporary and normal for the immediate postoperative period, but, nevertheless, a psychiatric consultation was requested.

The patient related to the psychiatric interviewer in a friendly, cooperative manner and was eager to talk about himself. He was a slender man who appeared younger than his age. His affect was appropriate and his mood, one of resignation. He had no history of illusions, delusions, or hallucinations. The patient denied ideas of hypochondriasis, reference, persecution, or grandiosity. There were no loose associations, and the patient's thought processes appeared to be intact. He was oriented to time, place, and person, and his memory was intact. He appeared to be extremely intelligent and to possess good judgment. Despite having had multiple physical difficulties for most of his life, the patient had made a successful adjustment. He had achieved success in his career, was happy with his life, and had warm, gratifying interpersonal relationships.

To summarize, the patient is an encouraging example of a man who has overcome a devastating physical handicap. His two-day period of mild anxiety represented a brief loss of his psychologic defense mechanisms, but these were rapidly reconstituted when his physician explained the exact nature of the problem. Fortunately, the patient has the ability and interest to be introspective, since there is the possibility that he may ultimately lose remaining vision. The patient is aware that his sight is a tenuous entity which could be lost at any moment. He has prepared himself psychologically as well as physically for this eventuality.

The patient who responds with acceptance to his visual handicap can be treated with supportive measures by the ophthalmologist, the members of the nursing staff, and the social workers. Such a patient may have a period of emotional stress, but usually all that is required at this time is the reassuring support of the physician and, on very rare occasions, mild tranquilizing medication such as diazepam (Valium® — Roche) or chlordiazepoxide hydrochloride (Librium® — Roche). Rarely will these patients have problems of such magnitude as to require psychiatric referral.

Denial

The second type of patient uses denial as a defense against the reality of partial or total visual disability. Unconscious denial is a type of reality distortion which allows one to negate threatening facts about the self or about the existence of external dangers such as illness (1). Denial is usually an unhealthy defense mechanism, but there are instances when denial can perform useful adaptive functions (2). For example, the dying patient uses denial in a healthy manner to maintain emotional stability and to avoid psychic decompensation. In a similar manner, some patients facing partial or total visual loss will use denial in a nonpathologic way to maintain emotional equilibrium. One does not initially wish to break down this defense as it allows the patient to cope with his disability. After a period of time, in most patients, the use of denial disappears, allowing acceptance and ultimate rehabilitation. If not, then psychiatric referral is indicated.

This kind of patient appears stoical, typically stating that he has always taken things "like a man." Occasionally, he will have difficulty with self-image and identity, conflicts in this area not having been totally resolved. This patient is typically aggressive, rigid, and demanding of himself. The contemplation of threatened or actual visual impairment accentuates his feeling of inadequacy and low self-esteem. Such a patient, therefore, must deny the existence of his disability to some extent in order to "bear up to grim reality." Many of these patients will not ask for practical information concerning rehabilitation and will make no plans to rearrange their lives. The patient who employs denial of illness has a reaction opposite to hypochondriasis. He may take his illness lightly, neglecting prevention as well as therapy. (A typical example of the latter is the glaucoma patient who does not use his medication and, as a result, eventually loses his vision.) With time, however, these patients accept their predicament more readily and seek help. Time is in their favor and, gradually, they are able to cope with their loss of vision and to accept it.

Case 2. The patient is a 31-year-old man who states he has been in good health all of his life. Nevertheless, 3 years prior to admission at the Jules Stein Eye Institute, he sustained a cleat injury of the right calf while playing soccer. Since that time, he has had three episodes of thrombophlebitis. Furthermore, he had two episodes in which he felt faint and became diaphoretic, with cold skin and dyspnea. Although the patient did not seek medical consultation, his physician felt that, on at least one of these occasions, a small pulmonary embolus may have existed.

Three days prior to admission, the patient was pressing weights, an activity which he performed daily. While doing so, he lost a portion of the lower visual field of his left eye. Because he felt this was unimportant and that time would resolve the condition, he continued his weight-lifting exercises. After the exercises were completed, some vision returned, but he still had visual loss in the left eye. Two days later, when his vision did not improve, the patient decided to seek medical advice. Examination confirmed loss of a portion of the lower visual field of the left eye. There was congestion of the superior temporal vein and slight attenuation of the superior temporal artery with adjacent retinal edema.

The patient was not overly concerned about the loss of vision and was confident that he would be able to continue in law school. He seemed unaware of the implications his condition had for his future. The patient had never been anxious about his health despite the two episodes of dyspnea, diaphoresis, cold skin, and faintness. At the time of admission, his electrocardiogram revealed evidence of a four- to six-week old myocardial infarction. When informed of his cardiac status, he showed the same lack of concern displayed toward his eye problem. Throughout his hospitalization, the patient was quite stoical. As in the past, he dealt with problems "from day to day" and stated the desire to "face life squarely."

The patient was uncertain about his identity as a man and felt the need to establish his masculinity continually. He expressed the desire to date many girls and his pleasure in multiple sexual conquests. He had joined the Marines in an effort "to reassert his masculinity." Throughout his hospital stay, the patient denied that his visual handicap would be detrimental to his intellectual, social, or physical activities. Consistent with his assertive, aggressive personality and somewhat rigid (obsessive-compulsive) life pattern, the patient never considered any alternative course of action.

In most circumstances, the patient who uses denial as emotional protection against the threat of partial or total visual loss can be managed by the ophthalmologist. It is not always desirable to force the patient to accept his situation. Initially, the physician should not try to break down the defense mechanism of denial. He should support the patient and, if possible, gradually attempt to demonstrate alternate courses of action. Support can be given by listening patiently and responding confidently. Occasionally, a mild tranquilizing agent may be necessary to reduce anxiety. In rare instances, the mechanism of denial may break down and an anxiety state or depression may occur. Under these circumstances, psychiatric consultation is indicated. Generally, the patient using denial can eventually accept his condition and be directed toward more realistic goals without psychiatric intervention. In rare instances where the use of denial does not disappear, psychiatric consultation is also indicated.

Depression

The third type of patient responds to the stress of his visual loss by depression with or without a concomitant anxiety state. For the most part, such a patient has been unable to cope with major stresses in his life. He is usually a chronic complainer with low self-esteem. He has had high aspirations which may not have been attained and which will probably be unobtainable now owing to the visual handicap.

In the initial stages of depression, the patient may not demonstrate overt symptoms. Some aspect of the patient's behavior may indicate that he is depressed and that he may require psychiatric help. The patient behaves as if everything is a tremendous effort but at times covers up this feeling with a forced humorous attitude. Self-punitive, self-abasing acts and the patient's neglect of his own interest may point to the proper diagnosis. Some depressed patients complain about other symptoms, usually of a minor nature, although no organic basis for them can be found.

As a rule, depressed patients suffer from feelings of helplessness, sadness, and lasting guilt (3). Depression is deepened by the slightest indication of the loss of love, by disappointments, criticisms, misgivings, and real or imagined threats — all of which tend to increase the patient's feeling of helplessness (4). Thus, the depression becomes a mode of response, constantly reactivated by experiences of further loss and by frustration or humiliation or both. Depressed patients have a pessimistic view of the world and of their own worth; they find it difficult to asset themselves. Physical symptoms of fatigability, insomnia (usually in the form of early morning awakening), anorexia, constipation, and decrease in sexual activity accompany depression. Depressed patients may become irritable and have occasional explosive outbursts. They have poor impulse control and are extremely demanding of those they love or of those who are caring for them. In more severe states of depression, the despair is paralleled by a general inhibition of intellectual and motor function. Although sadness is the most notable aspect of depression, concomitant anxiety is sometimes present. The patient may become extremely restless and agitated, often to the point of exhausting hypermotility.

The involutional patient is more apt to suffer from depression after loss of vision. In middle-aged women, typical secondary symptoms of menopause are frequent but not invariably present. Many of these patients report they are sad, gloomy, and unable to enjoy anything; they feel helpless and hopeless; their self-esteem withers. In mild cases or in prodromal stages, the harder the patient tries to combat his mood, the worse he feels. Involutional patients are more likely to become self-punitive and to neglect their own interests. They narrow, restrict, and distort the world. Judgment and self-image are impaired, and there is deterioration of interpersonal relationships.

Case 3. The patient is a twenty-eight-year-old woman who was in good health until January 1968, at which time she had bilateral intraocular hemorrhage without loss of vision. In October of the same year, she began having partial loss of vision and first came to the Jules Stein Eye Institute with a complaint of floaters in both eyes. Visual acuity at the initial examination was 20/40 in each eye. Within one year, her vision decreased to hand motion discrimination in the right eye and to 8/200 in the left eye. A diagnosis of extensive retinitis proliferans with vitreous hemorrhage was made. Extensive diagnostic testing failed to show evidence of generalized disease.

With the onset of nearly total blindness, the patient became extremely depressed. For approximately two weeks she stayed in bed, contemplating suicide. She did not commit suicide, she said, because such an act "would kill my mother". Her appetite diminished with a resulting fifteen-pound weight loss. She did not sleep well at night and frequently awakened at an early hour of the morning to pace around the room. She sought psychiatric aid from the Department of Vocational Rehabilitation; they also provided financial help while she undertook a retraining program. She studied Braille but, when her vision continued to improve, she stopped the study of this technique.

The patient stated that she had no confidence in her physicians because they were unable to explain what was wrong with her vision or what the prognosis would be. She added that she has come to accept her disability with resignation and that in some respects her life has improved since her loss of vision. She clarified this statement by saying she might never have gone to college or have realized "there are some wonderful people in this world" had she not undergone this traumatic experience.

To summarize, the patient had bilateral ocular hemorrhages in January 1968. In October of the same year, she began having loss of vision until she became totally blind in February 1969. When she lost her vision, she grieved for her eyes and became extremely depressed. The depression was manifested by suicidal ideation, extreme lethargy (to the point of being bedridden for two weeks), decreased appetite with weight loss, and inability to sleep. She felt sorry for herself and mourned the loss of her sight. Then she started thinking about people who were more unfortunate and began accepting her visual handicap. Her first step toward help was to seek psychiatric aid and to contact the Department of Vocational Rehabilitation. Approximately four to five weeks later, she started regaining some vision, which further enhanced her recovery from depression.

The patient who becomes depressed after total or partial visual loss usually goes through an abnormal grief for his eyes (reactive depression). In many instances, the ophthalmologist can care for this type of patient with the consultation of a psychiatrist. At other times, particularly when the patient has a psychotic episode or an extremely severe depression, it is best to consult a psychiatrist and have the patient in some type of psychiatric therapy (psychotherapy, chemotherapy, or both). In a severe depression where there is a threat of suicide or a concomitant severe anxiety state, the psychiatrist can be of utmost help to the ophthalmologist and to the patient. Short- or long-term psychiatric therapy may become imperative.

The loss or threatened loss of visual function is inevitably accompanied by serious emotional stress, although this stress may not always be evident. The way in which a patient handles this stress can be of great benefit or hindrance to his physical and mental health. The foregoing discussion is presented in an effort to show the ophthalmologist the various modes of response to stress engendered by visual loss and to indicate when professional psychiatric consultation would be beneficial.

REFERENCES

1. Waelder, R.: *Basic Theory of Psychoanalysis*, Intl Univs Pr, New York,

1960.
2. Weinstein, E. A. and Kahn, R. L.: *Denial of Illness,* Thomas, Springfield, 1955.
3. Bebring, E.: "The mechanism of depression", in Phyllis Greenacre, Ed., *Affective Disorders,* Intl Univs Pr, New York, 1953.
4. Freud, S.: *Mourning and Melancholia,* Hogarth, London, 1955, p. 14.

Chapter 10

FACTITIAL EYE PROBLEMS

Sherwin H. Sloan, M.D.

Every so often in our practice of ophthalmology we encounter a perplexing patient with a persistent or recurring problem the nature of which is puzzling. I am speaking of the patient with a persistent or recurrent conjunctivitis, corneal abrasion, "irritable eye", loss of lashes or tearing that reveals definite signs of an altered ophthalmic anatomy and physiology.

Many of these patients have seen a number of our colleagues, have undergone repeated cultures, scrapings and more exotic laboratory diagnostic tests, and yet remain an enigma. This is not a very large group of patients, but just one or two in every practice can create uncertainty, feelings of inadequacy and hostility on the part of the physician towards the patient.

Whenever one encounters such a problem the possibility of factitial etiology must be kept in mind. Frequently, and probably in the majority of cases, this will prove not to be the diagnosis, but don't be surprised at the occasional case in which a diagnosis of a self-induced problem will bring relief to all parties concerned except perhaps the patient and his family.

In the study of a particular external eye problem that resists diagnosis and treatment in my practice, the possibility of factitial etiology remains high and must be included in the differential diagnosis.

The two following cases will illustrate the types of problems that are encountered.

> Case 1: A fifty-year-old female was seen with the complaint of loss of lashes. The symptoms varied in the number of lashes lost and at times was either unilateral or bilateral. There was no previous history of eye disease. The patient had been examined by several ophthalmologists. Previous diag-

noses of blepharitis and meibomitis were made and diagnostic tests for leprosy and pituitary insufficiency were in progress. The general ophthalmic examination revealed only mild presbyopia in addition to the striking loss of lashes bilaterally. After several supportive visits slowly confronting the patient with our diagnosis, she admitted to the fact that she was epilating the lashes herself. Psychiatric referral indicated a diagnosis of severe depression. The patient continued under psychiatric care for several weeks only and then was lost to follow-up.

Case 2. A forty-five-year-old woman was first seen with the complaint of a repeated painful right eye and lid swelling. The history revealed two years of recurrent episodes in which the right eye became painful, red and the lids became swollen. She had been seen by several ophthalmologists and no definitive diagnosis was made. She had been given numerous medications for topical use as well as pain and sleeping medications.

Examination revealed swelling and ptosis of the right upper lid. The conjunctiva was severely injected and there was diffuse stippling of the cornea. No discharge was present. A preauricular node was not palpable. The intraocular findings were all normal. Because recent studies and cultures were negative the patient was hospitalized. The right eye was patched in the manner to be described. In twenty-four hours the signs of swelling and conjunctival injection were markedly cleared although the patient continued to complain of severe pain. During her hospital stay hysterical visual fields were elicited. After removing the patch in the hospital, the patient was observed instilling what proved to be salt crystals in the lower fornix of the right eye. After psychiatric consultation with attempts to handle the situation tactfully, the patient left the hospital and did not follow up with recommended care.

When we encounter problems of this type the natural question that arises is how to handle the situation, both in making a diagnosis and the ensuing treatment once a diagnosis is made. I will try to present the course of action I follow with these difficult problems.

(1) There is no substitute for a thorough ophthalmic reex-

amination beginning with an extremely careful history. The history alone may give one clues as to the etiology by the number of previous ophthalmic examinations without satisfaction. In the history it is important to elicit the types of medications used in the past to relieve symptoms because it is here that one finds the chronic narcotic, barbiturate or tranquilizer addict.

(2) Once a thorough history and examination is completed, the decision regarding repeat cultures, scrapings or other diagnostic tests will rest with the ophthalmologist and should include previous testing, the accuracy of these tests, what laboratory was used, etc. Remember that excessive and unnecessary testing only enhances the patient's and his family's uncertainty as to a diagnosis of factitial etiology.

(3) Once the previous examination and tests are completed and reveal no organic basis, the patient should be hospitalized and placed in a semicontrolled atmosphere.

(4) While in the hospital certain tests and observations should be made. Ancillary hospital personnel are extremely valuable in this endeavor and they should be forewarned of the problems and observations that would be helpful.

(5) While in the hospital, if the problem is conjunctival or corneal, a *firm* pressure patch should be applied over the eye in question and markings made on the tape and face, *without the knowledge of the patient,* that might indicate the patient's tampering with the patch (Figs. 10-1 and 10-2). We have found that an occasional problem that has persisted for weeks or months suddenly "clears" after twenty-four to forty-eight hours of patching.

(6) The ancillary hospital personnel, at times, have observed the patient's manipulations of the patch and eye in the middle of the night. A search through the patient's belongings has revealed the offending substance the patient was instilling in his eye to produce the problem. Substances that have been used are salt, urine, semen, various seeds and purposeful abrasions with pins, etc.

(7) Other testing that may add substance to a diagnosis of factitial injury, but by no means "proves" it, are the elicitation

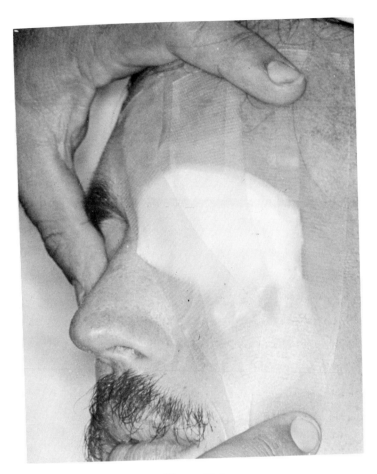

Figure 10-1.

of hysterical ambloypia or hysterical visual fields. These possibilities definitely require testing.

(8) Once a diagnosis is established, and it should be with positive evidence, and not by exclusion only, the patient should not be confronted directly and punitively by the ophthalmologist. At this point competent psychiatric consultation is mandatory and the approach must be discussed with the appropriate psychiatric colleague. This is an extremely difficult situation and must be handled with caution. At least the

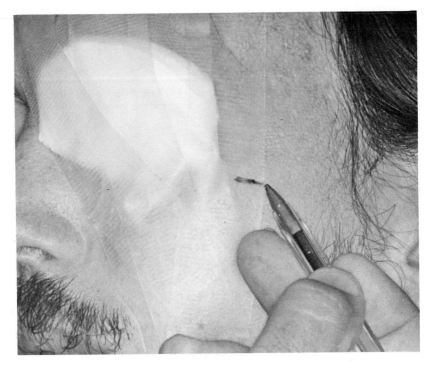

Figure 10-2.

ophthalmologist usually has been relieved of the headache and it now becomes the psychiatrist's turn. We have found the most profitable results are achieved when ophthalmologist and psychiatrist work in conjunction with the treatment plan. These patients usually do not stop their factitial mutilation immediately, but may continue even while in treatment and thus require the ophthalmologist's continued care and interest. Some of these patients may disappear from your practice once the diagnosis is made and look for someone new to supply them with drugs, etc.

From the two cases depicted it is evident that these patients are difficult to deal with. The ophthalmologist may have to be satisfied only with the fact that a true diagnosis has been made and may have to accept the frequent poor results in resolving the basis of the problem.

An even more exasperating and shocking problem to deal with is that of attempted or accomplished self-enucleation.

The term Oedipism is attached to this grotesque form of self-mutilation and is derived from the classic Greek play in which Oedipus gouges out his eyes when he discovers that he has been married to his own mother. The act has been described as both a symbolic self-castration and an actual elimination of visual truths of life.

I have seen several such cases and each time the horror of the act is terrifying. All of the cases I have consulted on have occurred in psychotic males, some of whom are teenagers. One such case occurred in a teenager, a young recruit in the army, who attempted to enucleate his eye by shoving a pen into his orbit, missing the eye but severing the optic nerve. The profound significance of the psychic importance of his eyes is seen in two drawings he made several years before he actually attempted the self-enucleation (Figs. 10-3 and 10-4).

Figures 10-3 and 10-4.

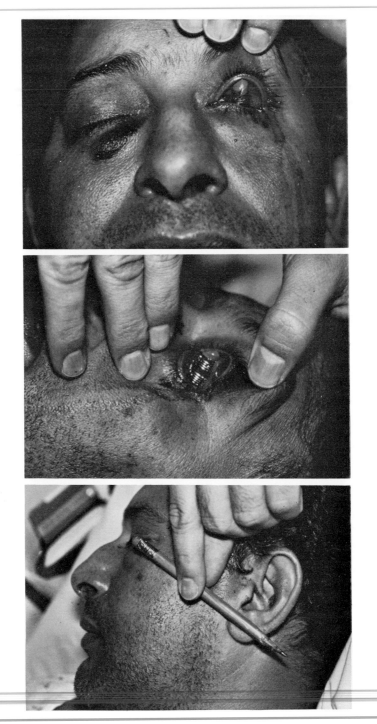

Figures 10-5, 10-6, and 10-7.

Figures 10-5, 10-6 and 10-7 show a patient who attempted to enucleate his right eye and was unsuccessful. He was admitted to a psychiatric ward and while being interviewed by the psychiatric resident asked to borrow a pencil. He then proceeded to pound the pencil into his left orbit, miraculously missing the eye and recovering with 20/20 vision in each eye!

Why do individuals do this sort of thing to themselves? The reasons are complex, and yet if we listen to what the patients say at the time we can learn a lot. All these patients are in acute psychotic states. However, they all at least give a glimpse of their reasons. Most of the patients' comments center around their guilt for sexual thoughts or acts which they experienced as sinful. This is an extremely important fact and has been present in every case I have seen or heard of through other reports.

Once the ophthalmologist has had the misfortune of encountering such a case, the following procedures are essential: (1) The patient must be immediately hospitalized in a psychiatric ward following the necessary ophthalmic surgical procedures, and (2) the psychiatrist *must* be warned that there is an excellent chance that the patient may attempt to destroy the other eye!

AUTHOR INDEX

A

Abraham, K., 88, 107
Adams, G. I., 141
Adams, G. L., v, 81, 82, 142
Adams, G. W., 137, 140
Alexander, F., 89, 107
Apt, L., v, 113, 119, 125

B

Bebring, E., 151
Beckwitt, M. C., v, 84, 113
Benjamin, J. D., 103, 107
Billinghurst, L., 124
Blone, G. E., 124
Braverman, S., 67
Breuer, J., 89, 102, 107
Bridgeman, G. J., 88, 107
Bruner, A. B., 140

C

Carroll, T. J., 67
Cassidy, W. I., 72, 74, 82
Chevigny, H., 67
Cholden, L. S., 49, 67
Clayton, P. H., 82
Cohen, M. E., 82

D

Dayton, G. O., Jr., 141
Deutch, F., 89, 107
Ditcham, H., 124
Dombro, R. H., 116, 124
Drews, R. C., 69, 82

E

Ekstein, R., 103, 107

Ellis, R., 136, 141
Emerson, P. F., 100, 108
Engel, G. I., 81, 82

F

Fenichel, O., 88, 107
Ferenczi, S., 88, 107
Filante, W., 141
Finch, S., 124
Finestone, S., 67
Flanagan, N. B., 82
Flynn, W. R., 141
Foley, J. M., 124
Freud, S., 88, 89, 102, 107, 151

G

Gailey, W., 124
Gesell, A., 87, 101, 102, 107
Gifford, E. S., Jr., 8, 11, 22
Goldberg, J., 141
Greenacre, P., 68, 82, 88, 107
Greenman, G. W., 99, 100, 107
Greenwood, A., 141
Grinker, R., 37
Gross, M. P., v, 68
Gunter, I. M., 141
Guze, S. B., 72, 81, 82

H

Hackett, T. P., 135, 136, 138, 139, 141
Haller, J. A., 124
Hart, H. H., 68, 82, 107
Hartman, E., 124
Heiman, J., v, 126
Hollender, M. H., 37
Hughey, G. A., 141

I

Illingsworth, R. S., 124

161

Wahl, C. W., vi, 3, 109, 110, 111, 112
Waltfogel, S., 124
Weckowitz, E., 102, 108
Weinstein, F. A., 151
Weisman, A. D., 135, 136, 138, 139, 141
Werner, H., 102, 108
Wheeler, E. O., 72, 74, 82
White, P. D., 82

Wolf, 100
Woodruff, R. A., 72, 82

Z

Ziegler, F. J., 81, 82
Ziskind, F., 141
Zubek, J. P., 141

SUBJECT INDEX

Twayne's United States Authors Series

Sylvia E. Bowman, *Editor*

INDIANA UNIVERSITY

Kurt Vonnegut, Jr.

TUSAS 276

Kurt Vonnegut, Jr.

KURT VONNEGUT, JR.

By STANLEY SCHATT

University of Houston

TWAYNE PUBLISHERS
A DIVISION OF G. K. HALL & CO., BOSTON

1 S

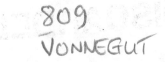

Library of Congress Cataloging in Publication Data

Schatt, Stanley.
    Kurt Vonnegut, Jr.

    (Twayne's United States authors series ; TUSAS 276)
    Bibliography: p. 167 - 71.
    Includes index.
    1.   Vonnegut, Kurt — Criticism and interpretation.
PS3572.05Z85   813'.5'4   76-41754
ISBN 0-8057-7176-X

Once again, for Jane

Contents

About the Author

Stanley Schatt served as a teaching assistant at the University of Southern California while working on his Ph.D. He taught briefly at the University of Southern California after receiving his doctorate and then moved to the University of Houston. While at the University of Houston, Dr. Schatt served as Director of Lower Division Studies in English, responsible for forty-five teaching assistants and the largest composition program in the Southwest.

Dr. Schatt has published widely in the fields of contemporary American literature and ethnic studies. His interest in Kurt Vonnegut, Jr., has resulted in a number of publications and bibliographies on Vonnegut as well as the Directorship of two Modern Language Association seminars on Vonnegut. His interest in ethnic studies has resulted in many scholarly articles and papers on Afro-American and Jewish-American literature as well as the co-authorship of *A Concordance to the Poetry of Langston Hughes* which was published by the Gale Research Company in 1975.

Dr. Schatt spent the 1974 - 75 academic year as Fulbright Visiting Professor to Japan. He lectured on American studies at Tokyo University, Keio University, and Hiroshima University. During this period Dr. Schatt completed *Understanding Modern American Literature: Cultural and Historical Perspectives* which will be published in 1976 in Japan by the Cultural Review Company.

Preface

Kurt Vonnegut, Jr., has been labeled at various times as a mediocre science-fiction writer, a social satirist, a Black Humorist, and a major novelist. The critical confusion concerning exactly what mode he represents reflects the complexity of his deceptively simple tales. Self-taught by years of free-lance writing, Vonnegut has always been acutely aware of a Middle-American audience that has little sympathy for "art for art's sake." While his sharply honed prose style and his grim, staccato jokes have attracted a wide range of readers, his innovative uses of narrative masks and of various cinematic techniques have made his novels required reading in many creative writing classes.

At the very center of Vonnegut's fiction is a concern with the age-old question of free will and the meaning of life and love. Although he is able to treat the subject comically in his early novel, *The Sirens of Titan*, Vonnegut returns to it with deadly earnestness in his latest novels, *Breakfast of Champions* and *Slapstick*. His consistent use of Jonah and Christ figures in his fiction is but one manifestation of his fascination with the problem of how human destiny can be reconciled with divine will.

While other critical studies have primarily concerned themselves with Vonnegut's style or with his philosophy, I have tried to trace the development of the two simultaneously since Vonnegut's medium is often closely related to his message. My plan has been to trace Vonnegut's development from his earliest novels to *Slapstick*; but, because many of his early short stories, first published in the now out-of-print *Canary in a Cat House*, were reprinted in *Welcome to the Monkey House*, I have chosen to devote an entire chapter to the major motifs and techniques found in Vonnegut's short stories rather than to consider throughout the book the relationship of the stories in regard to his other fiction. I have also devoted an entire chapter to

Vonnegut's plays since his career as a playwright is a logical extension of his changing attitude toward his relationship with his audience and since the serious flaws in these plays reflect, for the most part, the increasingly polemical nature of his work in recent years.

My final chapter is devoted to Vonnegut as a public man who chooses to speak about such issues as the Vietnam conflict, the space program, and human misery wherever it is found. In a Foreword to his first novel, *Player Pianos*, Vonnegut warned readers about the possibilities of a nightmarish future, yet he removed in *Breakfast of Champions* all narrative masks and spoke directly to his readers about the problems of his day. His tour of Biafra during the Nigerian civil war and his statements at New York City's celebration of the first Earth Day suggest that Vonnegut realized the communication barriers that fiction establishes between artist and audience. He has turned to journalism in an effort to communicate a Humanist philosophy that stresses kindness and love. In *Slapstick*, Vonnegut strips away his masks to discuss his feelings about his family, especially his sister Alice and his concern for America's lonely ones; but this fictional autobiography also functions as a coda of all his previous fiction and may mark a turning point in his career.

I am indebted to Professor Max F. Schulz in more ways than it is possible to acknowledge for first introducing me to Vonnegut's novels and for his later reading parts of this book and offering me consistently good advice. Professors Glen Meeter, Jerome Klinkowitz, and John Somer have graciously offered suggestions and hours of enlightening conversation about all facets of Vonnegut's career and family background.

I also wish to thank Kurt Vonnegut, Jr., for answering my questions and for providing me with an early draft of *Happy Birthday, Wanda June*. Mr. Seymour Lawrence has been kind enough to furnish me with galley proofs of *Slapstick*.

I am grateful to the University of Houston for a grant that defrayed the costs of typing the final manuscript, and I wish to thank Mrs. Chris Morris for typing it. Finally, I wish to extend my deepest gratitude to my wife, Jane, who provided moral support beyond the call of duty.

In quoting from Vonnegut's works, I have used the standard editions published by Seymour Lawrence/Delacorte Press exclusively. I

Preface

am grateful to the editors of *Southwest Review* and *Critique* for permission to use material that appeared previously in slightly altered form.

STANLEY SCHATT

Chronology

1922   Kurt Vonnegut, Jr., born November 11 in Indianapolis, Indiana. Son of architect Kurt Vonnegut and Edith (née Lieber).

1936 -   Attended Shortridge High School in Indianapolis. Served
1940   on the staff of the school's daily newspaper.

1940 -   Attended Cornell University and wrote columns for the
1942   *Cornell Sun*.

1943 -   Briefly attended Carnegie Institute of Technology. Served
1945   in the United States Army infantry. Captured after the Battle of the Bulge and sent to Dresden to work in a factory producing vitamin supplements for pregnant women. Awarded the Purple Heart.

1945 -   Married Jane Marie Cox. Attended the University of
1947   Chicago. Wrote a master's thesis on *Fluctuations Between Good and Evil in Simple Tales* which was rejected unanimously by the anthropology department. Worked as a police reporter for the Chicago City News Bureau.

1947 -   Worked as a public-relations official for General Electric
1950   Company, Schenectady, New York.

1950   Resigned from General Electric to do free-lance writing.

1951   *Player Piano* published by Charles Scribner's Sons.

1952 -   Wrote a number of short stories that appeared in such mass-
1958   circulation magazines as *Saturday Evening Post, Colliers,* and *Ladies' Home Journal.*

1959   *Canary in a Cat House* published by Fawcett as a Gold Medal paperback original.

1961   *Mother Night* published by Fawcett as a Gold Medal paperback original.

1963   *Cat's Cradle* published by Holt, Rinehart and Winston.

1965   *God Bless You, Mr. Rosewater* published by Holt, Rinehart and Winston.

1965 - Teaches at Hopefield School, Sandwich, Massachusetts.
1967   Teaches at Writer's Workshop, University of Iowa.
1967 - Guggenheim Fellowship enabled Vonnegut to travel to
1968   Dresden, Germany, to research *Slaughterhouse-Five*.
1968   *Welcome to the Monkey House* published by Seymour Lawrence.
1969   *Slaughterhouse-Five* published by Seymour Lawrence.
1970   *Happy Birthday, Wanda June* opens in New York at the Theatre de Lys.
1971   *Happy Birthday, Wanda June* published by Seymour Lawrence.
1972   *Between Time and Timbuktu, or Prometheus*-5 published by Seymour Lawrence.
1973   *Breakfast of Champions* published by Seymour Lawrence. Awarded an honorary LHD by Indiana University.
1974   *Wampeters, Foma, & Granfalloons* published by Seymour Lawrence. Awarded an honorary Litt.D. by Hobart and William Smith College.
1975   Named a vice-president of the National Institute of Arts and Letters.
1976   *Slapstick, or Lonesome No More!* published by Seymour Lawrence.

CHAPTER 1

Of Man and Machines: Player Piano and The Sirens of Titan

I *Literary Apprenticeship*

IN 1913 a young architect named Kurt Vonnegut married Edith Lieber in one of the largest and costliest weddings in Indianapolis history.[1] The Vonneguts were young, glamorous, and relatively affluent; and they loved travelling and entertaining. They were able to send Barnard and Alice, their two older children, to expensive private schools; but, by the time Kurt Vonnegut, Jr., was an adolescent, they had exhausted their fortune and heavily mortgaged their home. As a result, the youngest Vonnegut attended Shortridge High School where he edited the daily newspaper, *The Echo*, and discovered that he enjoyed writing about real events and real people.

In 1941 Vonnegut enrolled at Cornell University where he majored in chemistry to satisfy his father's stipulation that he major in something useful. He gravitated to the *Cornell Daily Sun* where he began editing the college humor column "Innocents Abroad." As a fourth-generation German, he was very sensitive about the growing anti-German sentiment on campus; and he felt compelled to write a column critical of the growing war hysteria: "Whether anyone else gives a hang or not about keeping out of World War II, we do, and from now on, readers may rest assured that material appearing in this column has been carefully edited so as to exclude anything smacking in the slightest of propaganda."[2]

Shortly after transferring to the Carnegie Institute of Technology, Vonnegut enlisted in the army and became an infantry combat scout. He obtained leave to visit his parents on Mothers Day, 1944; but the night before his arrival his mother took a fatal overdose of sleeping pills. Almost thirty years later, he expressed his painful feelings about this suicide in *Breakfast of Champions*. After his mother's funeral, Vonnegut returned to his regiment in time for the Battle of the Bulge where he was captured. As a prisoner of war, he was sent to the open city of Dresden where he was expected to earn his keep by working in a factory that produced vitamin supplements for pregnant women. Vonnegut heard the Allied fire-bombing of the city from the safe confines of an underground slaughterhouse locker. This holocaust colored Vonnegut's entire career, and it took him twenty years to achieve the esthetic distance necessary to describe the event without tears.

After the war was over, he returned to the University of Chicago where he majored in anthropology; his master's thesis "Fluctuations Between Good and Evil in Simple Tales" was unanimously rejected by his department. Twenty-five years later Vonnegut accepted an honorary degree from the University of Chicago for his contributions to the field of anthropology. The difficulty in distinguishing what is good from what is evil is a major theme in virtually all Vonnegut's novels, and the tension generated between these two forces becomes the cornerstone of Bokononism, the religion he invents for his novel, *Cat's Cradle*.

II   Player Piano *and the Anti-Utopic Tradition*

From 1947 to 1950 Vonnegut worked as a public-relations official for General Electric in Schenectady, New York. He quit the job to become a free-lance writer because he felt compelled to write a novel about people and machines "in which machines frequently got the best of it, as machines will."[3] *Player Piano* (1952) is a novel about a future America in which machines determine human destiny on the basis of computer "Achievement and Aptitude Profiles." It is the story of Paul Proteus, the young manager of the Ilium Works and the son of the late George Proteus who had served as Director of National Industrial, Commercial, Communications, Foodstuffs and Resources. As a brilliant administrator who is only thirty-five, Paul has an excellent chance to assume a major position in America's technocracy; but he becomes more and more disillusioned with a system that seems intent upon automating people out of jobs and eliminating any semblance of human dignity.

This loss of dignity is illuminated through a series of subplots that are linked to the adventures of Paul Proteus. The Shah of Bratpuhr, for example, is an Eastern spiritual leader who, accompanied by the State Department's Dr. Ewing J. Halyard, watches an army parade given in his honor. One of the soldiers marching is Private Edgar Rice Burroughs Hagstrohm. The Shah immediately notices the emptiness of American life, particularly for Halyard and Hagstrohm. Shortly after this parade, a computer discovers that Halyard never completed the physical education requirement for his B.A.; therefore he is not entitled to his M.A. or his Ph.D. and is a nonperson in a society where machines respond only to the trained hands of those possessing advanced degrees.

Similarly, Hagstrohm rebels against his technocracy by destroying his home and running naked into the woods; his name suggests that he is returning to the heroic Tarzan mold cast by the first Edgar Rice Burroughs. The removal of both Halyard and Hagstrohm from the technocracy occurs at the critical moment when Paul Proteus becomes involved in an abortive attempt to create a new society in which people are more important than machines, a society that would hold people as sacred as the Shah of Bratpuhr.

By setting this novel in Ilium, New York, Vonnegut deliberately contrasts the demeaning and unheroic role of man in a technocracy with the glory and grandeur of Homer's Troy. The major computer for the country is EPICAC which suggests that the only epic to which man can look forward in his post-Christian technological age is one found on computer paper. Vonnegut opens his novel by parodying Julius Caesar's *Commentary on the Gallic Wars*:

ILIUM, NEW YORK, IS DIVIDED INTO THREE PARTS.
    In the northwest are the managers and engineers and civil servants and a few professional people; in the northeast are the machines; and in the south, across the Iroquois River, is the area known locally as Homestead, where almost all of the people live. (1)

It soon becomes clear that the managers and engineers are the modern-day Romans, while the people who have been automated into early retirement and into reliance on public doles serve as counterparts of the non-Romans, or savages. Such a society is far more rigid than Caesar's, for it is stratified on the basis of intelligence.

Player Piano was ignored by most literary critics because it was science fiction; unfortunately for Vonnegut, many science-fiction critics dismissed it as good satire but bad science fiction.[4] In an essay written for *The New York Times Book Review* section, Vonnegut did express an admiration for science-fiction writers and editors because these men "are uniformly brilliant and sensitive and well informed. . . . They feel that it is their duty to encourage any writer, no matter how frightful, who has guts enough to include technology in the human equation.''[5] Vonnegut also pointed out, however, that the academic community refused to take his work seriously for years because science fiction was considered "the very lowest grade of fiction."[6] He has confessed that "I was classified as a science-fiction writer because the novel I did included machinery and all I'd done was write about Schenectady in 1948: So, I allowed this to go on, I thought it was an honor to be printed anywhere. . . . But I would run into people who would downgrade me."[7] Perhaps it is appropriate then that, twenty years after Vonnegut began work on *Player Piano*, he appeared on network television with two scientists to discuss the effect of man's first landing on the moon. While science fiction is an element in almost every Vonnegut novel, the blurring of the fine line between science and fiction during the past two decades is one of the reasons he has become acceptable to academe.

   Player Piano is an anti-utopic novel, a very respectable genre that includes such classics as E. M. Forster's *The Machine Stops*, Eugene Zamiatin's *We*, and George Orwell's *1984*. Vonnegut has admitted that he "cheerfully ripped off the plot of *Brave New World*, whose plot had been cheerfully ripped off from Eugene Zamiatin's *We*."[8] Characteristically, such novels usually are concerned with a government that considers itself utopic while it really functions in a totalitarian manner. Such a government cannot tolerate change since a utopia by definition is already perfect. In such a society science usually has already conquered nature. In John Campbell's short story "Twilight," for example, a scientist travels to the distant future and discovers that all domestic animals and all plants have disappeared from an environment that is totally sterile; but in *Player Piano* a cat is destroyed by a mechanical sweeper. In virtually all anti-utopic novels a concerted effort is also made by the government to remove its citizens' sense of personal identity. Frequently, such a government uses history to justify its existence by pointing out how dreadful conditions were before it assumed power. Ultimately the hero is forced to choose between happiness and freedom.[9] Paul Proteus, the protagonist in *Player Piano*, chooses freedom; and Vonnegut's novel is really the story of Paul's movement toward freedom.

III *Paul Proteus*

   Although Paul Proteus is the most important man in Ilium, New York, and the manager of the Ilium Works, he feels vaguely discontented. Paul feels dissatisfied because machines have made humans almost obsolete, and he tries desperately to reassert the value of human love and compassion in a world that lauds the ruthless machinelike, single-minded precision of his rival, Shepherd. It soon becomes apparent that Paul finds it necessary periodically to visit Thomas Edison's old laboratory in order to receive a "vote of confidence from the past . . . where the past admitted how humble and shoddy it had been, where one could look from the old to the new and see that mankind really had come a long way" (6). He loses any feelings of reassurance that the monument to technological progress should give him when he observes the efficient, utterly inhumane fashion in which his plant's mechanical sweeper disposes of his cat. Vonnegut carefully describes the cat's natural antipathy for the machine. When the machine mangled the cat and spewed it high in the air, the animal "dropped to the asphalt — dead and smoking, but outside" (12). It is only by dying that the cat is able to escape the scientific community's electronically guarded compound.

In a way, Paul faces the same problem as the cat. Unable to feel happy living in a machine-dominated society, he feels compelled to decide whether he wants to leave it and how he can do so. Paul finally decides to leave because of his job "wasn't getting anybody anywhere. Because it was getting everybody nowhere" (247). He occasionally thinks about an experiment that he and his colleagues Shepherd and Finnerty had conducted when they were younger and more eager to automate. They had managed to immortalize the skilled workman Rudy Herz on computer tape and ". . . this little loop in the box before Paul, here was Rudy as Rudy had been to his machine that afternoon — Rudy, the turner-on of power, the setter of speeds, the controller of the cutting tool. This was the essence of Rudy as far as the machine was concerned. . . . The tape was the essence distilled from the small, polite man. . ."(9 - 10). Obviously what the young engineers had overlooked was the uniqueness of Rudy as a human being; no machine could quite capture that quality. Vonnegut included this episode in his novel because he had witnessed a similar experiment at General Electric's Schenectady plant and had felt that "it was too bad for the human beings who get their dignity from their jobs."[10]

The pride Paul feels when his experiment works with Rudy Herz is indicative of the danger he faces if he remains in such an environment. His Doctor Frankenstein-like pride in creating a machine that functions like a man ultimately could deaden his feelings of human compassion and turn him into another Berringer, the dull young

engineer who feels nothing but irrational enthusiasm for the wonders
of technology. By the skillful use of metaphors Vonnegut seems to indicate that Paul and his wife Anita have already become two
automatons; for "Anita had the mechanics of marriage down pat,
even to the subtlest conventions. If her approach was disturbingly
rational, systematic, she was thorough enough to turn out a credible
counterfeit of warmth. Paul could only suspect that her feelings were
shallow. . ." (16). The key words here are *mechanics, rational,* and
counterfeit; for quite apparently Paul thinks Anita to be calculating,
precise, and cold as a machine. Anita has similar feelings about Paul;
she sobs and tells him that "I wasn't any damn use to you at all! . . .
All you need is something stainless steel, shaped like a woman,
covered with sponge rubber, and heated to body temperature. . . .
I'm sick of being treated like a machine!" (216). It is not surprising
that, when Paul is sleeping with a prostitute and she mumbles
something, "he utters an *automatic* reply, 'And I love you, Anita!' "
(118) (italics added).

Proteus realizes that he is becoming more and more inhuman and
finds that he must make a decision: he must either accept his age of
science as a paradise and be content to live as an automaton or leave
such a society. He slides into "the fantasy of the new, good life ahead
of him. Somewhere, outside of society, there was a place for a man
and wife — to live heartily and blamelessly, *naturally,* by hands and
wits" (126). What Paul seeks is a separate peace, a farm on which he
can live and ignore the demands of an unjust society. Unfortunately
for him, the farm in reality proves to be inadequate. When he attempts to grasp the "hand of nature," he soon discovers it is "coarse
and sluggish, hot and wet and smelly" (224). Paul finds he cannot be
a farmer because the conditioning he has received from an in-
dustrialized society has not only prepared him to work with machines
but completely divorced him from nature.

The only avenue remaining open for him is armed rebellion. Vonnegut suggests that Proteus's decision is really not surprising; it is
just that the young manager has not let himself consciously realize
his growing disillusionment. When he first learned that his good
friend Finnerty had quit his job, he was delighted but did not know
why. When his wife revealed that his boss Kroner felt that Proteus
was not really sure about following the path of his father by assuming a greater position of power and responsibility, Paul replied "he's
got more insight into me than I do. . . . I'm not sure. He apparently
knew that before I did" (15). When Finnerty comes to visit Paul, he

studies him and then says "I thought you'd be pretty close to the edge by now. That's why I came here" (35). Actually, his intuition is correct; Paul is close to resigning his position, but he does not yet realize this fact because he does not understand the depth of his own dissatisfaction.

Vonnegut provides another example of Paul's divided loyalties when he describes the young manager's desire to drive occasionally across the river to that part of Ilium that engineers never visited — the area where the people displaced by machines live. When Paul removes his engineer's coat for an old leather one, he symbolically rejects the values of his own society; for he tells Finnerty that a psychiatrist would label such an action as a "swat at my old man, who never went anywhere without a Homburg and a double-breasted suit" (72). While such a judgment may very well be accurate, Paul's father may also symbolize the very technological oligarchy that he managed. His choice of clothes suggests a surrender to the mores of a society that demands conformity. Obviously Paul cannot move from the values of his society to those of another as easily as he can change coats. When he sees unemployed workers who have been organized into a Reconstruction and Reclamation Corps, "his skin began to itch as though he had suddenly become unclean" (21). Later, his feelings would change; he would have a

feeling of newness — the feeling of fresh, strong identity growing within him. It was a generalized love — particularly for the little people, the common people. God bless them. All his life they had been hidden from him by the walls of his ivory tower. Now . . . he had come among them, shared their hopes and disappointments, understood their yearnings, discovered the beauty of their simplicities and their earthy values. This was *real*, this side of the river, and Paul loved these common people, and wanted to help, and let them know how they were loved and understood, and he wanted them to love him too (88).

While Paul feels love for the useless people in much the same way that Eliot Rosewater does in *God Bless You, Mr. Rosewater*, Vonnegut's presentation is ambiguous. Paul is very drunk when he describes his feelings of love for the common people. In light of the irresponsible actions of the members of the Ghost Shirt Society during the abortive revolution, in the narrative, Vonnegut is suggesting that Paul not only does not understand the struggle within himself but is also unable to distinguish between appearance and reality on either side of the river: he does not understand either the common

people or the engineers. Proteus' knowledge of himself does grow;
for, when he reaches the point that he no longer wants that part of
his social self identified with management to exist, he watches it die:
"He felt oddly disembodied, an insubstantial wisp, nothingness, a
man who declined to be any more" (117 - 18). Paul is quite capable
of such a change since his name Proteus suggests the ability to assume different forms, and Vonnegut has remarked that the myth of
Proteus is perhaps the paramount one for writers today.[11]

The new Proteus is encouraged to join the revolution about to take
place by a minister with an anthropology background, the Reverend
Lasher. Echoing many of Vonnegut's own sentiments, Lasher offers
Paul membership in the Ghost Shirt Society, a revolutionary group
that likens modern man's situation to that of the Indians when the
white men began to impose their values upon them since "Indian
ways in a white man's world were irrelevant" (250). To Lasher,

. . . the Ghost Dance religion . . . was the last, desperate defense of the old
values. Messiahs appeared, the way they're always ready to appear, to
preach magic that would restore the game, the old values, the old reasons for
being. There were new rituals and new songs that were supposed to get rid
of the white man by magic. And some of the more warlike tribes that still
had a little physical fight left in them added a flourish of their own — the
Ghost Shirt. . . . They were going to ride into battle one last time . . . in
magic shirts that white men's bullets wouldn't get through (250).

Lasher finds the analogy valid because "People are finding that
because of the way the machines are changing the world, more and
more of their old values don't apply anymore" (274). Paul notices
that a half-wit, Luke Lubbock, is wearing a Ghost Shirt; and when
he asks Finnerty if Luke really believes that it is bullet proof, Finnerty replies that "It's the symbolism of the thing" (250).

The fact that it is Luke who is wearing the shirt should remind
Paul of the time when he saw the costumed Luke leading the parade
of a secret fraternal order. When he had stepped out of one costume
to change into another, Paul noticed that Luke looked "ragged and
drab, and none-too-clean. And Luke had somehow shrunk and sad-
dened and was knobbed and scarred and scrawny. He was subdued
now, talking not at all, and meeting no one's eyes" (82). Desperately,
Luke began to put on his other costume; and he was suddenly
"growing again, getting his color back" as he dressed. When he
finished, he "was talkative again — important and strong" (82).

Lasher, who is much better able to distinguish between appearance and reality than Paul, tells the young manager that Luke's actions are "Harmless magic: good old-fashioned bunkum" (82). It is "bunkum" that Paul wants to believe as fervently as Luke.

Paul wants to believe that the Ghost Shirt Society is a positive force for changing an America dominated by machines. When the organization has been destroyed, Vonnegut reveals that, of all the conspirators, Paul is "the one most out of touch, having had little time for reflection, having been so eager to join a large, confident organization with seeming answers to the problems that had made him sorry to be alive" (289). He finds it simpler to transfer from one organization to another and is not really ready, therefore, to change his life. Lasher tells Paul that, since he knew all the time that the movement would fail, he didn't "let himself lose touch with reality" (289). Paul feels a moral responsibility to search for a solution to the problems posed by an unjust society, but he chooses unwisely because of his own insecurity. When Paul is questioned by the government at his trial, he is encased in electronic gadgets to the point that he resembles a machine more than a human being.

In answer to this dehumanization Paul declares that the "main business of humanity is to do a good job of being human beings . . . not to serve as appendages to machines, institutions, and systems" (273). One of the telling ironies in *Player Piano* is that Paul nobly declares his humanity at the very moment that a completely rational, unemotional, heartless government seems to dehumanize him. Yet, immediately afterwards, he joins an organization that is based completely upon emotion, the kind of irrationality revealed in the intentional destruction of sewage plants and food facilities by people who hate any and all machines and who fail to use their rational powers of discrimination.

IV *The Shah of Bratpuhr*

One of the many subplots in *Player Piano* centers around the Shah of Bratpuhr, who is the spiritual leader of six million Kolhouri, and who visits the United States. When he asks to see how average Americans live, he is taken to the home of Edgar R. B. Hagstrohm who is a member of the Reconstruction and Reclamation Corps. The manager of Hagstrohm's subdivision proudly shows the Shah the microwave oven, the ultrasonic dishwasher and clotheswasher, and the automatic ironer. Since the Shah cannot understand why everything must be done so quickly, he wishes to know "What is it she is in such a hurry to get at? What is it she has to do, that she mustn't waste any time on these things?" (159). Wanda Hagstrohm confesses that she uses her free time to watch television. The Shah leaves her home and chuckles as he gives the Hagstrohms his final message: Live! His advice is ironic, of course, because he realizes that the family is incapable of really living because it lacks any sort of spiritual foundation; its life is built on a foundation of materialism. At one point, Vonnegut provides his readers with a stream-of-consciousness passage to reveal what the thousands of Edgar Hagstrohms actually think about. The thoughts of a Private Hacketts who is marching in a parade honoring the Shah indicate the accuracy of the Shah's observation:

And Hacketts wondered where the hell he'd go in the next twenty-three years and thought it'd be a relief to get the hell out of the states for a while and go occupy someplace else and maybe be somebody in some of these countries instead of a bum with no money looking for an easy lay anyway but still a pretty good lay compared to no lay at all but anyway there was more to living than laying and he'd like a little glory by God and there might be laying *and* glory overseas and while there wasn't any shooting and wasn't going to be none either probably for a good long while still you got a real gun and bullets and there was a little glory in that. . . . (58)

Hagstrohm senses that there is more to life than what he has, but his imagination is so limited that he cannot grasp what the Shah represents.

The Shah also is taken to see EPICAC XIV, the massive computer that determines what intelligence levels separate the useful men from the useless rejects. When he is told that in the small section of EPICAC visible to him there is enough wire to circle the moon four times, he replies in characteristically human terms that people in his poor land sleep with smart women and thus make brains cheaply. Then he goes up to the massive computer and asks it a riddle because his religion believes that "a great, all-wise god will come among us one day . . . and we shall know him, for he shall be able to answer the riddle . . . (106). The fact that the computer cannot answer the sphinx-like riddle indicates to the Shah that technology is not the god that will liberate mankind. Before he leaves America for home, the State Department offers to send engineers and managers with him to "Study your resources, blueprint your modernization, get it started, test and classify your people, arrange credit, set up the machinery" (277). The Shah replies that, before he can accept such an offer, he wants EPICAC to tell him what people are for. This same question Billy the Poet ponders in a later Vonnegut short story entitled "Welcome to the Monkey House," and Vonnegut also considers it in his later novels *The Sirens of Titan* and *God Bless You, Mr. Rosewater.* He has little sympathy with people who consider money or machinery to be more important than people.

V *The Meadows*

One of the key scenes in *Player Piano* takes place at The Meadows, an executive retreat where managers annually spend two weeks playing team sports, drinking, and renewing their faith in the system. Some critics have scoffed at Vonnegut's description of the "goings on" at The Meadows as being sophomoric and ridiculous, but Vonnegut has confessed that General Electric used to hold such a ceremony annually at Association Island. The one-week stint served as a "morale-building operation for General Electric, and deserving young men were sent up there for a week and played golf and there were archery contests and baseball contests . . . and plenty of free liquor, and so forth."[12] Not surprisingly, General Electric abandoned this tradition shortly after *Player Piano* was published.

The Meadows section has been called "corny" and "trite," but this tone is precisely what Vonnegut tries to capture. The young managers arrive on the island serenaded by a medley of "Pack Up Your Troubles," "I Want a Girl," "Take Me Out to the Ball Game," and "Working on the Railroad." The élite then gather around a gigantic oak tree that has become a symbol of "courage, integrity, perseverance, beauty" (172). They then sing a hymn to the tree:

> Fellows at the Meadows,
> Lift your tankards high;
> Toast our living symbol, reaching toward the sky,
> Grown from but an acorn,
> Giant now you are;
> May you never stop growing;
> Rise to the stars!
> Proud sy-him-bol a-bov (173).

The only man to cry because of this ceremony is Luke Lubbock, the imbecile who has been hired to wash dishes. Luke is moved by the ceremony and believes what he hears and sees; later, he will embrace the Ghost Shirt Society with the same credibility.

The Meadows incident serves as a spiritual climax for Paul Proteus. He finds himself relaxing and having fun even though laughing is wholly out of character for him. He realizes that "for the first time since he'd made up his mind to quit, he really hadn't given a damn about the system, about the Meadows, about intramural politics. . . . Now suddenly, as of this afternoon, he was his own man" (182). Freed of any lingering doubts, he can enjoy the ludicrousness of The Meadows and chuckle at the ridiculous allegory that depicts the conflict between Radical and Young Engineer. The Radical quizzes John Average-man about how unimportant he now feels and about his paltry take-home pay. The Young Engineer points out that John is better off than Julius Caesar because all his medical and dental expenses are paid by the government and because he has every electronic appliance at his fingertips. John comes to realize how fortunate he is that the star of technology shines brightly in the heavens. The Star of Bethlehem has been replaced by the Star of Technology, and the allegory ends with a hymn to a new god:

Thirty-one point seven times as many television sets as all the rest of the world put together!
    (music gets louder)
Ninety-three per-cent of all the world's electrostatic dust precipitators! Seventy-seven per-cent of all the world's automobiles! Ninety-eight per-cent of its helicopters! Eighty-one point nine per-cent of its refrigerators! (189)

The allegory reflects the superficiality of the men who believe it. Later, Paul Proteus learns that the mighty oak tree has been destroyed by a disgruntled manager whose son failed his crucial placement examinations. When the Ghost Shirt Society stages its revolt, Proteus finds the same oversimplifications, the same concern with wearing costumes, the same concern with symbols. The managers believe in the invincibility of the machines. Finnerty and his followers also believe that they cannot possibly fail. The Meadows reflects Vonnegut's distrust of any large organization that expects blind devotion from its members even at the cost of their individuality.

VI *Fathers and Sons*

Paul Proteus eventually realizes that, while Finnerty rebelled against the government because it was a "close little society that made no comfortable place for him" (320), his own rebellion may represent a childish attempt to rebel against the memory of his famous father by attempting to destroy the very society he had helped create. At the trial, Vonnegut supplies electronic proof of Paul's feelings of hatred for his father. Paul angrily lashes out that, as for his father, "the editor of *Who's Who* knows about as much as I do. The guy was hardly ever home" (72). After leaving his job, Paul awakens from a dream to see "his father glowering at him from the foot of the bed" (224). This vision of his father apparently represents Paul's guilt feelings that result from his leaving and thus repudiating all that the elder Proteus had worked to build.

Doctor Proteus is the first of a long line of Vonnegut fathers who are so preoccupied with their own affairs that they ignore their children and psychically wound them. Vonnegut frequently has lamented his father's insistence that he ignore the "silly" arts and concentrate on chemistry since it was a practical subject in which to major.[13] Vonnegut portrays two kinds of father figures in his fiction: the very common domineering, career-minded kind represented by George Proteus *(Player Piano)*; Senator Rosewater *(God Bless You, Mr. Rosewater)*; and Felix Hoenikker *(Cat's Cradle)*, the less frequently appearing, loving, gentle, fantasy-father figure illustrated by Edgar Derby *(Slaughterhouse-Five)*. Often in Vonnegut's fictive universe there is a yearning for a God resembling a gentle, fantasy-father figure, but there is the realization that He is probably more like George Proteus or Felix Hoenikker — too busy with other projects to concern Himself with his earthly children.

VII   *The Conclusion of* Player Piano

As *Player Piano* concludes, Paul Proteus observes that the common people who took part in the revolution against machines are now seeking to reassemble the very machines that made them obsolete. Paul would like to drink to a "better world"; but, when he thinks of "the people of Ilium, already eager to recreate the same old nightmare," he merely says "To the Record" (295). He is unable to improve or even to change his society, but he is at least able to distinguish between appearance and reality. When Paul sees men driven by hysteria and frenzy racing through the streets destroying all machines indiscriminately, he moans that he "never thought it would be like this. . . . It had all the characteristics of a lynching" (286). And, in a sense, a lynching is all Paul has to look forward to as the novel concludes. It is quite clear that he realizes when he surrenders that he will be executed. Lasher declares that, even though they failed to destroy the technology-oriented society, the important thing is that they registered their protest and took the "one chance in a thousand." According to Lasher, then, Paul's struggle is not in vain but is a noble struggle that will pave the way for later rebels to alter the entire American social structure.

Vonnegut is not so optimistic as Lasher is because he sees the mob's attempt to reassemble the orange drink machine not as a random whim but as a reflection of the American psyche, which is characterized by "the restless, erratic insight and imagination of a gadgeteer."[14] Perhaps this characterization is the germ of an idea that later becomes a major theme in Vonnegut's fiction — the possibility that man has a tragic flaw that relentlessly moves him in the direction of self-annihilation.

VIII *Technique and Style in* Player Piano

Although *Player Piano* in many ways is Kurt Vonnegut's most conventional novel, it does foreshadow his later development as a major innovative novelist. The novel's structure consists of a series of intricate plots and subplots reminiscent of Aldous Huxley's *Point Counterpoint;* but, unlike the English novelist, Vonnegut never ties his subplots together. Although it is ironic and thematically quite appropriate that Paul Proteus is always near the Shah of Bratpuhr, the meeting which might fill Paul's spiritual void never occurs.

Rather than progressing in a strictly linear fashion, Vonnegut's plot evolves into subplots and then into digressions. Dr. Ewig Halyard, the State Department guide for the Shah of Bratpuhr, learns that he has been stripped of his degrees because a computer discovered that he never fulfilled his undergraduate physical education requirement. Vonnegut sets aside the Shah's story while he pauses to ridicule misplaced values in academe, particularly the excess importance of college athletics. While Peter Reed has criticized this technique because "the subplots and digressions often weaken the central narrative,"[15] such criticism overlooks the possibility that Vonnegut has consciously broken the rules for a conventionally structured novel in an attempt to find a narrative mode more conducive to his story and his temperament. Indeed, James Mellard has gone so far as to suggest that in *Player Piano* the object of Vonnegut's technique is "the overthrow of the accepted literary conventions of visual imagery, continuous plotting, connected characterization, uniform point of view — all the mechanical aspects of pictorialism associated with Henry James and the mimetic novel."[16]

In fact, Vonnegut creates caricatures rather than characters in *Player Piano* and focuses in this manner the reader's attention on what the characters represent. Paul's boss Kroner, for example, represents the technocracy's simple-minded faith in the myth of progress through technology; he tells Paul that "Our job is to open new doors at the head of the procession of civilization. That's what the engineer, the manager does. There is no higher calling" (111). Paul's subordinate, Bud Calhoun, on the other hand, represents the self-destructive American love for gadgetry that results in his automating his job out of existence. Bud, shown always in a sitting position, is passively, mechanically, willing to accept the computer's decision concerning his faith. Vonnegut portrays virtually all his characters as mechanical, lifeless, and passive, while his machines become hideous parodies of humanity. At times, the machines dance in human fashion: ". . . he turned in his delight to watch a cluster of miniature maypoles braid bright cloth insulation about a black snake of cable. A thousand little dancers whirled about one another, unerringly building their snug snare about the cable" (10). Immediately after observing this dance by the machinery, Paul is horrified to see a monstrous mechanical sweeper attack a cat, gobble her up, and hurl her into "its galvanized tin belly" (11).

Vonnegut symbolizes the central conflict in his novel between technology and nature with his description of both the player piano and the ghost shirt. When Paul Proteus visits Homestead, the area reserved for the men automated out of jobs, he is cornered by a senile Rudy Hertz, the man whose lathe motions had been captured years earlier on computer tape by Paul. Hertz is fascinated by the movement of the piano keys and tells Paul, "you can almost see a ghost sitting there playing his heart out" (28).

Paul's initials suggest his partial responsibility for the plight of the men in Homestead. It is precisely the notion that there is more to humanity than the mere mechanical motions able to be captured on computer tape that results in the formation of the revolutionary Ghost Shirt Society, for medicine men told their braves that those men wearing ghost shirts could not be harmed by bullets. With a double-edged irony, Vonnegut suggests that the engineer's belief in technology and the revolutionaires' belief in mankind are both overly zealous. The revolution fails because the group responsible for the destruction of the central computer EPICAC XIV displayed too much love for gadgetry. Their plan to place nitroglycerin in the "coke" bottles in a vending machine was too complicated, and it resulted in their own destruction.[17]

When the revolution fails, a robot helicopter flies over the ruins of the destroyed machinery and plays a message demanding that the Ghost Shirt Society leaders surrender. The helicopter is wounded, however, and its message becomes a garbled "Beeby dee bobble de beezle! Nozzle ah reeble beejee" (287). *Player Piano* is filled with descriptions of machines that do not work properly from the one in Thomas Edison's old laboratory to the microwave oven in a home the Shah of Bratpuhr visits. With telling irony, Vonnegut suggests that in the world of *Player Piano* the humans have replaced themselves with machines that contain their ghosts, their essences; and, perhaps because of this touch of humanity, the machines are imperfect and mortal. Like his Greek namesake, Paul Proteus is amorphous enough to become both a player piano and a Ghost Shirt Society leader although neither role satisfies him. In the nightmarish world of Ilium, New York, Vonnegut, like Paul Proteus, is unable to toast the possibilities of a better world. In his next novel, Vonnegut turns completely away from the world of machinery and creates a fantasy world that remains one of his most unique achievements.

IX   The Sirens of Titan: *Plot and Structure*

While in *Player Piano* Vonnegut suggests the dangers man faces if he allows technology to usurp his role, he goes one step further in *The Sirens of Titan* (1959) and considers the possibility that man is merely a machine whose destiny is already controlled by other machines. In many ways this novel is Vonnegut's most complex one since it functions simultaneously as a parody of "hard-core" pulp science fiction, a description of the mythic journey of a modern-day hero, and, perhaps most importantly, as a tongue-in-cheek exploration of the meaninglessness of the universe. The plot is far more complex than the mere counterpointing of Paul Proteus and the Shah of Bratpuhr in *Player Piano*.

The plot of *The Sirens of Titan* revolves around Winston Niles Rumfoord, a millionaire member of the Eastern establishment that is responsible for "a tenth of America's presidents, a quarter of its explorers, a third of its Eastern seaboard governors, a half of its full-time ornithologists . . ." (26). Vonnegut has confessed that Rumfoord is a portrait of Franklin D. Roosevelt and that Roosevelt is "the key figure of the book."[18] Rumfoord runs his spaceship into a chronosynclastic infundibulum, and he and his dog are transformed into wave phenomena. The result of this collision is that both dog and master are scattered both temporally and spatially throughout the solar system. Using his knowledge of the future, Rumfoord concocts a plot to bring peace and harmony to Earth with the unwilling aid of a jaded playboy named Malachi Constant.

Malachi Constant, a very familiar literary figure, is the profligate who abandons all the physical pleasure of the world and becomes a holy man searching for truth. He begins as a multimillionaire playboy who has become jaded by too many women and too much alcohol; he longs for only one thing, "a single message that is sufficiently dignified and important to merit his carrying it humbly between two points" (17). Throughout the novel Malachi functions as a Jonah figure; and Rumfoord serves as a vengeful Old Testament God. Malachi's name means "faithful messenger," and, when he visits the Rumfoord estate to receive his message, he disguises himself as Mr. Jonah Rowley in order to avoid the wrath of the crowd that longs to see Rumfoord appear as a wave phenomenon. The Jonah name is an appropriate choice for Constant since Rumfoord manipulates him into a spaceship named *The Whale* after first informing him that, despite any efforts to escape his fate, he would eventually mate with Mrs. Rumfoord and travel to Mars, to Mercury, and finally to Titan.

On Mars, Malachi and Beatrice Rumfoord find themselves part of a Martian army composed of ex-earthlings who are forced to obey the commands they receive from the radio antennae implanted in their heads. As part of Rumfoord's master plan, the Martian army attacks Earth and is virtually annihilated in a thermonuclear war designed by Rumfoord to end all wars. While the army is being destroyed, Malachi Constant (known on Mars as Unk) finds that his spaceship takes him and his Black companion Boaz to Mercury. The ship buries itself far beneath the planet's surface in a region inhabited by primitive creatures known as harmoniums. While Malachi spends three years searching for a way to escape, Boaz dedicates himself to playing music to satisfy the harmoniums' appetite for the vibrations they feed upon.

When Malachi discovers how to return to Earth, Boaz refuses to go. Like the famed anthropologist Franz Boaz who specialized in primitive cultures, he decides to dedicate his life to the harmoniums. Malachi returns to Earth at just the appropriate moment to become the scapegoat for Rumfoord's new Church of God the Utterly Indifferent. He is exiled with Beatrice Rumfoord and their son Chrono to

Titan where they meet Salo, the Tralfamadorian robot, and his disabled spaceship. Malachi learns that all human history has been manipulated by the Tralfamadorians in order to convey to Salo information about when to expect the replacement part for his ship.

As the novel concludes, Malachi dies imagining (with the aid of Salo's hypnosis) that he once again sees his best friend from Mars, Stony Stevenson, who reveals to him that they are going to Paradise. When asked why, Stony replies "Don't ask me why, old sport, but somebody up there likes you" (319). Thus Malachi's last act, albeit under hypnosis, is to turn away from reality and to indulge himself with a comforting illusion. While Constant opens the first chapter with the statement, "I guess somebody up there likes me" (7), in his final vision, Stony changes this statement for him having removed the words "I guess." Since Malachi now feels only love and compassion for all humanity, the question of whether or not he is actually going to Paradise is really irrelevant. Ironically, Rumfoord created and sold Malachi dolls as an object of scorn, a symbol of the worst traits of humanity. By being forced to journey in *The Whale* and suffer, the passive Malachi, like Jofa', lbsessallsfeelings of selfishness and callousness. He finds he can no longer hate anyone.

There is also a political dimension to Malachi's journey in *The Sirens of Titan*. At one point on Mars, after he has had his mind "cleaned out" of all previous thoughts, he is able to read a letter he had written earlier without even suspecting that he had done so: "Before turning to the signature, Unk tried to imagine the character and appearance of the writer. The writer was such a lover of truth that he would expose himself to any amount of pain in order to add to his store of truth. He was superior to Unk and Stony. He watched and recorded their subversive activities with love, amusement, and detachment" (132).

Until he reads the letter, Malachi feels contented after his operation; he knows what his purpose in life is: the destruction of Earth. The question of why Malachi is dissatisfied with his life on Mars before his operation is crucial to an understanding of Vonnegut's concept of man's role in society. Before his operation, Malachi views Martian society as essentially democratic with all men equal in the Martian army. Malachi learns the same painful lesson that Paul Proteus does; he realizes that he is being used. By taking away Malachi's power to govern his own destiny, Rumfoord has made him feel that he no longer has any human dignity.

When Malachi discovers that, during the period that his mind was "cleaned out," he had killed his best friend Stony Stevenson, he deals with the question of his moral responsibility for his actions. After weeping, he has a "thorough understanding now of his own worthlessness, and a bitter sympathy for anyone who might find it good to handle him roughly" (260). No longer split into the Malachi and Unk identities, Constant is faced with the same choice that confronted Paul Proteus: should he try for a separate peace? While his companion Boaz is happy remaining with his pet harmoniums on Mercury far away from the pressures of human society, Malachi finds that he wants to live with people; but he cannot bear to return to Earth. His wife perhaps best expresses his sentiments when she sarcastically bids adieu to "all you clean and wise and lovely people." Man is not clean, sweet, or lovely; but Malachi learns to love him at a distance and realizes that the "purpose of life, no matter who is controlling it, is to love whoever is around to be loved" (312).

Malachi Constant's movement from ignorance to knowledge can also be viewed in mythic terms. As John Somer has indicated, Constant's search for spiritual unity follows the three stages of departure, initiation, and return that Joseph Campbell describes in *The Hero with a Thousand Faces* as the basic mythic-adventure pattern.[19] Vonnegut begins the fourth chapter of *The Sirens of Titan* with the following:

> Rented a tent, a tent, a tent;
> Rented a tent, a tent, a tent.
> Rented a tent!
> Rented a tent!
> Rented a, rented a tent.

SNARE DRUM ON MARS

The chant represents eventually the limits imposed upon Unk (Malachi) while he is a soldier in the Martian army. The martial drumming and the pain that can be piped through his antenna condition him to obey blindly all orders. When he is ordered to kill his best friend Stony Stevenson, he does so without hesitation. This chant, which is repeated four times in the chapter, represents what could be Vonnegut's Unpardonable Sin — the deliberate dehumanization of a fellow human being.[20]

The army experience on Mars is only one stage of Malachi's initia-

tion, and it is followed by his three-year stay deep beneath the surface of Mercury. During this period he struggles to free himself from
his womb-like cave. On Titan, Unk once again becomes Malachi
Constant; but this time he no longer pines for a message to carry; he
knows now that the secret of human life is to love whomever is
around to be loved. His earlier strangulation of Stony Stevenson was
really the death of a very important part of himself since it had
destroyed any hope he might have had for mankind's perfectability.
Later on Mercury, he constantly thought about how, once he was
united with Stony, the two of them would be invincible. Malachi
returns to Indianapolis, Indiana, to die.

Beatrice Rumfoord is the bridge that connects Winston Niles
Rumfoord and Malachi Constant. When Malachi first arrives at the
Rumfoord estate, he sees a picture of her as a little girl:

> . . . a huge oil painting of a little girl holding the reins of a pure white pony.
> The little girl wore a white bonnet, a white, starched dress, white gloves,
> white socks, and white shoes.
>   She was the cleanest, most frozen little girl that Malachi Constant had
> ever seen. There was a strange expression on her face, and Constant decided
> that she was worried about getting the least bit dirty (23).

Rumfoord later tells Malachi that Beatrice suffered from a
"congenital coldness" (163); her marriage with Rumfoord was un-
consummated. Forced to mate with Malachi and then to become a
small cog in the Martian invasion, Beatrice gradually grows in
stature. Working as an instructor of Schliemann breathing, the
technique that permitted Martian soldiers to acquire oxygen from a
pill rather than from the atmosphere, Beatrice writes a sonnet that
begins:

> Break every link with air and mist,
> Seal every open vent;
> Make throat as tight as miser's fist,
> Keep life within you pent.
>
>   . . . .
>
> Yes, every man's an island:
> Island fortress, island home (152 - 53).

This sonnet, which parodies John Donne's seventeenth-century
"Holy Sonnets" and his sermon "No Man is an Island," reflects

Beatrice's spiritual isolation on Mars: she is told she may visit her son Chrono, but her feelings of love for the boy were removed during her brain cleansing. Malachi Constant's movement from rake to holy man is paralleled by Beatrice's movement from a cold, virginal statue to a warm earth goddess. Signs of this movement appear even on Mars where her job requires her to be a bee, going from one frozen soldier to another plugging noses, ears, and mouths.[21] She provides a life-giving service since her soldiers will be able to survive without oxygen after they have mastered the technique she is teaching.

When she lands on Titan, she and Malachi lean against a statue of Saint Francis of Assisi, an appropriate figure since Malachi is in the process of becoming a holy man. Beatrice looks like a "gypsy queen smoldered at the foot of a statue of a young physical student" (228). Beatrice's earth-goddess role becomes apparent when Vonnegut points out that a closer look at the young scientist reveals that "the young truth-seeker had a shocking erection" (289). Before she dies and is buried beneath Titantic peat, she suddenly has an idea: she turns to Malachi to tell him that "the worst thing that could possibly happen to anybody . . . would be to not be used for anything by anybody" (310). Since she makes this observation after looking at the painting of her as a little girl, the implication is that she realizes that had she continued as detached and virginal as she was as a little girl, her life would have been a living death. This truth relaxes her, and she dies apparently as contented as her husband.

X *Science Fiction, Future History, and Meaninglessness* in The Sirens of Titan

The early lurid paperback covers that adorned *The Sirens of Titan* are ample proof that at least some publicists read the novel strictly as science fiction and completely missed the satiric elements. In reality, Vonnegut manages to parody the traditional elements of "hard-core" pulp science fiction while utilizing the future-history framework used successfully in such science-fiction classics as Isaac Asimov's *Foundation* trilogy and Frank Herbert's *Dune* and *Dune Messiah*. Moreover, Vonnegut's often-expressed love for the novels of H. G. Wells is reflected in the comic contrasts between his novel and Wells's *The War of the Worlds*. While Wells's Martians are completely inhuman and possess superior weaponry, Vonnegut's Martians are the dregs of human society equipped with single-shot rifles. Four other elements of traditional science fiction not found in *The War of the Worlds* but treated mock seriously in *The Sirens of Titan* include the use of robots with the suggestion that Salo, the robot, is more human than his human friend, Rumfoord; the kidnapping of Earthlings by extraterrestrials; the use of superior spaceships able to exceed the speed of light by some version of "space warp," in Vonnegut's novel the powerful force is the "Universal Will to Become"; and a trip beneath the surface of a planet where strange creatures are encountered.

The Sirens of Titan begins with Vonnegut revealing that "the following is a true story from the Nightmare Ages, falling roughly, give or take a few years, between the Second World War and the Third Great Depression" (8). The story is told retrospectively, as are many science-fiction stories; and, since the story examines the distant past, it not only allows Vonnegut to provide background material that otherwise might seem obtrusive, but also makes the story more believable. History is the major subject of *The Sirens of Titan* since Vonnegut's focus is on whether or not human history is meaningful.

Vonnegut suggests that historians such as Arnold Toynbee and Oswald Spengler have wasted their time trying to discover patterns and meaning to a human history that has been the result of Tralfamadorians' efforts to send a message from one end of the universe to the other. Vonnegut points out that the Tralfamadorians manipulated the people of Earth in order to communicate with Salo on Titan:

> Stonehenge wasn't the only message old Salo had received.
> There had been four others, all of them written on Earth.
> The Great Wall of China means in Tralfamadorian, when viewed from above: "Be patient, we haven't forgotten about you."
> The Golden House of the Roman Emperor Nero meant: "We are going the best we can."
> The meaning of the Moscow Kremlin when it was first walled was "You will be on your way before you know it."
> The meaning of the Palace of the League of Nations in Geneva, Switzerland, is "Pack up your things and be ready on short notice" (271 - 72).

Hundreds of times Salo watches civilizations begin to bloom on Earth only to "poop out without having finished the message" (273). When the President of the United States makes a speech about the need for progress and for space research, his statement is ironical because history is not linear and because mankind is not moving toward a City of God. The message that precipitated all human history is the word "Greetings" which, ironically, was until recently the United States government's call to arms to its young draftees. They were drafted, trained, fought, and died for no human purpose.

Later a distraught Vonnegut returns to the theme of free will in *Breakfast of Champions;* but his tone in *The Sirens of Titan* is still playful with a touch of cynicism. Malachi Constant, Beatrice Rumfoord, and Malachi's companion Boaz are each able to accept the idea of being used by some unknown force. They are able to accept their lack of free will in determining their destinies because they find that what is important is not *why* they live but *how* they live. Only the millionaire Winston Niles Rumfoord is unable to accept this harsh truth.

Vonnegut frequently describes Rumfoord as supernatural, as almost godlike. When he "staged a passion play, he used nothing but real people in real hells" (329). More importantly, following the terrible destruction of the Martians, Rumfoord reveals to the people of Earth that they should accept his Church of God the Utterly Indifferent because he "as head of the religion can work miracles as the head of no other religion can. What miracles can I work? I can work the miracle of predicting with absolute accuracy the things that the future will bring . . . The next time I come to you, I shall bring a Bible, revised so as to be meaningful in modern times" (180 - 81). Rumfoord manipulates the inhabitants of Earth and Mars in his godlike way because he "wished to change the world for the better by means of the great and unforgettable suicide of Mars" (174). On Titan, he resembles a halo-clad deity: "Rumfoord held his hands tight and his fingers were spread. Streaks of pink, violet, and pale green, Saint Elmo's Fire, streamed from his fingertips. Short streaks of pale gold fizzed in his hair, conspiring to give a tinsel halo" (279).

Vonnegut may very well be using the word *tinsel* to indicate the dubious nature of Rumfoord's divinity, for the millionaire is merely a small cog in a vast machine that is beyond his control. At one point, he tells his wife Beatrice "life for a punctual person is like a roller coaster. . . . All kinds of things are going to happen to you! I can see the whole roller coaster you're on. And sure — I could give you a piece of paper that would tell you about every dip and turn, warn you about every bogeyman that was going to pop out at you in the tunnels. But that wouldn't help you any. . . . Because you'd still have to take the roller-coaster ride . . . I don't own it, and I don't say who rides it and who doesn't. I just know what it's shaped like" (57 - 8).

If his wife's fate is inevitable, it is not clear why Rumfoord finds it necessary during this conversation to lie to her when she asks about her future relationship with Malachi Constant. She will eventually be mated with him and become his loving wife on Titan. Vonnegut stops the narrative at the very moment Rumfoord lies to reveal that "this cock-and-bull" story is one of the few known instances of Winston Niles Rumfoord's having told a lie (58). He may have lied because he had to since Beatrice's inevitable destiny is to wind up on Titan with Malachi, or this lie might be one link in a chain of events that eventually leads her there. It is apparent that Rumfoord feels helpless and realizes with a certain horror that the Tralfamadorians have manipulated him when he tells Beatrice that "Tralfamadore . . . picked me up, and used me like a handy dandy potato peeler! I take a certain pride, no matter how foolishly mistaken that pride may be, in making my own decisions for my own reasons" (285).

Is it possible to reconcile Vonnegut's contention that Rumfoord can see into the future with his shock at discovering that he is being used? If he can see far enough into the future to be able to tell his wife that "Some day on Titan, it will be revealed to you just how ruthlessly I've been used, and by whom, and to what disgustingly paltry ends," why should he be so angry when he tells Salo, the Tralfamadorian, about his shock at learning he was being used? In his anger, Rumfoord hurls the ultimate insult at Salo when he calls him a mere machine. Salo has revealed earlier to his friend that all Tralfamadorians were machines:

> Once upon a time on Tralfamadore there were creatures who weren't anything like machines. They weren't dependable. They weren't efficient. They weren't predictable. They weren't durable. And these poor creatures were obsessed by the idea that everything that existed had to have a purpose, and that some purposes were higher than others.
> These creatures spent most of their time trying to find out what their purpose was. And every time they found out what seemed to be a purpose of themselves, the purpose seemed so low that the creatures were filled with disgust and shame. And, rather than serve a low purpose, the creatures would make a machine to serve it. This left the creatures to serve a higher purpose, the purpose still wasn't high enough. . . . So the machines were made to serve higher purposes too. . . . The machines reported in all honesty that the creatures couldn't be said to have any purpose at all.
> The creatures thereupon began slaying each other because they hated purposeless things above all else (274 - 75).

Rumfoord feels the same degree of disgust and shame when he realizes that man is also seemingly without a purpose although he does have a Tralfamadorian purpose. All human history has been merely a vast billboard upon which the Tralfamadorians have placed messages for their messenger, Salo. The narrator echoes Rumfoord's feeling of disillusionment when he states in reference to himself that "An explosion on the sun had separated man and dog. A Universe schemed in mercy would have kept man and dog together" (295). Rumfoord is doomed to travel forever in a merciless universe without even his dog for companionship.

In *The Sirens of Titan* there is no evidence of God's mercy; the only merciful act in this novel is a Tralfamadorian machine's hypnotism of Malachi which permits him to die contented, not disillusioned like Paul Proteus. Like Finnerty's manipulation of Paul Proteus, Rumfoord guides Constant because the millionaire is motivated by a selfish reason, basically a psychological need to change his society. Rumfoord knows that "Thus, fly this way and that . . . with or without messages — It's chaos, and no mistake. . . ." (39). Because he is a proud man, though, he creates the Church of God the Utterly Indifferent because he cannot tolerate the thought that he does not control his own destiny. Rumfoord eagerly manipulates Malachi Constant in his efforts to create an institution that expounds his own views, The Church of God the Utterly Indifferent; but he himself is in reality being manipulated by Tralfamadorians in just the way he finds intolerable. Like Finnerty in *Player Piano*, Rumfoord is self-deceived. Even as he leaves the solar system, he can ignore his treatment of Malachi, Beatrice, the thousands of people he killed during the war he started between Mars and the Earth, and his formation of a Church that preaches his peculiar, personal doctrines. His last words are, "I have tried to do good for my native Earth while serving the irresistible wish of Tralfamadore" (298).

XI *Technique in* The Sirens of Titan

Vonnegut provides numerous pictures of broken machinery in *Player Piano* with the implication that mankind has replaced himself with machinery that reflects human fallibility. In his second novel he focuses on patterns that defy human comprehension and suggests that humanity still suffers from Sir Francis Bacon's "idols of the tribe," the human need to observe order in a universe even when there is none. This tendency is apparent in the vast number of hallucinations in *The Sirens of Titan*. In the first chapter Malachi Constant climbs a forty-foot cylindrical fountain in order to "see whence he had come and whither he was bound" (17). He imagines how happy the crowd outside the estate would be watching "the teenyweeny bowl at the tippy-tippy top brimming over into the next little bowl. . . . And yawning under all those bowls was the upturned mouth of the biggest bowl of them all . . . a regular Beelzebub of a bowl, bone dry and insatiable . . . " (19). The crowd would enjoy watching the fountain because it is harmonious and because it does suggest order and meaning. Constant imagines that the fountain is running only to discover its doing so is merely another of his hallucinations.

In a similar way Constant learns that Biblical scholars also have hallucinations. When Malachi turned twenty-one, his father showed him the secret to his great success in the stock market. Rather than study the financial history of corporations, Noel Constant merely broke the Book of Genesis into two-letter combinations and invested sequentially in the companies that corresponded to the abbreviations. Thus Vonnegut suggests, tongue in cheek, that theologians have overlooked the real meaning and the real pattern of the Old Testament: it is a guide to financial and not to spiritual success.

When Malachi's spaceship lands beneath the surface of Mercury, he observes that the harmoniums have only two messages to convey: "Here I am, here I am, here I am," and "So glad you are, so glad you are, so glad you are" (186). He ignores these simplistic messages and searches for a meaningful pattern on the walls of the cave because he sees the message, "It's an intelligence test!" (145). The messages on the wall are placed there by Rumfoord, and they are linked to the meaninglessness of human history since ultimately they will help Salo get the replacement part for his spaceship. Perhaps the really meaningful message is the harmonium's since Malachi and his wife Beatrice both become convinced as the novel concludes that the real meaning of human existence is to love and comfort whoever is around.

The hallucination theme in *The Sirens of Titan* is reinforced by the fantasy-like quality of the novel. In by far the most detailed analysis of this novel David Ketterer has likened it to *Alice in Wonderland*;[22] for the parallels include the "Alice in Wonderland" door to the Rumfoord estate, the well-like infundibulum that Rumfoord falls through, and the grinning countenances and disappearances of both Carroll's Cheshire cat and Vonnegut's Rumfoord.[23]

Vonnegut makes his novel even more fantastic by frequent references to drugs, including the narcotics Malachi mixes with alcohol, the sedatives Beatrice takes, and the Schliemann "goof balls" that the Martian army takes to enable it to breathe in any environment. It is not surprising that *The Sirens of Titan* joined Robert Heinlein's *Stranger in a Strange Land* and Frank Herbert's *Dune* as counterculture favorites. In *The Making of a Counterculture* Theodore Roszak indicated that the counterculture can be defined as a group in society that opposes a technocratic society and embraces such causes as the dialectical philosophy of Herbert Marcuse and Norman Brown, the validity of the psychedelic experience, and the need for a shamanistic world view.[24]

At one level, *The Sirens of Titan* is a revolutionary novel as ideological as John Steinbeck's *The Grapes of Wrath*. The Constant family fortune is made without any hard work or particular skill on the part of either Noel or his son. Malachi spends the first half of the novel revelling in the dissipation that leads to a climactic fifty-six-day party. It is only when he loses everything that he begins to grow spiritually. Similarly, Winston Niles Rumfoord exhibits the class consciousness of the wealthy; at one point, he can tell his wife "that was a pretty scene to play before a servant" (55). His army that is destined for almost total destruction is composed almost entirely of the poor and the oppressed, yet he deems his goal well worth the sacrifice.

While the presence of class struggle and psychedelic drugs in *The Sirens of Titan* is quite apparent, there is also a marked counterculture rejection of technocracy's reliance upon science and an acceptance of a shamanistic view of the world. The scientists in Vonnegut's novel are bewildered by the chrono-synclastic infundibulum and cannot design a way to eliminate this problem. Their only success in the novel is the arsenal of thermonuclear weapons they assemble and detonate to annihilate the Martian army. In many ways *The Sirens of Titan* describes a pre-scientific magical world in which ritual is far more important than scientific knowledge; in fact, the ritualistic appearances of Rumfoord reoccur periodically. Theodore Roszak has pointed out that members of the counterculture long for a shaman/artist of sorts who will use his magic to help them see the meaningful patterns to the world:

. . . the artist lays his work before the community in the hope that through it, as through a window, the reality he has fathomed will be witnessed by all who give attention. For the shaman, ritual performs the same function. By participating in the ritual, the community comes to know what the shaman has discovered. Ritual is the shaman's way of broadcasting his vision; it is his instructive offering. If the artist's work is successful, if the shaman's ritual is effective, the community's sense of reality will become expansive; something of the dark powers will penetrate its experience.[25]

The most detailed community ritual in *The Sirens of Titan* is Malachi's return to Earth, the community's recognition of what he represents, and its subsequent rejection of him as a scapegoat. Rumfoord prepared the community for this ritual by writing his own Bible. Consequently, Vonnegut reveals that Rumfoord is a false shaman/artist who manipulates the community for his own purposes. Thematically, this incident effectively re-emphasizes once again the inherent meaninglessness of the universe and the pathetic human need to see a divine purpose. While Vonnegut's novel attacks many of the same targets that counterculture writers such as Richard Brautigan have, he concludes that the major tenets of the counterculture are impossible to realize. While the science and technology associated with the technocracy certainly do not provide all the answers to the ills of American society, neither does the rhetoric of revolution, the escape from the everyday world provided by psychedelic drugs, or a return to a pseudo-American-Indian tribal structure. In his next novel, *Mother Night*, Vonnegut abandons the fantasy mode to consider the advantages and limitations of a schizophrenic's decision to create a separate "nation of two" and to ignore the problems of the real world.

CHAPTER 2

That Way Lies Madness: Mother Night

I   *Howard W. Campbell, Jr., and Schizophrenia*

M*other Night* (1961) represents a marked change for Kurt Vonnegut, Jr., in terms of both subject matter and narrative technique. Instead of writing another social-science fiction novel, he decided to write about World War II. Howard W. Campbell, Jr.,[1] is an American dramatist living in Germany and married to a beautiful German actress. He is recruited by the United States as a secret agent, and he spends the war years making propaganda broadcasts that contain hidden messages for the Allies in the form of coughs, pauses, and burps. After the war he is sought in the United States as a Nazi war-criminal — and is also idolized by a strange collection of aging fascists. Campbell surrenders himself to Israel to stand trial with Adolph Eichmann, but he concludes by declaring that he will kill himself instead of waiting for trial because he is guilty of crimes against himself. The novel is written in the form of *The Confessions of Howard W. Campbell, Jr.*, with an editor's note explaining the textual problems. The point of view is very similar to that found in Vladimir Nabokov's *Lolita* since both Humbert Humbert and Campbell are imprisoned monsters by society's standards who resolutely declare that they have been sinned against much more than they have sinned; and both are extremely unreliable narrators.

World War II was doubly traumatic for Vonnegut; not only was he captured in the Battle of the Bulge and forced to listen to the fire-bombing of Dresden and subsequently view the horror, but he was also disturbed about fighting against many of his relatives and his parents' friends.[2] At the time he began writing *Mother Night*, Israel had just captured Adolph Eichmann. As Tony Tanner has pointed out, another impetus for the novel might have been Charles Norman's biography of Ezra Pound which had appeared in 1960; for

Norman revealed that the Italian government had "mistrusted the [Pound] broadcasts, even suspecting that they hid a code language."[3] When Vonnegut was asked what prompted the novel, he answered "I began with the idea of an American Lord Haw Haw and there really wasn't one, but the idea interested me so I began pursuing it. . . . What started me on the book was a cocktail party where I met a man. . . . He said every spy is a double agent because otherwise he can't survive. Also, he's a very sick man; he's a schizophrenic."[4] In an introduction written in 1966 Vonnegut revealed that the moral of the novel is "We are what we pretend to be, so we must be careful about what we pretend to be" (v); and this point is made again and again in *Mother Night*.

Vonnegut indicates in his "Editor's Note" that to state that Campbell is a playwright is to warn the reader that "no one is a better liar than a man who has warped lives and passions onto something as grotesquely artificial as a stage" (ix). Campbell, who will not even admit that he is ill, declares at one point that "it was my world rather than myself that was diseased" (194). One of the classic symptoms of simple schizophrenia is the "gradual withdrawal of interest and a progressive decline of responsible behavior with absence of commitment to a definite way of life."[5] After the war Campbell lives in an attic apartment in New York and thinks only of his dead wife: "Always alone, I drank toasts to her, said good morning to her, said good night to her, played music for her, and didn't give a damn for one thing else" (37). At one point he freezes on a New York street corner because he realizes that what had kept him alive for so many years was curiosity and that "now even that had flickered and there was not a single other satisfaction to be had" (97). When Helga (his wife) dies, Howard declares that he is now a stateless person; and appropriately, Vonnegut placed Sir Walter Scott's "Breathes there the man with soul so dead/Who never to himself hath said" on the page facing the novel's opening chapter. Campbell retreats to a stateless position in an attempt to ignore the realities of the atrocities around him, but he cannot escape the stench from the concentration camps and battlefields.

It is significant that one of the games Howard plays with his wife in their "nation of two" is an adult version of "This-Little-Piggy" and that he defends doing so on the grounds that "Everybody's supposed to play games for mental health" (33). While the games of obfuscation that Cambell plays fail to prevent him from ultimately having to face his responsibilities for his actions as a Nazi propagandist,

Vonnegut feels that Howard's plays and his childishness are symp-
tomatic of one of the major reasons wars occur. His medieval plays
are constructed upon the principle that people are either pure good
or pure evil. Later, when he is confronted by a vengeful American
legionnaire named Bernard B. O'Hare, the benign half of Howard's
schizophrenic personality innocently points out to O'Hare that

"There are plenty of good reasons for fighting," I said, "but no good
reason to hate without reservation, to imagine that God Almighty Himself
hates with you, too. Where's evil? It's that large part of every man that wants
to hate without limit, that wants to hate with God on its side. It's that part of
every man that finds all kinds of ugliness so attractive."
"It's that part of an imbecile," I said, "that punishes and vilifies and
makes war gladly" (190).

It is difficult to determine when Campbell is playing the role of Doctor Jekyll and when he is playing Mr. Hyde. He is able to "strut like
Hitler's right-hand man" (31), yet he is surprised that "nobody saw
the honest man I hid so deep inside" (31). He is quick to admit that
he has always "been able to live with what I did. How? Through that
simple and widespread boon to modern man — schizophrenia"
(136). This disease is particularly disturbing to Campbell when he
learns that he broadcast without even knowing it the fact that his
wife Helga had disappeared: "It represented, I suppose, a wider
separation of my several selves than even I can bear to think about"
(140).
   Many of the facets of Campbell's complex personality are illustrated in the opening chapter of *Mother Night* when he describes
the various Israeli guards who minister to his needs. One of the
guards is Arpad Kovacs, a Jew in Nazi Hungary who managed to survive by obtaining false papers and by joining the Hungarian S.S.
When Campbell asks Kovacs if anyone had suspected him of being a
Jew, Kovacs replies " 'How would they dare. . . . I was such a pure
and terrifying Aryan that they put me in a special detachment. Its
mission was to find out how the Jews always knew what the S.S. was
going to do next. There was a leak somewhere, and we were out to
stop it,' He looked bitter and affronted, remembering it, even
though he had been that leak" (10).
   While Kovacs illustrates Campbell's schizophrenia, the middle-
aged Andor Guttman exhibits many of the same guilt feelings that
afflict Vonnegut's protagonist. Guttman worked as a corpse carrier at

Auschwitz and thus, like Campbell, managed to survive the war;
but, when he is questioned about this experience, he replies,
"Shameful . . . I never want to talk about it again" (7). Campbell
managed to bury many of his guilt feelings by anesthetizing himself
to the point that only his wife Helga can stir his emotions. Similarly,
the Israeli guard Bernard Mengel managed to survive the war by
dulling all his senses. He once played dead while a German soldier
pulled three of his teeth to get his gold inlays. He confesses to
Campbell that he got so he couldn't feel anything since "every job
was a job to do, and no job was any better or any worse than any
other" (12).

A sxhizophrenic person traditionally becomes "incapable of
blending feeling, thought, and action in a meaningful and constructive fashion."[6] The line between "fact and fiction grows blurred,"
and the patient "becomes careless in appearance, sloppy in work
habits, and impervious to responsibility. As the illness grows in
strength, he may show an incredible indifference to his own fundamental physical comforts and needs."[7] One of the most vivid pictures in Vonnegut's novel is the death-worshipping Campbell who is
sitting in his attic apartment surrounded by twenty-five army surplus
kits — apparently unconcerned about his own physical condition and
about the world outside his room.

II   *The Forces of* Mother Night

When Howard W. Campbell, Jr., hides from his enemies in New
York City, he refers to the city as his purgatory. If purgatory is
thought of in the traditional sense of a place for souls "who have died
without repentance for venial sins or who have not yet paid for their
sins, the guilt of which has been removed,"[8] it is quite clear that
Campbell absolves himself of any guilt feelings; and it is equally
clear that he does not repent. He glances out of his window toward
what he describes as "a little private park, a little Eden formed by
joining backyards" (17). The reason that the park seems like an Eden
or Paradise to Campbell is that he observes children who play hide-
and-seek crying "Olly-olly-ox-in-free." He too, "hiding from many
people who might want to hurt or kill me, often longed for someone
to give that cry for me, to end my endless game of hide-and-seek
with a sweet and mournful — 'Olly-olly-ox-in-free' " (18).

When Howard indicates that he is going to commit suicide for
crimes committed against himself, he is not being completely honest.
The reason that he wants to kill himself is that it is becoming in-

creasingly more difficult for him to rationalize the actions of that part of himself that is dark and evil. The title of the novel, "Mother Night," comes from a speech by Mephistopheles in Goethe's *Faust:* "I am part of the part that at first was all, part of the darkness that gave birth to light, that supercilious light which now disputes with Mother Night her ancient rank and space, and yet can not succeed; no matter how it struggles, it sticks to matter and can't be free. Light flows from substance, makes it beautiful; solids can check its path, so I hope it won't be long till light and the world's stuff are destroyed together" (xi). Mephistopheles' optimism that darkness and evil will succeed before long in destroying the light of the world apparently is justified in Campbell's case. Since there are two Howard W. Campbell, Jrs., he would like to believe that the part of him that accepts what the Nazis do to the Jews and that calmly writes Nazi propaganda is only the side of himself that he presents to the world; the *real* Howard W. Campbell, Jr., he believes, is secretly virtuous and is well aware of the difference between right and wrong.

Campbell's desire for a world in which he can cry "Olly-olly-ox-in-free" is a desire to escape reality. Children can take a break from the games they play, but Campbell cannot escape the reality of his position as a twentieth-century man; in his case, he has the additional burden of being a Nazi war-criminal living in New York. At one point, he tells a policeman that he expects another war because "each person does a little something . . . " (178). Rather than face this problem of the "Mother Night" forces at work within man, Campbell seeks escape by creating his own world — one in which he can watch his actions as a Nazi with detachment and even with smug amusement, secure in the knowledge that he is actually only acting. He consistently lies to himself even though at one point he proudly declares that he "can no more lie without noticing it than he could unknowingly pass a kidney stone" (126).

Campbell is disturbed when the Israelis fail to distinguish between Adolph Eichmann and himself. He sees a very clear distinction; he remarks that Eichmann "actually believed that he had invented his own trite defense, though a whole nation of ninety some-odd million had made the same defense before him. Such was his paltry understanding of the God-like human act of invention" (126). Campbell, of course, is a writer, a man with an imagination. Erich Fromm has pointed out that the Bible uses the word *yetzer* to indicate the evil impulse. Since the word means "imaginings" (evil or good), "the most important fact is that evil (or good) impulses are possible only

on the basis of that which is specifically human: imagination. For
this reason, only man . . . can be evil or good."[9]

III   *The Role of the Artist*

As a man of imagination, Campbell is the first of a series of Vonnegut characters who ponder the role of the artist in the modern
world. During the time when Hitler was beginning to prime the Nazi
war machine, Campbell seemed perfectly contented to write
medieval romance. In recruiting him to become a spy, Frank Wirtanen tells Campbell that a reading of his plays reveals that "you ad-
mire pure hearts and heroes. . . . That you love good and hate evil
. . . and that you believe in romance" (30). Later, when contemplating escape to Mexico, Campbell chooses Don Quixote as his
code name, one more indication of his romantic streak. Campbell
confesses that Wirtanen "didn't mention the best reason for ex-
pecting me to go on and be a spy. The reason was that I was a ham.
As a spy of the sort he described, I would have the opportunity for
some pretty grand acting. I would fool everyone with my brilliant interpretation of a Nazi, inside and out" (31).

Unfortunately for Campbell, he becomes the very race-baiting
Nazi propagandist that he is pretending to be. This change is made
clear in the conversation he has with Frank Wirtanen:

"Three people in all the world knew me for what I was —" I said. "And all
the rest —" I shrugged.
"They knew you for what you were, too," he said abruptly.
"That wasn't me," I said, startled by his sharpness.
"Whoever it was —" said Wirtanen, "he was one of the most vicious sons
of bitches who ever lived."
I was amazed. Wirtanen was sincerely bitter (193).

Vonnegut counterpoints Campbell, the artist who is really a spy,
with George Kraft, the Russian spy who turns out to be one of the
greatest modern artists and a very mediocre spy. Kraft, in reality
Colonel Ioana Potapov, tells Howard that

"future civilizations — better civilizations than this one — are going to
judge all men by the extent to which they've been artists. You and I, if some
future archaeologist finds our works miraculously preserved in some city
dump, will be judged by the quality of our creations. Nothing else about us
will matter."
"Um," I said (43).

Kraft's real artistry can be found in his masterful paintings, but Howard Campbell can only reply a monosyllabic "um" because he realizes that he will be judged on the Nazi role that he played too well.

IV   *Howard W. Campbell's Pluralistic Universe*

Since Campbell is not only the narrator of *Mother Night* but also a playwright, an artist who uses his imagination to construct a more pleasant world, it is very difficult to determine what is real in his universe. The very fact that this Nazi war-criminal is comforted by his apparent imaginative transformation of the real world into a morality play of sorts suggests that Vonnegut assumes a philosophical stance that closely resembles the pragmatic pluralism of William James who wrote in *Pragmatism* that: "What we say about reality thus depends on the perspective in which we throw it. The 'that' of it is its own; but the 'what' depends on the 'which' and the 'which' depends on us. Both the sensational and the relational parts of reality are dumb; they say absolutely nothing about themselves. We it is who have to speak for them. . . . We receive in short the block of marble, but we curve [sic] the statue ourselves."[10] In carving the sensational and relational parts of his marble block of reality, Howard W. Campbell, Jr., tries his utmost to rationalize away his feelings of guilt caused by his actions as a Nazi and by his realization that the sinister forces of "Mother Night" are a very real part of man's nature. As is the case with all of Vonnegut's protagonists, Campbell lives in a pluralistic universe in which it is impossible to determine just what is real. The reader can never completely resolve the disparity between Howard's actions and thoughts and his view of reality. His point of view is most succinctly summarized in his statement that it is his world rather than himself that is diseased.

There is, however, one touchstone that can be applied to Campbell's actions — William James's concept that, in a pluralistic universe, "evil, whenever it occurs, becomes the occasion for acting; it poses a task to be performed, a defect to be removed, a situation to be improved. Pluralism, therefore, finds immediate pragmatic verification in moral experience."[11] Howard pragmatically eases his pain by assuming the role of spectator and by observing his two identities, representing evil and goodness, perform in a morality play. At first glance, Campbell's actions appear to fail James's test since they bring more pain than comfort. He declares, as the novel concludes, that he will "hang Howard W. Campbell, Jr., for crimes against himself" (202). Yet, since Vonnegut apparently conceives of a pluralistic universe, it is impossible to know if Campbell's statement is a sincere one. Admittedly, he has failed to construct a reality for himself that is both esthetically pleasing (a play possessing a beginning, a middle, and an end, and a moral) and morally palatable.

What, then, is real in *Mother Night?* For the pluralist, "reality is known through a number, potentially infinite, of systems of knowledge. Each of these systems reveals the essence of reality from its point of view."[12] Thus, in order to discover what is real, it is necessary to reconcile a number of different views of reality even though some of these may be contradictory. Because of the difficulty inherent in such an approach, T. S. Chang has gone so far in his study *Epistemological Pluralism* as to declare that the "external world is relatively, though not absolutely unknowable."[13] While Campbell's reality is not verified by his experience, Vonnegut does not suggest what is actually real in this novel; instead he clouds reality in an ambivalent mist. Is Campbell, for example, no better than Eichmann and Dr. Jones, or is he, as Kraft suggests, innocent by virtue of his "inability to distinguish between reality and dreams" (198)? The very form of *Mother Night* suggests that reality is unknowable since the novel's narrative structure leads the reader through the complex maze of Campbell's mind and deposits him, on the final page, in a corner facing a blank wall.

V   *The Totalitarian Mind*

Much of the macabre humor in *Mother Night* results from Kurt Vonnegut's treatment of right-wing extremists who range from neo-Nazis to Bernard B. O'Hare, the American legionnaire who imagines he is like Saint George and is on a holy quest to destroy the pure evil that Howard Campbell represents. Campbell and many of the minor characters in *Mother Night* are able to serve evil too openly and good too secretly because they have what Campbell himself calls "the classic totalitarian mind" which he likens to a cuckoo clock in hell:

. . . Hence the cuckoo clock in Hell — keeping perfect time for eight minutes and twenty-three seconds, jumping ahead fourteen minutes, keeping perfect time for six seconds, jumping ahead two seconds, keeping perfect time for two hours and one second, then jumping ahead a year.

The missing teeth, of course, are simple, obvious truths, truths available and comprehensible even to ten-year-olds, in most cases.

The willful filing off of gear teeth, the willful doing without certain obvious pieces of information — (169).

Campbell conveniently ignores the effect his broadcasts have on bolstering Germany's sagging morale. He is shocked and surprised when his father-in-law tells him that the broadcasts gave him and thousands of other Germans the courage to continue the struggle. In a similar way, the Reverend Doctor Lionel J. D. Jones, founder of the scurrilous *White Christian Minuteman,* can write a book entitled *Christ Was Not a Jew* in which he proves his point by "reproducing in the book fifty famous paintings of Jesus. According to Jones, not one painting showed Jewish jaws or teeth" (51). One of Jones's companions is Robert Wilson, the "Black Fuehrer of Harlem." With the same totalitarian logic of Jones or of Campbell, he can announce to Campbell that

The colored people gonna have hydrogen bombs all their own. . . . They working on it right now. Pretty soon gonna be Japan's turn to drop one. The rest of the colored folks gonna give them the honor of dropping the first one.

Where they going to drop it? I said.

China, most likely, he said.

On other colored people? I said.

He looked at me pityingly. Who ever told you a Chinaman was a colored man? he said (68).

Another companion of Jones is his bodyguard, August Krapptauer whose greatest achievement in life was the joint meeting he arranged in 1940 between the Ku Klux Klan and the German-American Bund. At the meeting he revealed that the "Pope was a Jew and that the Jews held a fifteen-million-dollar mortgage on the Vatican" (54 - 5). Krapptauer was working to establish an organization known as The Iron Guard of the White Sons of the American Constitution when he died. Jones's companion, a renegade priest named Father Keeley, laments Krapptauer's loss since the bodyguard was so good with "kids who would ordinarily be at loose ends and getting into trouble" (66). Krapptauer was leading his youngsters into far more trouble than they could possibly find in any poolroom, but Jones and Keeley cannot understand this since their totalitarian minds function with all the precision of a cuckoo clock in hell.

This totalitarian logic is not limited to Doctor Jones's companions. Bernard B. O'Hare, the man who first captured Campbell in Germany, sees himself as Saint George to whom Campbell is the Dragon to be slain. What Vonnegut finds so repulsive about the totalitarian mind is its tendency "to imagine that God almighty hates . . . too. Where's evil? It's that large part of every man that wants to hate without limit, that wants to hate with God on its side" (190). O'Hare's life has been filled with failure, and he is reduced to serving as a radio dispatcher for frozen-custard trucks. Yet he can rationalize his destroyed dreams as long as he can see himself as pure good and Campbell as pure evil and thus believe that his mediocre life has a noble purpose to it.

VI   *The Conclusion of* Mother Night

Throughout *Mother Night* Campbell's statements about his love for Helga are pathetically self-deceiving. His "nation of two" is really such a selfish, ego-centered love that it is quite appropriate that the diary of his private life with Helga becomes a best-selling pornographic book. When Campbell discovers that he has been deceived by Resi Noth and has been sleeping with her rather than with her sister Helga, he readily accepts her; he does so because her love provides him with ego-gratification. After his first night with Resi, he even boasts to his readers that he is still as virile as a youth.

At the conclusion of the novel Campbell is no longer capable of love, even of self-love. Resi Noth describes him as "so used up that he can't love anymore. There is nothing left of him but curiosity and a pair of eyes" (173). Like William Golding's Pincher Martin, Campbell strips himself of everything that is human; and what is left is merely a caricature of his particular crime — his willingness to view his sins with the smug detachment of a schizophrenic. Even his final decision to commit suicide illustrates this curious detachment; for as has been cited elsewhere, he tells his readers that "I think tonight is the night I will hang Howard W. Campbell, Jr., for crimes against himself" (202). Describing himself in the third person, Campbell apparently finally realizes that he has become the insensitive automaton he pretended to be. As Jerome Klinkowitz has suggested, Campbell, by in effect destroying his self, has destroyed the only meaningful object in his godless universe.[14] The physical act of hanging himself is really anticlimactic since Campbell has already cut himself adrift from the roles that gave his life meaning; he is a patriot curiously without a country, a man who lived for love who is no longer capable of loving, and a dramatist who can no longer write.

VII   *The Movement toward Black Humor*

When Vonnegut wrote his first two novels, *Player Piano* and *The Sirens of Titan,* he used a conventional narrative style and a third-person point of view. Paul Proteus and Malachi Constant lack a three-dimensional quality perhaps because Vonnegut has always been more concerned with ideas than with characterization — in common with many of the science-fiction writers he admires. *Mother Night* is different, however, because Vonnegut uses a first-person point of view to build Campbell's characterization, also a series of very short chapters that build his novel around a series of jokes. In order to understand how these jokes function, it is necessary to consider the distinction between social satire and Black Humor. In *Player Piano,* an excellent example of social satire, Vonnegut shows the horrors that could result from overvaluing technology and efficiency and from undervaluing people. By satirizing what is wrong with the present direction of American society, Vonnegut hopes to prevent the events in his novel from actually taking place.

After *The Sirens of Titan* Vonnegut's fiction does not contain simple implicit or explicit solutions to the problems he presents. Robert Scholes concludes that the basic difference between satire and Black Humor is that Black Humor

> . . . is generally more playful and more carefully constructed. . . . It is more certain esthetically and less certain ethically than its ancestors. . . . The spirit of playfulness and the care for form characteristic of the best black humorists operate so as to turn the materials on satire into comedy. . . . These writers reflect quite properly their heritage from the esthetic movement of the nineteenth century and the ethical relativism of the twentieth. They have some faith in art but they reject all ethical absolutes. Especially they reject the traditional satirists' faith in the efficacy of satire as a reforming instrument. They have a more subtle faith in the humanizing value of laughter.[15]

Bruce Jay Friedman, the acknowledged father of Black Humor, has further clarified the distinction between Black Humor and social satire by pointing out that, since the satirist has had his "ground usurped by the newspaper reporter," he has had to "sail into darker waters somewhere out beyond satire. . . ."[16] Furthermore, Friedman believes that the best way to examine society is to begin by examining its "throwaways, the ones who can't or won't keep in step. . . ."[17] By examining outsiders like Adolph Eichmann and Howard W. Campbell, Jr., Vonnegut probes the question of why men commit atrocities and how they are able to live with their own consciences. Perhaps because there are no easy answers to such questions, Black Humorists usually view the world as so complex and so fragmented that any answers can only be tentative; and the best advice they can offer their readers is how to smile through their tears at the absurdi-

ties of the world. *Mother Night* ends with Campbell's decision to
commit suicide; and the novel, while comic, certainly does not represent Northrop Frye's New Comedy which would include a mythic
victory of spring over winter and life over death.[18]

Black Humor stops short of any such Frye victories. Rather than
triumph, Black Humor characters are fortunate merely to survive
their ordeals. Vonnegut has confessed to an interviewer that he does
see the similarity of his work and that of other Black Humorists to
what Freud called "gallows humor" — Jewish jokes about hopeless
situations — such as "a small people being pushed this way and that,
enormous armies and plagues and so forth, and still hanging on in
the face of hopelessness."[19] Vonnegut softens this feeling of hopelessness by focusing his novel on Howard W. Campbell, Jr., a man
who observes hilarious incidents but is incapable of understanding
the jokes. The result is much the same as the later *Slaughterhouse-
Five*, a novel that is simultaneously very sad and very funny.

The jokes that provide the scaffolding for *Mother Night* rarely run
more than three chapters. Vonnegut has admitted, "I build jokes. I
find sections of my book constructed like jokes and then they're not
very long and I suddenly realize the joke is told, and that it'll spoil
the joke if I were to go past. The tag line is where the joke paid off
and so . . . I'll begin again, and it'll essentially build as another
joke."[20] Two typical Vonnegut joke sequences illustrate how this
technique works in *Mother Night*. Campbell's diary of his life with
Helga is discovered by a Russian writer named Bodovskov[21] who
plagiarizes it and publishes it as *Memoirs of a Monogamous
Casanova*. Later, Campbell learns that Bodovskov had become
famous by plagiarizing all this work. Finally, Campbell learns that
when Bodovskov has been arrested and executed, his crime had not
been plagiarism but originality. When he ran out of Campbell's
material, Bodovskov wrote a two-thousand page satire on the Red
Army, written in a style "distinctly un-Bodovskovian" (157). In
another joke sequence, Resi Noth throws away a noose that the
American Legion had left in Campbell's mail box. A garbage man
named Szombathy finds it the next morning and hangs himself.
Szombathy kills himself because he is not permitted to practice
veterinary medicine. Finally, Vonnegut casually reveals that the real
reason the garbage man was despondent was because he had a cure
for cancer that the world had ignored.[22]

The Nazis in *Mother Night* are comic rather than frightening, and
this effect is heightened by Campbell's detached narration. At one

point, for example, Paul Joseph Goebbels asks Campbell to write a pageant honoring the German soldiers who died during the Warsaw uprising by Jews. When Campbell responds by translating Abraham Lincoln's Gettysburg Address into German, Goebbels is so impressed by such a "very fine piece of propaganda" that he gives it to Hitler to read; but he does so with a certain amount of apprehension — he fears Lincoln might have been Jewish. Hitler responds by writing that "Some parts of this almost made me weep. All northern peoples are one in their deep feelings for soldiers. It is perhaps our greatest bond" (16). Campbell does not seem to see the ironic contrast between Lincoln's efforts to free slaves and Hitler's efforts to eradicate Jews. Also, he cannot see the similarity between Hitler's use of Lincoln's speech and Bodovskov's use of Campbell's own material. The "greatest bond" of which Hitler speaks that holds all Northern peoples together is to a great extent responsible for the war raging in Europe at the time.

The esthetic distance Vonnegut establishes in *Mother Night* makes the jokes in the novel work. Schizophrenic Campbell can comment about his ludicrous poisonous broadcasts with the same detachment that the Tralfamadorian robots exhibit in *Slaughterhouse-Five*. Vonnegut uses this technique in both novels to enable him to deal with subjects too painful to handle in any other way. He has indicated that he would like to believe that, as one critic has suggested, he has found in "laughter an analgesic for the temporary relief of existential pain."[23]

CHAPTER 3

Saints and Sinners: Cat's Cradle *and* God Bless You, Mr. Rosewater

I   Cats Cradle

*I*N *Cat's Cradle* (1963) Vonnegut once again explores many of the same problems found in *Mother Night* including the dangers of role playing and the nature of evil. The major focus of the novel is, however, on epistomology: the narrator John, who finds it increasingly difficult to determine what is real and what is illusory, discovers that life is very much like the children's game of cat's cradle. John, a former Christian and a twice-divorced alcoholic writer, comes to the Caribbean republic of San Lorenzo in search of the Schweitzer-like Julian Castle who had set up the House of Hope and Mercy in the Jungle. John becomes a Bokononist, a religion founded on truthful lies; he then watches as the world ends by freezing.

Cat's Cradle is a *tour de force* and it is stylistically Vonnegut's most unusual novel. The book is written as a *Book of Bokonon*, a Bokononist Bible. John learns that Bokonon placed a warning at the beginning of his *Books of Bokonon* that "nothing in this book is true," and this is precisely the statement Vonnegut places at the beginning of *Cat's Cradle*. The novel consists of 127 chapters; and, like the Bible, it contains both parables and poetry, saints (Bokonon and Julian Castle) and sinners (Earl McCabe and Papa Monzano). All the book's characters are flat, and in many ways it is an anti-novel. In *The Sirens of Titan* human history turns out to be merely a contrivance to get the word "greetings" from one end of the universe to the other; in *Cat's Cradle*, Vonnegut minimizes the meaning of history; and, as Glen Meeter has pointed out, he thus rejects the "novel — the Western act which, more than any other, finds meaning in history."[1] San Lorenzo is an isolated Caribbean island far outside of the mainstream of history, but the world ends here by accident. In the later *Slaughterhouse-Five* Vonnegut has a robot reveal that the universe will eventually end by accident when a robot scientist miscalculates while testing a new rocket fuel.

When John has arrived in San Lorenzo, he looks out the window of his beautiful hotel room and sees the Boulevard of the Hundred Martyrs to Democracy (San Lorenzo's one paved street), the Monzano Airport, and Boliver Harbor. These showplaces are only an illusion of the real San Lorenzo, for the "Casa Mona was built like a bookcase, with solid sides and back and a front of blue-green glass. The squalor an misery of the city, being to the sides and back of the Casa Mona were impossible to see" (131).

II *The Hoenikker Family*

Virtually all the characters in this novel suffer from this same myopic vision. Gathered together on the island are Angela, Frank, and Newt Hoenikker, the grown children of Felix Hoenikker, the father of the atomic bomb, who died and left the secret ice-nine as a legacy for his children. The substance has a boiling point of 114.4 degrees Fahrenheit and has the ability to alter the structure of water so that all water that comes in contact with it will also freeze.[2] When Hoenikker died, his children divided the ice-nine and bartered it for what seemed to be happiness. Vonnegut is careful in each case to distinguish between reality and the mere appearance or illusion of happiness that each Hoenikker so desperately desires.

Dr. Hoenikker, a scientist more concerned with developing the doomsday device, ice-nine, than with rearing normal children, sired three "Grotesques," humans distorted emotionally and even physically by social, political, and parental forces. With a single-minded devotion to his own interests, Felix Hoenikker removed his daughter Angela from high school in her sophomore year to serve as his housekeeper. As Marvin Breed points out, "All she had going for her was the clarinet she'd played in the Ilium High School band. Nobody ever asked her out. She didn't have any friends, and the old man never thought to give her any money to go anywhere. . . . She'd lock herself in her room and she'd play records, and she'd play along with the records on her clarinet" (66). Denied the normal experiences of a normal young girl, Angela sought happiness so desperately that she did not feel any qualms when handsome Harrison C. Connors asked her to marry him in return for her share of her father's death dealing ice-nine. It is quite apparent that Angela did not feel any moral doubts about such an action because her father and mentor was amoral and had once with perfect sincerity asked a fellow scientist, "What is sin?"

Frank, Felix Hoenikker's middle child, presents another but far more complicated example of how the famous Nobel-prize-winning scientist's amorality and complete devotion to science distorted his children into Grotesques. Jack, the owner of Jack's Hobby Shop where Frank worked as a young man, explained that the boy "didn't have any home life" but accepted the shop as his real home. Unable to find any love at home from his detached, disinterested father, Frank no doubt sought love from an older woman, one who would ameliorate his feelings of inferiority and rejection. He began having sexual relationships with the wife of his good friend, Jack. Evidently this life style proved unsatisfactory because Frank soon began to seek a newer, better world to live in. One solution to his inability to adjust to the real world was to create a "fantastic little country built of plywood, an island as perfectly rectangular as a township in Kansas" (68). Such a world, unfortunately, was too small for the boy to lose himself in. Perhaps as a defense mechanism that would enable him to avoid any more pain, Frank began to pattern himself after his father; for only by being as coldly detached and indifferent to the rest of humanity was it possible to live without feeling any pain. He recognizes the similarities between himself and his father, and at one point Frank declares that he has a "lot of very good ideas" like his father, and "he is no good at facing the public and neither was his father" (162).

Just as it is impossible for Felix Hoenikker's wife to communicate with her husband, John, the narrator of *Cat's Cradle*, finds it impossible to communicate with the scientist's son Frank. After ice-nine had wreaked havoc on the world, John notices that Frank is very attentively observing a group of ants whom he had trapped in a glass prison. The young scientist gave John "a peevish lecture on all the things that people could learn from ants" (226). When John finds him unable to explain who had taught the ants how to survive in a world ravished by ice-nine, he offers the suggestion that God had done so. Frank's reaction was simply to "grow madder and madder" (227). Walled in within his world of science and unable to find love or to accept the solace religion offered, Frank represents the automaton that Paul Proteus would have become if he had not fled from Ilium and from all that its complex technological society represented. Yet, ironically, both Paul and Frank are finally destroyed by technology.

The youngest Hoenikker child, Newt, is perhaps an even sadder case than Frank. He was psychically wounded at a very early age by his disinterested father who for some unexplainable reason, perhaps instinct, had decided one day to play with his son. When he approached Newt in order to show him a cat's cradle, however, the child screamed in horror at what he saw. Looking at his father at close range, Newt observed that his father's "pores looked as big as craters on the moon. His ears and nostrils were stuffed with hair. Cigar smoke made him smell like the mouth of Hell." He was "the ugliest thing Newt ever had seen" (21). Significantly, Newt points out that he still dreams about this incident — a disquieting episode that obviously had a profound effect upon him. His father increased his son's discomfort and deepened this wound by sending the midget-sized Newt to a "special school for grotesque children" (228). The very last thing Newt needed was to be made to feel different, but this realization probably never occurred to Felix Hoenikker who was so engrossed with science that anything else in life was of secondary importance.

After Felix Hoenikker dies, his children try to find happiness. The homely Angela chooses a handsome husband; Frank finds the glory and power he has always desired by assuming the position of Minister of Science and Progress on San Lorenzo; and the midget Newt selects a beautiful Russian dancer. When Newt reveals to John that his sister Angela gave her portion of ice-nine to her husband in return for marrying her and that the two are not happily married, he responds to John's astonishment by asking, "See the cat? See the cradle?" (148). Frank does not really command the respect in San Lorenzo that he so earnestly seeks. When he tries to make John like him, the narrator points out that the "effect was dismaying. Frank meant to inspire camaraderie, but his head looked . . . like a bizarre little owl, blinded by light and perched on a tall white post" (160). When Newt, with the same degree of earnestness as his brother, barters his portion of ice-nine to a Russian midget in return for her assurances of love and devotion, he too is doomed to be disappointed. In reality, she is a Russian spy who, at forty-two, is old enough to be his mother.

III *Science and Scientists in* Cat's Cradle

Like Nathaniel Hawthorne, Vonnegut scorns those people who sin against the human heart. Each Hoenikker child is a Grotesque precisely because he was reared by his famous father with scientific curiosity rather than with love. Newton is a midget who draws paintings which cynically depict the meaninglessness of life. Named after Sir Isaac Newton, Newt's painting proves the law of gravity still is operative when Julian Castle throws Newt's picture down a waterfall. Frank, a morally irresponsible technician named after Benjamin Franklin, refuses to accept responsibility for his share of ice-nine and prefers to work on an electrical generator that would have fascinated his namesake. Angela is a homely woman denied the normal pleasures of adolescence by her selfish father.

To Newt, his father "just wasn't interested in people" (22). He was not even interested in people enough to attend his own child's high school commencement; and so, with the same missionary zeal for science as Felix Hoenikker, Doctor Asa Breed had substituted and had told the audience that "science was going to discover the basic secret for life someday" (30). A bartender later reveals to John that science finally has discovered that the basic secret of life is protein. Such a simple resolution to the complexities of life seems to infuriate Vonnegut as much as the reduction of Rudy Herz to a stack of computer cards by Finnerty, Shepherd, and Proteus in *Player Piano;* in both cases, proud scientists essentially deny the uniqueness of man.

Such a callous attitude goes hand in hand with a tendency to consider men as mere numbers rather than as faces, to use W. H. Auden's terminology.[3] A fine example of such an attitude is Breed's reaction to an old stockade where men once held public executions, for he cannot understand the mentality of one criminal who was hanged in 1782 for killing twenty-six people. When John declares in answer that "The mind reels" (34), he is ridiculing the callousness and detachment of Breed, Hoenikker, and all the other scientists who had worked on the atomic bomb but who had felt absolutely no sense of guilt when it killed thousands of people. Perhaps Vonnegut's attitude toward science is illustrated most clearly when he has Hoenikker answer a young colleague who observed the successful testing of the first atomic bomb and declared "Science has now known sin" (25). Hoenikker responded by asking quite seriously "What is sin?" (25).

In answer to this very question, Vonnegut introduces a secretary, Miss Faust. While the legendary Faust was an over-reacher who felt that it was worth the sacrifice of his immortal soul if he could obtain knowledge, this young woman tells John that she disagrees with Hoenikker's preoccupation with gaining new scientific knowledge because she has trouble understanding "how truth, all by itself, could be enough for a person" (52). Her solution to the complexities of the modern world is "God is love." Hoenikker's response, "What is God? What is love?" (53), indicates the complete lack of real communication or understanding between those who rely on God to solve their problems and Breed's scientific community which is totally divorced from any concern for the spiritual or moral problems concomitant with the invention of the atomic bomb.

Because the scientists ignore these spiritual and moral problems, those like Hoenikker and Breed are shown to be not only irresponsible schoolboys who never grew up but also charlatans. Hoenikker's Nobel Prize acceptance speech consists of "I stand before you now because I never stopped dawdling like an eight-year-old boy on a spring morning on his way to school. Anything can make me stop and look and wonder, and sometimes learn. I am a very happy man" (20). While he does have the usual test tubes and other scientific equipment available, Hoenikker makes most of his discoveries by playing with kites, turtles, bubble pipes, and other cheap toys. Much like Bud Calhoun in *Player Piano*, Felix loved to tinker with gadgets; it is more than mere coincidence that his twin brother is a music-box manufacturer. Even when Hoenikker made ice-nine, Vonnegut describes it as the scientist's "last batch of brownies" (50). Ice-nine is created by the scientist because "Admirals and generals . . . looked upon him as a sort of magician who could make America invincible with a wave of his wand" (43). The ice-nine that the marines desire to make it easier to wage war becomes, ironically, the doomsday weapon that eliminates the need for marines by destroying all humanity. Just before Papa Monzano dies by swallowing the ice-nine Frank had given him, he declares that "science is magic that works" (178).

While Vonnegut pictures the scientists as carefree, amoral children who allow the public to view them as magicians, what irritates him is their naïve belief in the myth of progress. Asa Breed tells John that the underlying assumption behind the General Forge and Foundry Company where Hoenikker worked is that "New knowledge is the most valuable commodity on earth. The more truth we have to work with, the richer we become" (43). John points out that "Had I been a Bokononist then, that statement would have made me howl" (43). Vonnegut further undercuts Breed's reliability by having him observe the Girl Pool singing Christmas carols and remark "They serve science too . . . even though they may not understand a word of it. God bless them, every one!" (41). The substitution of science for God in an echo of John Milton's famous "On His Blindness" and the yoking of this phrase with one from Charles

Dickens' "A Christmas Carol" indicates that new scientific knowledge may not be the most valuable commodity on earth.

Frank Hoenikker's gift of ice-nine to Papa Monzano is responsible for the death of all humanity; yet, when John questions him, the young technician is able to dissociate himself from the moral consequences of the act and to identify himself with "growing pride and energy, with the purifiers, the world-savers, the leaners-up" (197). Perhaps the one person who best summarizes Vonnegut's feelings concerning the callous indifference and the myopic vision of scientists and technicians is the last person one would expect to feel human compassion, the former camp physician at Auschwitz. Doctor Schlicter Von Koenigswald confesses to John that he is "a very bad scientist" because he "will do anything to make a human being feel better, even if it's unscientific. No scientist worthy of the name could say such a thing" (180). Yet, with a Black-Humor touch, Vonnegut points out that Von Koenigswald will have to save patients night and day until the year 3010 to equal the number of people he had let die during the war.

IV Bokonon and Bokononism

It is not surprising that John, as a typical Vonnegut protagonist, should reject the callous scientific view of Asa Breed and Felix Hoenikker for the man-centered religion of Bokononism. The religion was created by a Negro named Lionel B. Johnson and by an American Marine deserter named Earl McCabe when, shipwrecked off the coast of San Lorenzo, the two came ashore naked and were reborn as a holy man and as a tyrant, respectively. The two adventurers decided that the only way to keep the unhappy, poverty-stricken natives of San Lorenzo from staging a revolution was to create a religion, Bokononism, and then to outlaw it and its founder. Then, as "the living legend of the cruel tyrant in the city and the gentle holy man in the jungle grew, so too did the happiness of the people grow. They were all employed full time as actors in a play they understood, that any human beings anywhere could understand and applaud. 'So life became a work of art' . . ." (144).

Bokonon, like Campbell in *Mother Night*, transformed life into a work of art, a morality play; but, while Campbell's "work of art" is linked to his insanity, Bokonon (Johnson) played the role of a saint and also became "for all practical purposes, insane" (145). In his lunacy, Bokonon writes *The Books of Bokonon*. Although this false messiah, like Finnerty in *Player Piano* and Rumfoord in *The Sirens of Titan,* does have a sordid purpose for founding his religion, Vonnegut suggests ambivalently that this religion that is founded upon deception actually contributes to the mutual love and enjoyment of life by the natives of San Lorenzo. Bokonon preaches a doctrine of love and conceives *boko-maru,* a ritual in which two Bokononists unite their souls by rubbing the soles of their feet together:

> We will touch our feet, yes,
> Yes, for all we're worth,
> And we will love each other, yes,
> Yes, like we love our Mother Earth (132).

In this mode of expressing *caritas,* the highest form of spiritual, not physical, love, Vonnegut may be expressing some doubt as to the effectiveness or even the possibility of human love. There are, for example, overtones of satire, of the *infra dig* in the sole/soul pun. Bokonon is using the most scorned literary device (the pun) with the highest spiritual content.

Julian Castle, the founder of the House of Hope and Mercy in the Jungle, reveals to John that *boko-maru* "works. I'm grateful for things that work. Not many things do work, you know" (142). Bokonon wrote in *The Books of Bokonon* that

> I wanted all things
> To seem to make some sense,
> So we all could be happy, yes,
> Instead of tense.
> And I made up lies
> So that they all fit nice,
> And I made this sad world
> A par-a-dise (109).

Since the citizens of San Lorenzo practice Bokononism, they thereby do create a paradise of sorts, a lotus land where love diverts their minds from their hunger and their poverty. The religion also works for John, for he rejects his former role as a chain-smoking, twice-divorced alcoholic and becomes a pleasant young man who is offered both the presidency of San Lorenzo and the beautiful Mona, the country's national sex symbol. Vonnegut appears to be parodying the American dream come true, but John's accomplishments lose all significance the moment Papa Monzano's ice-nine ravaged body strikes the water surrounding San Lorenzo and freezes the entire world. John, like Howard W. Campbell, Jr., in *Mother Night*, would like to ignore the horror around him; therefore, he tries to create a nation of two and to transform his bomb shelter into a hedonistic paradise. But his dream is shattered because Mona, as a devout Bokononist who believes in the sanctity of both man and nature, refuses to join him. She tells John that "It would be very sad to have a little baby now" (215).

Groping to understand man's handiwork, the senseless destruction caused by ice-nine, John considers the possibility of becoming a Nihilist. After observing what a Nihilist has done to his apartment and to his cat, John declares that . . . "after I saw what Krebbs had done . . . nihilism was not for me" (71); and Bokononism gradually begins to make more and more sense to him. Frank Hoenikker tells John that man is the only thing sacred to the Bokononists, for what their religion tries to do is to reconcile the Humanistic view of man as sacred with the harsh reality of man's actions. Bokonon believes that "good societies could be built only by pitting good against evil and by keeping the tension between the two high at all times" (90).

Vonnegut deflates this theory somewhat by pointing out that Bokonon got the idea from Charles Atlas' advertisements in comic books and by having Bokonon summarize his feelings on the subject of evil in a poem:

> 'Papa' Monzano, he's so very bad,
> But without bad 'Papa' I would be so sad;
> Because without Papa's badness
> Tell me, if you would,
> How could wicked old Bokonon
> Ever, ever look good? (90)

Bokonon, much like Vonnegut, believes that there is no such thing as absolute evil or absolute good; both are relative; and they can only be evaluated in terms of each other.

In *The Books of Bokonon*, the prophet reveals that people should "Live by the *foma* (harmless untruths) that make you brave and kind and healthy and happy" (v). As for people and nations, Vonnegut inserts his feelings of antinationalism when he has Bokonon caution that man should be able to distinguish between appearance and reality; moreover, he should realize that the conception of a nation is really meaningless, "a *granfalloon* which is a false *karass*, a seeming team that was meaningless in terms of the ways God gets things done . . ." (82). Such a doctrine comforts Bokononists since they can dismiss the horrors resulting from wars between nations as not a manifestation of something inherently wrong with mankind, but as merely an example of yet another misconception that man will rid himself of when he sees the truth in *The Books of Bokonon*. What is meaningful for Bokononists is the struggle between good and evil.

If the natives of San Lorenzo can only understand these forces by becoming involved in the *foma* of a staged morality play, then a lie helps them in a sense to understand a truth. Bokononism has been described as a "religion after alienation because it carefully removes evil from the self and deposits it in a finitude granted real existence."[4] It is a religion that sees evil and good as coexisting in a world filled with paradox. God, Bokonon reveals, created man because of His cosmic loneliness. Yet, when asked by man for the purpose of life, God replies, "I leave it to you to think of one for all this . . ." (215). One of Bokonon's last statements is a calypso:

> Someday, someday, this crazy world will have to end,
> And our God will take things back that He to us did lend.
> And if, on that sad day, you want to scold our God,
> Why go right ahead and scold Him. He'll just smile
>   and nod (218).

This cosmic coolness is precisely what Bokononism cultivates as a reaction both to the horrors created by modern science and to the realization that God does not intervene in human affairs. In many ways Bokononism is a comic version of the man-centered religion that Wallace Stevens proposed in "Sunday Morning": the sky is less frightening if it is only a sky and not a curtain that separates the helpless human from the omnipotent Divine.

If there is indeed a God, says Bokonon, he is a practical joker; and ice-nine is his final horrible joke. "If I were a younger man, I would write a history of human stupidity. . . . I would take from the ground some of the blue-white poison that makes statues of men; and I would make a statue of myself, lying on my back grinning horribly, and thumb my nose at You Know Who" (231). When the novel ends with this final message from Bokonon, John has finally come full circle. He began his journey as a Christian trying to write *The Day the World Ended*, and he ended as a Bokononist who was witnessing the event in San Lorenzo. The novel begins with John's parodying Herman Melville's Ishmael by declaring "Call me Jonah."

John is a Jonah figure much like not only Malachi Constant who

traveled in his spaceship *The Whale*, but also Eliot Rosewater in the
later *God Bless You, Mr. Rosewater* who confessed that, if he tried to
leave his office, a whale would swallow him and deposit him back at
his Destination. Vonnegut is fascinated by Jonah figures because
Jonah represents "someone forced to work for God even though he
doesn't much want to."[5] John, much like Jonah, is driven by forces
beyond his control to the island of San Lorenzo; and he finds there a
version of a Nineveh that is awaiting destruction. Glancing at Mount
McCabe that towers over the entire island, John notices that it is
shaped like a whale. God in his infinite mercy spared Nineveh, but
that is too much to expect in a Bokononist universe. John, like Jonah,
senses that "God Almighty had some pretty elaborate plans for me"
(64). Later, he comes to believe as a Bokononist that "humanity is
organized into teams . . . that do God's will without ever discovering
what they are doing" (14).

Bokonon loses his sanity when he is constantly compelled to live a
lie; as a result, perhaps, he is obsessed with the paradoxical concept
of truthful lies; and this obsession may account for his destruction of
his worshippers. Many of his ideas cannot be easily discounted,
however, for there must be some reasons why almost everyone in
Cat's Cradle is a devout Bokononist. One very good reason for
Bokononism's popularity is its concept that man's very nature is
"sacred" (73). As William James pointed out, it is possible in such a
universe for man to speak of himself as sacred precisely because he is
an integral part of the same system as God.[6] While such a view is
comforting, just as comforting is Bokonon's suggestion that, though
man constantly wonders "why" (150), he should not waste his time
trying to distinguish between truth and illusion, appearance and
reality, since the world will often appear meaningless.

In many ways Bokonon's religion resembles Christianity. The
precept that man should not waste his time trying to distinguish
between truth and illusion takes the form in Christian pulpits, of
"God works in mysterious ways," or "Man proposes, God disposes."
Foma actually are the same as the platitudes fed to the masses by the
Church on the grounds that such harmless untruths are necessary
because they work and do help people to accept their misfortunes
with equanimity. *Foma* do not, however, cure the inequities of life.
John is aware that Bokonon's boast that *foma* make people brave,
kind, healthy, and happy is a lie because he notices that the people of
San Lorenzo "were thin. There wasn't a fat person to be seen. Every
person had teeth missing. Many legs were bowed or swollen. No one

pair of eyes were clear. The women's breasts were bare and paltry . . ." (115). In *The Books of Bokonon,* the prophet declares that "Anyone unable to understand how a useful religion can be founded on lies will not understand this book either" (16). Obviously Vonnegut is suggesting that all religions are founded on lies, but that they may nevertheless be useful. Rumfoord's religion in *The Sirens of Titan,* for example, is also founded on lies; but it too serves a purpose, a Tralfamadorian purpose.

V   *The Apocalyptic Tradition*

John describes how he had once planned to write a book about the first atomic bomb. While *The Day the World Ended* was to describe the bombing of Hiroshima, its emphasis was going to be on the human rather than on the technical aspects. When he becomes a Bokononist, he is still concerned with the human rather than with the technical aspects of the destruction of the world, but his view of the Apocalypse does change. Traditionally, the Apocalypse represents a key moment in the linear movement of history from the Fall to ultimate redemption.[7] With the destruction of the physical world man will experience a revelation, a discovery of something heretofore hidden. American novelists have always been fascinated by the idea of the Apocalypse, and their treatment of it has taken a number of different forms. Often, like John, they have focused on the human aspect of mass destruction. Novels such as Pat Frank's *Alas, Babylon* and Samuel B. Southwell's *If All the Rebels Die* illustrate how a group of ordinary citizens react when they are faced with the end of the world as they have known it. Such novels usually emphasize man's courage and resourcefulness, but they also touch upon his pettiness and greed.

Rather than serving merely as a backdrop or as a setting in *Cat's Cradle,* the Apocalypse assumes thematic and structural significance. The novel is really a comic investigation of epistemology, for Newt Hoenikker draws a picture of a cat's cradle to illustrate the meaninglessness of life while Bokonon writes *The Books of Bokonon* to make life meaningful through truthful lies. While Newt may be correct in asserting the impossibility of ever knowing what is real or meaningful, there is no question that ice-nine is all too real. In many ways Vonnegut's treatment of the Apocalypse is similar to Mark Twain's apocalyptic vision in *The Mysterious Stranger,* for Twain's Satan reveals that Heaven and Hell are illusory and that the only way to account for the absurd world is to realize that it is only a

dream. Bokonon tells John that, given the absurdity of life and the
end of the world, the proper thing for man to do as the world ends is
to thumb his nose at God. *The Mysterious Stranger* ends with Satan's
revelation that the universe is empty except for the startled narrator
and that even he is only a useless thought. In *Cat's Cradle* Papa
Monzano swallows a capsule of ice-nine and proclaims that "Now I
will destroy the whole world" (193). In an absurd world where God's
existence is suspect and where there is no assurance of a Heaven or
Hell, the death of man is the death of the entire world.

In such an absurd universe the very moment of history which once
gave the end of the world philosophical and theological meaning
now becomes meaningless. Bokonon writes in his *Books of Bokonon*,
"History! Read it and weep!" (204). History is not the orderly linear
progression of man from beast to angel, nor is it the predictable
cyclic movement that Oswald Spengler and Mircea Elliade
described. Rather, history is a useless tool to explain, to predict, or to
justify human behavior because it reveals that man has not learned
anything which could help him survive. One of the many *Books of
Bokonon* is entitled "What Can a Thoughtful Man Hope for
Mankind on Earth, Given the Experience of the Past Million
Years?"; and the answer according to Bokonon is simply "Nothing"
(199).

The Apocalypse comes in *Cat's Cradle* because Science
(represented by Felix Hoenikker) concentrates on progress while it
ignores morality, responsibility, and Religion (represented by
Bokonon); it concentrates on happiness while it ignores the physical
reality. Art (Newt), Music (Mona), and Literature (John) are all
powerless to prevent the annihilation of mankind. John May has
categorized *Cat's Cradle* as an example of "humorous apocalypse . . .
imagined catastrophe that nevertheless provokes laughter"; and he
sees Vonnegut's hope for mankind as a desire that man will accept
himself as a moral midget.[8] Yet there is no suggestion in *Cat's Cradle*
that any of the characters really change as a result of the catastrophe.
In fact, Frank Hoenikker is still able to speculate about how ants survived ice-nine while ignoring his own role as the man who gave his
share of the substance to Papa Monzano and thus triggered the freezing of the entire world. Perhaps Robert Scholes's classic definition of
Black Humor explains the ending of *Cat's Cradle:* in the absurd
world Vonnegut draws, perhaps the best thing man can hope for is
not the answer to what he should do about his life but an understanding of the cosmic joke on himself.[9]

VI   *The Saga of*
Eliot Rosewater, Vonnegut's Schizophrenic Hero

In Vonnegut's next novel, *God Bless You, Mr. Rosewater*, he once again ponders what is required to make people "brave and kind and healthy and happy." If new scientific knowledge and if a religion based upon harmless untruths fail to achieve this goal, perhaps the answer lies in a combination of money and love. *God Bless You, Mr. Rosewater, or Pearls Before Swine* (1965) is the story of Eliot Rosewater, a millionaire who suddenly develops a social conscience, abandons New York, and establishes the Rosewater Foundation in Rosewater, Indiana, where he attempts to dispense unlimited amounts of love and limited sums of money to anyone who will come to his office. The experience drives Eliot insane; and, after a year in a rest home, he returns to Rosewater County and wills all his money to the fifty-seven children whose mothers have claimed that Eliot fathered them. Eliot is innocent of such charges; but, instead of being angry, he asks that his newly claimed children be fruitful and multiply.

The plot summary does not really do the book justice for in many ways it is Vonnegut's richest and most complex novel. The idea for the novel came from Vonnegut's experience in sharing an office over a liquor store with an accountant who "really is that kind. . . . I could hear him comforting people who had very little income, calling everybody 'dear,' and giving love and understanding instead of money. And I heard him doing marriage counseling and I asked him about that and he said that once people told you how little money they'd made they felt they had to tell you everything. I took this very sweet man and in a book gave him millions and millions to play with."[10]

Since Vonnegut rarely presents simple black-and-white situations, it is not surprising that the very title of this novel reflects some of its ambiguities. The phrase, "God Bless You, Mr. Rosewater" appears twice in the book. When Diana Moon Glompers, an unloved old lady who is "ugly, stupid, and boring," calls Eliot during a storm because she is afraid of lightning, her "God bless you" is obviously heartfelt and sincere, a tribute to Eliot's efforts to love those people nobody else cares about. The second occurrence of this phrase is suspect, however, because Fred Rosewater, Eliot's distant relative and an insurance salesman, is trying to sell some insurance policies. He approaches his prospective buyers and tells them about a young wife

who lost her husband and who confessed to him that "I don't know
how the children and I can ever thank you enough for what you've
done. God bless you, Mr. Rosewater" (104). Since this story is part of
Fred's salesmanship, its authenticity is questionable.

Eliot Rosewater's very name also suggests a yoking together of op-
posites. "Eliot" links the young altruist to T. S. Eliot and his depiction of modern life as a spiritual wasteland devoid of any love but
surfeited with lust. "Rosewater" also suggests a yoking together of
the liberal Franklin Delano Roosevelt and his conception of welfare
programs and the conservative Barry Goldwater. Mushari, the villian
in this novel, chooses to read Barry Goldwater's *Conscience of a
Conservative*. Eliot's father, Lister Rosewater, is also a very conservative senator, and it becomes apparent that Vonnegut was very
much aware of the 1964 election of a President while writing this
novel.

The paradoxical quality to Eliot's name suggests what a very complex character he is. He dedicates himself to becoming a special kind
of artist, for he tells his beautiful wife Sylvia that "I'm going to love
these discarded Americans, even though they're useless and unattractive. *That* is going to be my work of art" (47). On the stairs
leading to his office Eliot paints a William Blake poem which illustrates why he has established his office in Rosewater County:

> The Angel
> That presided
> o'er my
> birth said,
> 'Little creature,
> formed of
> Joy and Mirth,
> Go love
> without the
> help of
> Any Thing
> on Earth' (64).

Eliot believes that he must give uncritical love to the citizens of
Rosewater County and that no one will help him. Vonnegut deflates
some of Eliot's nobility, however, by linking the unwashed,
overweight altruist to the phrase "Little creature." Also, it is difficult
to think of any progeny of Senator Rosewater as being "formed of

Joy and Mirth." Indeed, Senator Rosewater refutes his son's martyr-
like concept of his role with another Blake poem:

> Love seeketh only Self to please,
> To bind another to its delight,
> Joys in another's loss of ease,
> And builds a Hell in Heaven's despite (65).

If Senator Rosewater is correct, then Eliot's God-like love is really
narcissistic, and what he really wants is a master/slave relationship
with the rabble.

As for some evidence to support this view, Eliot keeps a Domesday
Book in which he "entered the name of each client, the nature of the
client's pains, and what the Foundation had done about them" (93).
The book he keeps of his transactions with his clients is a record of
their spiritual and financial debt to him, and the very name
"Domesday" suggests that all accounts will be paid on Judgment
Day. There is something demeaning and demoralizing about coming
to Eliot's office to ask for help; people slink in and out as if they were
visiting a house of prostitution; and it is not mere coincidence that
Eliot advertises by scrawling messages on phone booths or that on
one phone booth is written "Eliot Rosewater is a saint. He'll give you
love and money. If you'd rather have the best piece of tail in
Southern Indiana, call Melissa" (90). Eliot's book may be an attempt
to ameliorate his guilt feelings not only about his unearned wealth
but also about the people he has inadvertently killed or maimed. At
the age of nineteen he took his mother sailing and killed her when
the ship's boom knocked her overboard. During World War II he
killed three unarmed firemen when he mistook them for German
soldiers. A psychiatrist concludes that Eliot has attempted to atone
for these deaths and for his unearned wealth by "channeling his
sexual drives into a utopic vision" (87).

Eliot spent a good deal of his childhood visiting the local fire station; for as his father confesses, "I told him it was home but I never
thought he would be dumb enough to believe it" (63). The only time
Eliot really becomes sexually excited is when he reads about fires.
When he reads about the fire-bombing of Dresden, Eliot's palms
sweat. In fact, Vonnegut points out that Eliot "had a book hidden in
his office, and it was a mystery even to Eliot as to why he should hide
it, why he should be afraid of being caught reading it. His feelings

about the book were those of a weak-willed puritan with respect to pornography, yet no book could be more innocent of eroticism than the book he hid" (175). When Eliot thinks about the fire-bombing of Dresden while riding a bus leaving Indianapolis, he suddenly has a vision of a firestorm over Indianapolis: "He was awed by the majesty of the column of fire, which was at least eight miles in diameter and fifty miles high. . . . Within the boundaries, helixes of dull red embers turned in stately harmony about an inner core of white. The white seemed holy" (201).

The firestorm takes, therefore, the form for Eliot of a gigantic phallus, but it appears also to be holy. Vonnegut uses fire imagery here to symbolize both lust and purification: to Eliot, the firemen represent the pure altruism needed for a utopic community; but mass destruction, such as the fire-bombing of Dresden, represents something so obscene that it has a pornographic effect on him. By channeling his sexual drives into a utopic vision, Eliot can only achieve sexual gratification by creating a utopia; but his schizophrenia clouds his ability to distinguish between appearance and reality in much the same way it affected Howard W. Campbell, Jr.

While Eliot's desire to help the poor is laudable, his methods are not. Although he pays people who are on the verge of committing suicide not to do so, such action does not solve these people's problems; it merely postpones them. By making the last payment on a motor scooter for a client and his girl friend, Eliot indirectly contributes to their death two days later in an accident. Vonnegut responded to the question of whether Eliot's altruism was a model that man should imitate by declaring that "the unselfish love of Rosewater certainly changes lives. Yes — what we need is a world filled with unselfish love. Everybody will be more comfortable."[11] Vonnegut's response is clouded, however, by his usual shades of ambivalence; the word "comfortable" contributes to this passage's sarcastic tone since Eliot, Malachi Constant, and Howard W. Campbell, Jr., all live in an illusory world that is far more comfortable than the real world.

The fact that Vonnegut intimates that Eliot's brand of altruism would result in a more comfortable world and not necessarily in a better one suggests that his schizophrenia is comfortable since it shields him from the harsh reality of the conditions around him, particularly the nature of the people found in Rosewater, Indiana, who "have neither pride nor self respect . . . are totally unreliable, not maliciously so, but like cattle who wander aimlessly" (138).

Rosewater argues that the people he helps are "the people who, in generations past, had cleared the forests, drained the swamps, formed the backbone of the infantry in time of war . . ." (69); but the readers learn that "The people who leaned on Eliot were a lot weaker than that — and dumber, too" (69). While Eliot professes to love the poor, he reacts differently when Senator Rosewater tells him that his "clients" "love you, they hate you, they cry about you, they laugh at you, they make up new lies about you every day. They run around like chickens with their heads cut off"; for Eliot "felt his soul cringe, knew he could never stand to return to Rosewater County again" (213).

Deep within the altruist Eliot lies the more aristocratic identity with its conventional disdain for the poor and the uneducated; and his father, who also feels this way, cannot bear the sight of Eliot's "clients." Eliot's schizophrenia becomes apparent when a client named Mary Moody calls him on the telephone he reserves for fire calls, for Eliot snarls "*God damn* you for calling this number! You should go to jail and rot! Stupid sons of bitches who make personal calls on a fire department line should go to hell and fry together!" (172). When a sobbing Mary calls back a few moments later on Eliot's other phone, he asks her, " 'What on earth is the trouble, dear?' He honestly did not know. He was ready to kill whoever had made her cry" (172).

While there are many more examples illustrating Eliot's mental illness, there are also many instances of his saintlike behavior. Mushari's fellow lawyers refer to Eliot as "The Nut," "The Saint," "The Holy Roller," and "John the Baptist" (18); and he actually does baptize babies according to his religion of love. He tells them, "Hello, babies. Welcome to Earth. It's hot in the summer and cold in the winter. It's round and wet and crowded. At the outside, babies, you've got about a hundred years here. There's only one rule that I know of, babies: God damn it, you've got to be kind" (110). Such a creed is vastly more superior to Vonnegut than the oath that a "Christian" orphanage requires its students to take once a week before Sunday supper:

I do solemnly swear that I will respect the sacred private property of others, and that I will be content with whatever station in life God Almighty may assign me to. I will be grateful to those who employ me and will never complain about wages and hours, but will ask myself instead, 'What more can I do for my employer, my republic, and my God?' I understand that I have not been placed on Earth to be happy. I am here to be tested. If I am to pass the test, I must be always unselfish, always sober, always truthful, always chaste in mind, body, and deed, and always respectful to those whom God has, in His wisdom, placed above me. If I pass the test, I will go to joy everlasting in Heaven when I die. If I fail, I shall roast in Hell while the Devil laughs and Jesus weeps. (154 - 55)

The respect orphans are supposed to feel for private property and for those above them in station is not surprising when it is realized that in *Cat's Cradle* the entire island of San Lorenzo once was run by Castle Sugar Incorporated and the Catholic Church, an unholy alliance between church and state that Vonnegut finds repugnant. Vonnegut attacks the Protestant ethic that presumes that the wealthy are God's chosen people and that the poor are guilty of sin or natural depravity. Why, Vonnegut asks, should the world be a moral gymnasium only for the poor while the rich enjoy the fruits of their inherited funds? He is not surprised that wealthy families support public institutions that require such oaths: it represents one way to assure social stability since it implies that any form of revolution or rebellion against America's moneyed interests really represents an attack on both God and the republic; therefore, such an attack would be both immoral and unpatriotic.

Behind the Rosewater Foundation is the Rosewater Corporation, another attempt by the "haves" to prevent the "have nots" from sharing in what Eliot calls "the money river"; for the corporation is dedicated "to prudence and profit, to balance sheets" (16). If Eliot Rosewater gives his money to the poor, Mushari reasons that the Rosewater Corporation will have to assume that he is crazy and remove him from the presidency of the Rosewater Foundation. The elderly McCallister, the lawyer for both the Rosewater and the Buntline family fortunes and a fierce advocate of the free-enterprise system, dismisses any suggestion that wealthy families share their fortunes by pointing out that "Giving away your fortune is a futile and destructive thing. It makes whiners of the poor, without making them rich or even comfortable. And the donor and his descendants become undistinguished members of the whining poor" (140). This lawyer's attitude is precisely what Eliot attacks by establishing his office.

VII   *Money, a Symbol*

God Bless You, Mr. Rosewater is a novel about money; for, as Vonnegut declares on the first page, "A Sum of Money is a leading character in this tale about people . . ." (15). When Eliot describes in his will just how the Rosewater fortune grew, it becomes clear that Vonnegut is presenting a Black Humor version of the Horatio Alger story to show the basic flaw in the American dream of rags-to-riches success. Noah Rosewater, unlike the Biblical Noah, not only survived the Civil War deluge on his hog farm, but actually prospered by selling his animals to the government at inflated prices. Instead of marrying the beautiful daughter of a banker or a clothing magnate, Noah, in Vonnegut's Black Humor version, marries Cloeta Herrick, "the ugliest woman in Indiana," who had four hundred thousand dollars.

The basic flaw in the American dream is that the Founding Fathers "had not made it the law of the Utopia that the wealth of each citizen should be limited" (20). As a result of this oversight, the "American dream turned belly up, turned green, bobbed to the scummy surface of cupidity unlimited, filled with gas, went *bang* in the noonday sun" (21). The growth of the Rosewater fortune becomes intertwined with the Rockefeller family since "Noah begat Samuel, who married Geraldine Ames Rockefeller" (21). The Biblical *begat* suggests the wealthy peoples' feelings of religious justification for their position. When Noah Rosewater cheats his blind brother George of his share of the family farm, George replies that "as the Bible tells us in no uncertain terms, business is business" (118). The Rosewaters spend thousands for paintings and then donate them to museums which are closed on Sundays; and, by this act of largesse, they ameliorate any guilt feelings they might have but really do not give anything to the poor.

Because of the rapaciousness of men like Noah Rosewater and his descendants, "the savage and stupid and entirely inappropriate and unnecessary humorless American class system was created" (21). The result of this class system is that men like the young lawyer Norman Mushari are willing to do anything to gain a fortune; therefore, money is clearly a dehumanizing force in Vonnegut's novel,[12] and Mushari is just as clearly the villain. He is only five feet and three inches tall, but he possesses "an enormous ass, which was luminous when bare" (17). Mushari characteristically always eats alone; and, like Noah Rosewater, he has no time for beautiful women or for literature. Even more serious is Mushari's inability to laugh while monomaniacally pursuing his fortune. The inequitable distribution of money in America creates Norman Mushari, but it rewards men like Bunny Weeks and ruins men like Harry Pena. Weeks, the homosexual great-grandson of Herman Melville's Captain Ahab, the man who finally killed Moby Dick, is flourishing because he caters to "stupid, silly, fat widows in furs" who are the inheritors — "benificiaries of boodle and laws that had nothing to do with wisdom or work" (151). Harry Pena, a Vonnegut version of Hemingway's old man in the sea, is a fisherman who works with his three sons killing the fish who swim into their traps. As director of the local bank, Weeks calls Pena a silly romantic and reveals that bankruptcy proceedings will soon begin against the fisherman. Surrounded by lesbians (Amanda Buntline), homosexuals (Weeks), impotent utopic dreamers (Eliot), and ambitious asexual lawyers (Mushari), Pena is the only heterosexual in the novel. Money is not only a dehumanizing force for Pena, but it has a sterilizing effect on everyone it touches in the novel.

VIII   *Kilgore Trout*

Eliot's guide in his efforts to redistribute his wealth is the science-fiction writer Kilgore Trout whom he refers to as "society's greatest prophet" (28). Destined to reappear in both *Slaughterhouse-Five* and *Breakfast of Champions,* Trout is "an old man with a full black beard. He looked like a frightened, aging Jesus, whose sentence to crucifixion had been commuted to imprisonment for life" (134). Trout himself acknowledges his resemblance to Jesus when he tells Rosewater that he had shaved off his beard when he had applied for a job at a stamp redemption center because "Think of the sacrilege of a Jesus figure redeeming stamps" (212). Vonnegut has admitted that Trout is based to some extent on his early career and on a number of science-fiction writers, particularly on Theodore Sturgeon who, like Kilgore Trout, has become famous for his marvelous ideas and his mediocre prose style. The very name Kilgore Trout also may have religious significance: *Kilgore* suggests the killing and the gore that result from living in a world where there is not enough love and human compassion. *Trout,* of course, is the name of a fish; and the fish was a symbol by which early Christians identified one another and of a religion based upon the need for human as well as divine love.

During Eliot's period of insanity he urged his father to summon Trout since this prophet and science-fiction writer could explain the meaning of everything the young altruist had done while in Rosewater County. Trout's explanation makes some sense. He points out that Eliot dealt with a very difficult social problem: "How to love people who have no use" (21). The reason he idolized firemen is because they were virtually the "only examples of enthusiastic unselfishness to be seen in the land" (211). According to Trout, the main lesson "Eliot learned is that people can use all the uncritical love they can get. . . . Thanks to the example of Eliot Rosewater, millions of people may learn to love and help whomever they see" (213). Besides such endorsements of Eliot's actions, Trout's stories help to explain the problems Eliot faces.

As a religious prophet of sorts, Trout writes stories that serve much the same function as Christ's parables. Vonnegut also uses excerpts from these science-fiction novels to unify his novel by providing authorial comment on Eliot's actions. "2BR0 2B" describes a time in the future when suicide parlors are established to accommodate the thousands of people who feel useless and unloved. Vonnegut later incorporated many of these details in his short story "Welcome to the Monkey House" in which an old man, forced to choose between uselessness and death, wonders what people are for; and this situation is precisely what Eliot tries to avoid by loving the discarded Americans who are useless and unattractive. Another Trout story entitled "The First District Court of Thank You" deals with ingratitude. If judged guilty of not being properly grateful for the deeds done for them, people have to choose between thanking the plaintiff in public or going into solitary confinement. The fact that almost all choose solitary confinement helps explain Eliot's insanity and lends credence to Matthew's warning, "Give not that which is holy unto the dogs, neither cast ye your pearls before swine, less they trample them under their feet and turn again and rend you."[13] Trout's story "The Pan Galactic Three Day Pass" describes a space cadet who learns that the entire Milky Way has disintegrated; and, in a way, this story not only foreshadows Eliot Rosewater's apocalyptic vision of a firestorm over Indianapolis, but may also be linked to Eliot's excited perusing of a book detailing the fire-bombing of Dresden.

Unlike Rumfoord and Bokonon, Trout firmly believes in his religion of love. Both Rumfoord and Bokonon created utterly indifferent gods: one does so in reaction to his discovery that man was a pawn of the Tralfamadorians; the other, in an act of political expediency. On the other hand, though, Vonnegut reveals that, although Senator Rosewater "admired Trout as a rascal who could rationalize anything," the prophet had in reality "never tried to tell anything but the truth" (212). Vonnegut never explains whether

Trout is both earnest and correct or merely sincere and misinformed. While this self-confessed Jesus figure expresses his full support for Eliot, he does not follow the young altruist's example. Instead, he shaves his beard and goes to work in a stamp redemption center. The difference between the two appears to be that, while Eliot lives by Trout's precepts and becomes an altruist, the science-fiction writer cannot stand the social pressures that the Senator Rosewaters, McAllisters, and even Musharis apply; he chooses to accept a job within a corrupt society and to receive something in return for the gifts he dispenses. Once again, Vonnegut is ambiguous; but it appears at this point that Trout is speaking for Vonnegut and that his words are far more important than his actions.

Vonnegut implies that whether or not man lives in a godless universe is really inconsequential. What man must do is seek to create a better world in which human love and compassion are paramount. Eliot Rosewater may seem quite mad to a world that admires Senator Rosewater and the upper-class Pisquontuit society composed of people like Bunny Weeks and Amanda Buntline; but, if all people acted with the young Rosewater's complete altruism, the social conditions that create prostitutes, drunkards, and suicides would be eliminated.

IX   *The Conclusion of* God Bless You, Mr. Rosewater

The conclusion of the novel is both comic and confusing. During the year Eliot spends in a private mental hospital, Mushari works to seize the Rosewater Foundation funds for Eliot's distant cousin Fred Rosewater because he knows that, as a lawyer, he "can often take as much as half the bundle and still receive the recipient's blubbering thanks" (18). All Mushari has to do is to prove that Eliot is insane since a provision of the Rosewater Foundation charter calls for the immediate expulsion of any officer so adjudged. When Eliot is confronted by his father, his financial counselor, and Kilgore Trout, his memory is hazy; and he is "careful not to cry out Trout's name again as he turned around. He understood this might betray how sick he was . . ." (209). Sick as he is, Eliot hears a bird's "Poo-tee-weet?" and suddenly remembers his plan "for settling everything instantly, beautifully, and fairly" (215). Aware that, if he has children, they will automatically inherit his money and it will not go to Fred Rosewater, Eliot writes a check to Fred Rosewater for a hundred-thousand dollars, smiles a "Madonna's smile," and claims as his own children the fifty-seven children whose mothers have claimed that Eliot is their father. Eliot waves his tennis racket "as though it were a magic wand" and declares "Let their names be Rosewater from this moment on. And tell them that their father loves them, no matter what they may turn out to be. And tell them . . . to be fruitful and multiply" (217).

The bird's "Poo-tee-weet?" has great significance for Vonnegut since he uses it a number of times in his fiction to represent the cool, detached way to deal with a catastrophe. When Eliot hears the bird, he suddenly knows what he must do; and he does it calmly. What Eliot does, in effect, is to take it upon himself to perform actively a divine act of mercy and love in an effort to make Kilgore Trout's suggestions for a heaven on earth a reality. The very fact that he echoes Genesis in this final proclamation may well indicate that Eliot is taking the first step toward creating a new and, hopefully, a better world. While such an interpretation is possible, Eliot's last act is shrouded in ambiguity. When he smiles to his father and to McAllister, his is a "Madonna's smile"; and, when he issues his instructions concerning the fifty-seven children, he raises his tennis racket as if it were a magic wand. Vonnegut paints such absurd pictures that the godlike Eliot evokes laughter rather than devotion. It is very difficult, if not impossible, to determine whether he is sane or not at this point.

Eliot's action can be viewed, however, as a very pragmatic solution to his problems. He prevents the money from going to the rapacious Mushari and gives it to a group of children who hopefully can use it after Eliot's death to escape the circle of poverty and stupidity that has entrapped their parents. Eliot may also have finally realized that he has hurt his clients far more than he has helped them since his monetary gifts were usually token ones: he never solved any problems; he merely postponed them. By willing his fortune to the poor, Eliot rids himself of his albatross-like burden that haunted him from the moment he developed a social conscience.

While one cannot be sure of Eliot's motives, *God Bless You, Mr. Rosewater* appears to fit into a pattern seen in Vonnegut's earlier novels that makes it possible to generalize concerning his view of man and society. Man, unable to work within the framework of an intolerable society to effect social reforms, may seek a separate peace; but he will find it unsatisfactory because it is he himself who is sick. In the disillusionment of Paul Proteus and Malachi Constant, in the suicide of Howard Campbell, Jr., in the destruction of the entire world in *Cat's Cradle,* and in the insanity of Eliot Rosewater, Vonnegut's characters react predictably when they recognize the

"Mother Night" forces at work within man. Each of these characters briefly becomes schizophrenic and assumes a new identity in an effort to cope with this problem. This new identity in each case involves a farther retreat from the real world and an unpleasant society into a more comforting illusory world. But does this mean Vonnegut has given up on his society? While *Player Piano* ends on a totally pessimistic note, *God Bless You, Mr. Rosewater's* conclusion is ambivalent. The novel's cosmic view is indeed dark, but whether it is totally black depends upon how the reader interprets Kilgore Trout, Rosewater's defender. If Trout is reliable, then Eliot should be lauded rather than condemned; and a world filled with people who practice a modified and more restrained form of his altruism would indeed be a more pleasant place than Rosewater, Indiana.

CHAPTER 4

Vonnegut's Dresden Novel:
Slaughterhouse-Five

I Slaughterhouse-Five: *Plot and Structure*

Slaughterhouse-Five (1969) is Kurt Vonnegut's "Dresden novel," the book that took him twenty years to write. Vonnegut writes in the first chapter that he would

hate to tell you what this lousy little book cost me in money and anxiety and time. When I got home from the Second World War twenty-three years ago, I thought it would be easy for me to write about the destruction of Dresden, since all I would have to do would be to report what I have seen. . . .

But not so many words about Dresden came from my mind then — not enough of them to make a book anyway. . . (2).

While money is a central character in *God Bless You, Mr. Rosewater*, death serves that role in this novel that is one without characters and, as Vonnegut admits, a book with "almost no dramatic confrontations, because most of the people in it are so sick and so much the listless playthings of enormous forces. . ." (140 - 41). The subtitle "The Children's Crusade: A Duty-Dance with Death" clearly represents Vonnegut's most serious statements about both war and death. On the title page of *Slaughterhouse-Five*, Vonnegut describes the book as "a novel somewhat in the telegraphic schizophrenic manner of tales of the planet Tralfamadore," and this description might very well be the best one of a work that abandons the novel's conventional linear plot for a Gestalt approach that asks readers to observe a series of seemingly unrelated episodes and then to share Vonnegut's view of both war and death.

In his opening chapter Vonnegut describes his efforts to gather information about the fire-bombing of Dresden from a "war buddy" who shared the experience with him. He promises his friend's wife that *Slaughterhouse-Five* will not be just another war book with potential roles for John Wayne and Frank Sinatra. By subtitling his novel "The Children's Crusade," Vonnegut relates all modern warfare to the original Children's Crusade of 1213 when thirty thousand children volunteered to go to Palestine but half of them drowned in shipwrecks while the remaining half were sold as slaves in North Africa. He concludes that all wars are fought by the young — usually for causes they cannot understand.

Vonnegut's story centers on an awkward young chaplain's assistant named Billy Pilgrim who returns from World War II to Ilium, New York, where he marries the fat, unattractive daughter of a wealthy optometrist. As a result, Billy becomes a wealthy optometrist with two healthy children. But Vonnegut's updated version of the traditional Horatio Alger rags-to-riches story does not end at this point, for it is described in the first two pages of the novel's second chapter. Billy finds that he has no control over time, and without warning he is frequently hurled through time and space away from his lush surroundings to the desolate German front. He is kidnapped by some Tralfamadorian robots and taken to the planet Tralfamadore where he is placed in a zoo with the movie star and sex symbol, Montana Wildhack. But this episode is only a short segment of his life, for Billy learns from the Tralfamadorians that all moments in a person's life exist simultaneously and that the best philosophy is to enjoy the good moments and to ignore the bad ones. Like Malachi Constant, he also learns that the concept of free will is uniquely human. The Tralfamadorians with their cosmic vision are puzzled by Billy's concern about finding a cure for the wars that plague Earth and result in atrocities like the fire-bombing of Dresden; they know that the universe always has and always will be destroyed by an accident, the result of a Tralfamadorian's experiment with a new rocket fuel.

Slaughterhouse-Five is constructed much like Joseph Heller's *Catch-22*. Just as that novel's Yossarian is compelled to think about Snowden's death yet finds it too painful and tries to avoid the memory, so too is a reluctant Billy Pilgrim forced to return again and again to the fire-bombing of Dresden. Only when Yossarian and Billy Pilgrim learn to cope with mankind's inhumanity and the horrors of war are they able to describe the atrocities they have repressed. Billy consistently retreats from Dresden just before the atrocity is to take place until he hears a group of optometrists singing, for the barbershop quartet reminds him of the group of German soldiers who shared the protection of Slaughterhouse-five with the American prisoners during the bombing. When Kilgore Trout, Vonnegut's archetypal science-fiction prophet and writer, observes Billy's strange expression, he asks Billy if he is looking through a time window, if he is observing either the past or the present. While Billy denies it, he is doing that, and his observation or recall of the past incident represents the climax of Vonnegut's novel since it is only after Billy has faced the past that he is able to return to Dresden and live through the holocaust once more. Vonnegut himself had blotted out his memories of the actual fire-bombing of Dresden, for he has admitted that "there was a complete forgetting of what it was like . . . as far as my memory bank was concerned the center had been pulled right out of the story."[1]

By naming the unheroic hero Billy Pilgrim, Vonnegut contrasts John Bunyan's *Pilgrim's Progress* with Billy's story. As Wilfrid Sheed has pointed out, Billy's solution to the problems of the modern world is to "invent a heaven, out of 20th century materials, where Good Technology triumphs over Bad Technology. His scripture is Science Fiction, man's last good fantasy."[2] In a review of *Slaughterhouse-Five* entitled "Requiem to Billy Pilgrim's Progress," Sheed speculates that Vonnegut is unable to write a novel of conventional form about the fire-bombing of Dresden perhaps because "in a sense he has been blinded by the glare of the fire bombs." Instead, Vonnegut "has turned his back on the raid and written a parable."[3] Although Sheed's title emphasizes the many similarities between *Slaughterhouse-Five* and *Pilgrim's Progress*, Vonnegut's novel is not a parable; indeed, the differences between these two works reveal Vonnegut's concern with his own personal reactions to his experience in Dresden.

While Bunyan's Christian begins a journey with Heaven as his goal, Vonnegut's Billy Pilgrim is a pilgrim who is not a Christian and who does not even think about Heaven. While Christian is warned that the City of Destruction will be burned by heavenly fire, Billy Pilgrim is shocked when he observes bombed Dresden, a city with a skyline that was "intricate and voluptuous and enchanted . . . like a Sunday School picture of Heaven . . ." (129) that has been burned by a hellish fire-bombing. Finally, when Christian and Hopeful are about to leave the plain, they see "a pillar of salt with the inscription 'Remember Lot's Wife.' They marvel much at this monument that seems to warn them against covetousness."[4] Vonnegut, on the other hand, interprets the action of Lot's wife as not covetousness, but as a very human concern for the welfare of the inhabitants of both Sodom and Gomorrah. He then goes one step farther and indicates that *Slaughterhouse-Five* in a sense does the same thing; it too looks back at a holocaust with feelings of human compassion and love.

The key to these differences between the views of Christian and Pilgrim becomes apparent when one realizes that, since *Pilgrim's Progress* is an allegory, a parable, it deals with "a re-examination of the objective norms of experience in the light of human ideality. It concludes the making of a new version of reality by means of an ideal which the reality of the fiction proves."[5] In *Slaughterhouse-Five*, there is no idealism — only shock and outrage over the havoc and destruction man is capable of wreaking in the name of what he labels a worthy cause.

II   *Vonnegut's Use of Esthetic Distance*

John Keats coined the term "negative capability" to describe the ability of the artist (in his case, the poet) to free himself from the confines of his own personality and ego and to adopt the identity of the person or persons he is writing about.[6] While an artist who is able to annihilate his own personality when writing a novel has Keats's "negative capability," such annihilation is surely not within Vonnegut's capability in *Slaughterhouse-Five*. Billy Pilgrim's reaction to the fire-bombing of Dresden is crucial to an understanding of Pilgrim's character. Because of the parallel in *Slaughterhouse-Five* between Vonnegut's experience in Dresden and that of Billy Pilgrim, Vonnegut creates a mask, a narrator who provides a certain distance between author and protagonist. Just as the first chapter of *Slaughterhouse-Five* is ending, Vonnegut introduces a note of science fiction when he tells his readers that "Somebody was playing with the clocks. . . . The second hand on my watch would twitch once, and a year would pass, and then it would twitch again. There was nothing I could do about it. As an Earthling I had to believe whatever clocks said — and calendars" (18).

Vonnegut then quotes a stanza from Theodore Roethke's "The Waking" that describes how it is possible to "wake to sleep" and "dream by going where I have to go." The key word in the poem for Vonnegut is *sleep. Slaughterhouse-Five* in a way is a vision, a dream, Vonnegut's version of James Joyce's *Finnegans Wake* in which he and the reader both learn by "going where I have to go." The very process of making this journey is so painful for Vonnegut that he has labeled this novel a failure. After the quote from "The Waking," a masked narrator continues Vonnegut's story for the next eight chapters with occasional interruptions by Vonnegut himself. This narrator has a Tralfamadorian philosophy of life which makes it painless for him to describe the fire-bombing of Dresden and Billy's suffering in a cold, detached, objective manner. Tralfamadorians, it should be remembered, are machines devoid of all human feelings of love and compassion. In the final chapter Vonnegut reappears and speculates on whether or not he can accept such a view of life.

Often, when an author uses a mask, its reliability may be questionable. In *Slaughterhouse-Five* Vonnegut is careful to distinguish his viewpoint from both Billy Pilgrim's and his narrator's. In the first chapter Vonnegut, speaking as himself, is not using a mask; and he explains that he loves the wife of Lot for expressing her feelings of love and compassion by turning to look back at the inhabitants of Sodom and Gomorrah even though doing so means being transformed into a pillar of salt. What may be confusing is the fact that Vonnegut's view that man must try to ameliorate the suffering of his fellow man, or at least show some concern, is not shared consistently either by his narrator or by Billy Pilgrim. An example of this disparity in point of view occurs when Billy Pilgrim drives through the Negro slum area of Ilium, New York:

The people who lived here hated it so much that they had burned down a lot of it a month ago. It was all that they had and they'd wrecked it. The neighborhood reminded Billy of the towns he had seen in the war.
"Blood brother," said a message in pink paint on the side of a shattered grocery store.
There was a tap on Billy's car window. A black man was out there. He wanted to talk about something. The light had changed. Billy did the simplest thing. He drove on.
Billy drove through a scene of even greater desolation. It looked like Dresden after it was fire bombed — like the surface of the moon. The house where Billy had grown up used to be somewhere in what was so empty now. This was urban renewal. A new Ilium government center and a high rise apartment building were going up soon.
That was all right with Billy Pilgrim (51).

The tone of this passage is confusing because the motives of both the narrator and the protagonist are shaded in ambivalence. It appears that, from the point of view of the narrator, Billy pragmatically takes the course of action most feasible, to do the "simplest thing," and drives away when a Negro tries to talk to him. Similarly, Vonnegut's narrator likens a section of Ilium under urban renewal to the condition of Dresden after its fire-bombing. He then reports that Billy is apathetic and does not really care whether or not there is urban renewal even though it results in the destruction of his childhood home. It is difficult for the narrator to understand Billy because Pilgrim's motives are quite different. While Billy, like Vonnegut, is torn between a desire to forget Dresden and the pain this memory brings and an obsession about finding a way to reconcile the human suffering he observed there, the narrator pragmatically adopts the Tralfamadorian philosophy of "ignoring unpleasant times and concentrating on the good ones" (102). He declares "so it goes" whenever he describes an unpleasant event such as the death of Billy's parents or the airplane crash that killed all the passengers except Billy. "So it goes" is a Tralfamadorian expression used by these robots to describe an unpleasant event which cannot be avoided since man and robot both live in a universe in which there is no such thing as free will.

While the novel's narrator reports that Billy turns away from a slight reminiscence of Dresden's fire-bombing, he does not appear to understand the motives behind such an action. Billy is not following the Tralfamadorian philosophy of indifference because, as a human filled with compassion, he cannot. Rather, his actions are a result of the equipoise between his painful memories of Dresden and his almost intolerable fixation about the suffering he observed there. While at one moment the memory of Dresden may make the urban renewal project in Ilium something he wants to pass through quickly — and the sight of a ghetto Negro equally unpleasant — he at other times marries a fat woman to alleviate her suffering and loneliness, and he also cries over the agony of a horse he has unwittingly mistreated. The question Vonnegut never answers in reference to Billy and his slogan is what young Pilgrim can and cannot change.

The major difficulty for the reader of *Slaughterhouse-Five* is that, while Vonnegut's narrator accepts the Tralfamadorian view of the universe wholeheartedly, Billy Pilgrim accepts this view intellectually but not emotionally. Emotionally, his view of the universe is much closer to Vonnegut's sentiments in the first chapter where the author speaks for himself: for Billy, like Vonnegut, cannot endure the sight of human suffering even though the Tralfamadorians tell him that there is nothing he can do about it. As a child Billy was forced to contemplate "torture and hideous wounds at the beginning and at the end of nearly every day of his childhood" since he had "an extremely gruesome crucifix hanging on the wall of his little bedroom in Ilium"

(33). When he sees a group of cripples selling magazine subscriptions in his neighborhood, he knows at the intellectual level that he should follow the advice he heard from a man from the Better Business Bureau and call the police; instead, he weeps although he does not know why. The narrator, who also does not understand Billy's weeping, declares that "Every so often, for no apparent reason, Billy Pilgrim would find himself weeping" (53). Billy is crying in despair for the plight of mankind even though his intellect refuses to recognize this fact.

Intellectually, at least, Billy tries to escape from the sight of human suffering by adopting the Tralfamadorian philosophy. When he meets a boy whose father died in Vietnam, he tells him "about his adventures on Tralfamadore," and assures the fatherless boy that his father "is very much alive still in moments-that boy would see again and again." He then asks, "Isn't that comforting?" (117). The boy and his mother flee the office convinced that Billy is insane. Eventually, Pilgrim realizes that he cannot comfort others with the Tralfamadorian philosophy; he cannot even ameliorate his own suffering. When Billy marries his fat wife Valencia, the narrator knows that "Billy didn't want to marry ugly Valencia. She was one of the symptoms of his disease. He knew he was going crazy when he heard himself proposing marriage to her, when he begged her to take the diamond ring and be his companion for life" (93). Pilgrim's "disease" is his inability to accept human suffering; during their honeymoon night Valencia tells him "I'm so happy . . . I never thought anybody would marry me" (103). Billy does not feel any love for her, but he is reconciled to the marriage since he "had already seen a lot of their marriage, thanks to time-travel, knew it was going to be at least bearable all the way" (104). A marriage that is "bearable" seems a small price for Billy to pay if it relieves the pangs he feels when he watches Valencia suffer as an unmarried, fat, unloved woman.

As noted, the Dresden holocaust made such an impression on Vonnegut that he devoted twenty-three years to trying to write a novel about it. It made such an impression on Billy Pilgrim that, as an optometrist who, by dint of his profession, should help people see more clearly, he frequently feels compelled to travel back in time and to relive the events leading up to the climactic day of the Dresden air raid. Although the novel's narrator can accept the destruction of this city with a Tralfamadorian "so it goes," Billy cannot because Vonnegut cannot. Both protagonist and author respond in characteristic

Vonnegut fashion — ambivalently. While Billy and Vonnegut would very much like to purge themselves of the painful memory, they find themselves fixated on the needless suffering they observed there. This condition of dynamic equilibrium seems irreconcilable; both are confronted with the very human conflict between man's desire for personal comfort and his desire to ameliorate another's suffering.

Crucial to an understanding of *Slaughterhouse-Five* is the realization that Billy's feelings concerning human suffering are directly linked to his experience at the fire-bombing of Dresden. In an article entitled "Time and the Modern Novel," Dayton Kohler may well have pinpointed why the Dresden holocaust is the key to the structure of this novel when he wrote that "the modern novelist is alert to that time sense which runs through all awareness of the relations between fact and meaning, objects and ideas, outward appearance and inner reality; and he tries to make the form of the novel correspond, at least in its technical aspects to his perception of reality."[7] The fire-bombing is at the center of Billy's consciousness and is much more real to him than his shallow life as an optometrist in Ilium, New York. Pilgrim frequently feels himself drawn to Dresden by what was by far the most traumatic experience of his life. When he does travel there, however, he utilizes the Tralfamadorian concept of time travel to jump away whenever he comes too close to the actual day of the bombing. On the night before the actual attack, for example, the narrator reveals that "Nothing happened that night. It was the next night that about one hundred and thirty thousand people in Dresden would die. So it goes. Billy dozed in the meat locker. He found himself engaged again, word for word, gesture for gesture, in the argument with his daughter with which this novel began" (142). It is less painful for Billy to sustain his daughter's scolding than it is to endure the fire-bombing once again.

III   *Stream of Consciousness in* Slaughterhouse-Five

Since Vonnegut has constructed *Slaughterhouse-Five* with the fire-bombing of Dresden at its center, all Billy's time travel and memories are linked to it by repression. Because Vonnegut apparently links the fire-bombing of Dresden with what to him is the very problem posed by man's seemingly unbounded proclivity for evil that he referred to in an earlier novel as the forces of "Mother Night," it is quite natural for him to show Billy trying to repress such a memory. Despite such efforts, however, Billy's repressed thoughts are part of his stream of consciousness though, even while in his sleep-like state, the actual holocaust is still too painful to face directly.

Vonnegut uses stream of consciousness, sensory impressions, and interior monologue to show that all of Billy's thoughts lead indirectly yet ultimately to Dresden and to the disturbing yet unanswerable question for him of why man destroys and kills. Billy begins one of his journeys through time as a German prisoner of war about to be given a shower in Dresden in 1944. When a German soldier turns on a master valve, the water is like "scalding rain." It "jangled Billy's skin without thawing the ice in the marrow of his long bones" (73). This sensation of being showered with hot water causes young Pilgrim to go back in time to his infancy. Suddenly he "was a baby who had just been bathed by his mother." In order to powder him, his mother takes him into "a rosy room . . . filled with sunshine" (73). The remembrance of that sunshine upon him causes Billy to jump forward in time to a point when he is a "middle-aged optometrist again, playing hacker's golf . . . on a blazing summer Sunday morning" (73). When he bends down to retrieve his golf ball safely trapped in the cup, Billy suddenly travels in time to the moment when he finds himself trapped by the Tralfamadorians, "strapped to a yellow contour chair . . . aboard a flying saucer, which was bound for Tralfamadore" (73 - 74).

The logic behind this time shift appears to be his association with the word *trapped*. A Tralfamadorian tells him that all men and all Tralfamadorians are like bugs trapped in amber, for "Only on Earth is there any talk of free will" (74). Billy has moved from taking a shower in Dresden in 1944 to talking to aliens on the planet Tralfamadore in 1967, but his focus is still on man's inhumanity exemplified by the Dresden holocaust; for, when he ponders the question of human free will, what he really is asking is, if man does indeed have free will, what rationale can he possibly have to explain his actions during the war, particularly his fire-bombing of Dresden.

While Vonnegut's use of a narrator with a personality all his own, his use of stream of consciousness, and his manipulation of the novel's time scheme and esthetic distance makes *Slaughterhouse-Five* a difficult book to follow, his strong feelings about the Dresden holocaust made such techniques necessary. Without such artistic sleight-of-hand, the novel might have turned into a political diatribe or perhaps into a maudlin, introspective look at war.

IV   *The Role of Science Fiction*

In *God Bless You, Mr. Rosewater*, Eliot Rosewater drunkenly praises science-fiction writers for their concern with human problems; and he singles out Kilgore Trout as America's greatest prophet. In *Slaughterhouse-Five*, Billy Pilgrim suffers a nervous breakdown and draws Eliot Rosewater as his roommate in the hospital. Billy comes to love Kilgore Trout's novels as much as Eliot Rosewater does because both men "were trying to re-invent themselves and their universe. Science fiction was a big help" (87). Trout's stories serve much the same purpose as Bokonon's *foma* in *Cat's Cradle* since they too function as bittersweet lies that reveal truths.

Trout's novels provide a comic commentary on the serious problems facing Billy Pilgrim. *Maniacs in the Fourth Dimension*, for example, is about people whose mental diseases could not be cured by doctors because the diseases — like Heaven and Hell, as Trout confides — existed only in the "fourth dimension." As an optometrist, Billy is expected to help people see better; but he is labeled insane because he sees Dresden as an example of what war does to the victors as well as to the vanquished. He also sees with the aid of his Tralfamadorian guides the futility and absurdity of traditional Christian views of death and free will. A second Trout novel entitled *The Gutless Wonder* is linked even closer to both Billy Pilgrim and Vonnegut, for the book describes a robot with bad breath who becomes popular after his halitosis is treated. Without a conscience, the robot drops napalm on people; but nobody complains about that act though "they found his halitosis unforgivable. But then he cleared that up and he was welcomed to the human race" (144).

A few pages following this Trout story Vonnegut quotes passages from David Irving's *The Destruction of Dresden* in which an officer attempts to justify the fire-bombing as a military necessity.[8] Seen in the context of Vonnegut's antiwar statements in the first and in the last chapters of *Slaughterhouse-Five*, Trout's story reflects the myopic morality of all apologists for war. To testify additionally about the absurdity of war, the climax of the novel, according to Vonnegut, is supposed to be the execution of gentle Edgar Derby who survives the fire-bombing and the Battle of the Bulge only to be tried and then shot for taking a teapot from the ruins.

Trout reiterates the absurdity-of-life theme in another novel entitled *The Big Barrel* in which an Earth man and woman are kidnapped by extraterrestrials and then taken to a zoo on a planet called Zircon-212. There they find a room equipped with a news ticker and a telephone that appears to be connected to a brokerage on Earth. The extraterrestrials stimulate the Earthlings to gloat, sulk, or cheer by manipulating the prices of stocks on the phony tickertape. The Earthlings would realize the absurdity of their actions if they could perceive reality, but they cannot. Similarly, they have no control over their destinies and are as much the playthings of fate as Billy Pilgrim.

Since Vonnegut's novels usually are constructed around two diametrically opposed points of view, it is not surprising that *Slaughterhouse-Five* is built around the irreconcilable conflict between free will and determinism. While Vonnegut urges his sons to exercise their free will and do what is morally and ethically justified (17), his Tralfamadorian robots point to the utter meaninglessness of such human actions. The Tralfamadorian sections of the novel may also serve another function since they provide a form of comic relief from the unbearable tension that builds as Billy approaches the day of the actual fire-bombing. Vonnegut likens these science-fiction passages to the clowns in Shakespeare's works: "When Shakespeare figured the audience had had enough of the heavy stuff, he'd let up a little, bring on a clown or foolish innkeeper or something like that, before he'd become serious again. And trips to other planets, science fiction of an obviously kidding sort, is equivalent to bringing on the clowns every so often to lighten things up."[9]

Perhaps the key Trout story in *Slaughterhouse-Five* is *The Gospel from Outer Space* in which a Visitor from outer space studies Christianity and concludes that Christians are cruel partly because of slipshod storytelling in the New Testament. Instead of getting the message across that people should be merciful even to the lowest of the low, the Gospels actually teach "Before you kill somebody, make absolutely sure he isn't well connected. So it goes" (94). The flaw in the Christ story is that, while Jesus appears to be just a poor harmless carpenter, he is in reality the son of the most powerful being in the universe. The moral of such a story unfortunately becomes not only that "they sure picked the wrong guy to lynch that time" but also that "There are right people to lynch" (94). According to Trout's extraterrestrial, there should be a new Gospel in which Christ really is a nobody. Only after he is executed do the heavens open and God reveals that he is "adopting the bum as his son, giving him the full powers and privileges of the Son of the Creator of the Universe throughout all eternity." God then declares that "From this moment on, He will punish horribly anybody who torments a bum who has no connections!" (95). Such a new Gospel hopefully would prevent any future children's crusades even if it might not eliminate the possibility of more Dresden-like holocausts.

Trout buttresses his new Christianity by adding a short novel about Christ that describes how a man builds a time machine and visits the twelve-year-old Jesus who is learning the carpentry trade from his father. Father and son gladly accept a contract to build a cross for some Roman soldiers anxious to execute a rabble-rouser. Later, when the time traveler checks to see if Christ really died on the cross, he discovers that the five-feet three-and-a-half inch Jesus "was dead as a doornail" (176). Trout's stories point toward a new Christianity in which Christ is far more human, is more like Vonnegut's Billy Pilgrim. Trout's view of God's relationship to man suggests the ending of Vonnegut's *God Bless You, Mr. Rosewater*; for God becomes Eliot Rosewater, all humanity becomes his adopted children, and each child has an equal share of the bounty.

Kurt Vonnegut, Jr., and Kilgore Trout share a view of a Humanistic Christianity, a religion in which man will consciously choose to love his brother. A number of theologians have attacked Vonnegut for trying to reject Christian theology but retain its ethics. To Peter Scholl,

His [Vonnegut's] books propose that absurdity lies at the heart of the cosmos, thus making any sort of moral statement is at the least a little foolish. Still, paradoxically, he insists that man must be treated with kindness and respect, as though he were the center of the universe and possessed of an eternal soul. . . . Vonnegut has lost the Faith, has repudiated Christianity, its creeds and assorted institutions, but he has retained all the ethical reflexes which sometimes embellish that religion. . . . He retains belief in the worth of man as an article of faith, though it is a faith he cannot justify intellectually, and which he sometimes only half-heartedly maintains.[10]

Vonnegut has always attacked massive institutions whether they be political, social, or religious on the grounds that they tend to dehumanize people; and, no matter how noble their goals, they eventually care more about their own survival than about the public welfare. In *Cat's Cradle* the Catholic Church conspires with a large corporation to enslave the entire island of San Lorenzo; and, in *God*

Bless You, Mr. Rosewater, the federal government strives to survive and to preserve the status quo by overlooking the immoral actions of the unprincipled rich while simultaneously ignoring the impassioned cries of the poor. Fort Jesus in *Cat's Cradle* and the innumerable children's crusades throughout history suggest the destruction and carnage that people have tried to justify in the name of institutionalized religion. Since the Tralfamadorian robots tell Billy Pilgrim that time is not a linear movement toward Heaven, then it becomes man's responsibility to create a Heaven on Earth. Ironically, the Tralfamadorians establish a Heaven of sorts on their planet for Billy and the movie star Montana Wildhacks. At one point in the novel Billy walks into a pornographic book store and sees a short film clip of Montana removing her clothes; later, the Tralfamadorians fulfill his wildest fantasies by bringing them together to their zoo for mating purposes. But life with the movie star is only one small part of Billy's existence which also includes the fire-bombing of Dresden. He is unable to escape the harsh realities of life by turning his back on Earth. Creation of a Heaven on Earth is predicated on whether or not humanity will have enough sense to stop trying to destroy itself.

But how much can man change? Vonnegut links both Billy Pilgrim and Montana Wildhacks to the motto of Alcoholics Anonymous:

> GOD GRANT ME
> THE SERENITY TO ACCEPT
> THE THINGS I CANNOT CHANGE,
> COURAGE
> TO CHANGE THE THINGS I CAN,
> AND WISDOM ALWAYS
> TO TELL THE
> DIFFERENCE (52).

The narrator confesses at this point that "Among the things Billy Pilgrim could not change were the past, the present, and the future" (52). Such a statement is true from a Tralfamadorian point of view since the robots live in a completely deterministic universe, but the major thrust of both the opening and concluding chapters of *Slaughterhouse-Five* suggests that Vonnegut is not content to excuse either the fire-bombing of Dresden or the Vietnam war as fate beyond the control of human free will. He reveals that he has told his sons that "they are not under any circumstances to take part in massacres, and that the news of massacres of enemies is not to fill them with satisfaction or glee" and that they should not work "for companies which make massacre machinery . . ." (17).

V   Vonnegut's View of War and Death

Slaughterhouse-Five is proof that Vonnegut kept his promise to write a war novel that does not glorify or glamorize killing. His novel does repudiate most of the stereotyped characters and patriotic bilge that has become standard movie fare. One of Billy's companions after the Battle of the Bulge is Roland Weary; he is stupid, fat, mean, and smells like bacon no matter how often he bathes; and he enjoys romanticizing the war until his daydreams blot out the reality of the frozen German landscape. While he is in reality unpopular, he imagines himself to be one of the three close war comrades who call themselves the "Three Musketeers." Vonnegut describes how Weary confronted Billy Pilgrim and "dilated upon the piety and heroism of 'The Three Musketeers,' portrayed, in the most glowing and impassioned hues, their virtue and magnanimity, the imperishable honor they acquired for themselves, and the great services they rendered to Christianity" (44).

Weary's fantasy is counterpointed by Vonnegut's earlier description about an early Christian crusade — by the shocking reality of a children's crusade in which young boys are butchered or sold into slavery because of a war they cannot even comprehend. Vonnegut further deflates the idea that war is glorious and fun by describing a group of English prisoners of war who live in a self-supervised camp that they keep immaculate and well stocked with goods. They exercise regularly, keep themselves well bathed and groomed, and manage to preserve an atmosphere of normalcy. It is not surprising that the German commander adores them because "they were exactly what Englishmen ought to be. They made war look stylish and reasonable, and fun" (81). The British prisoners are unaware that the soap and candles they use were made from "the fat of rendered Jews and gypsies and fairies and communists, and other enemies of the state" (83). It is more than coincidental that they entertain Billy Pilgrim's group of bedraggled American prisoners by performing an adult version of Cinderella. They reinforce the German commander's justification for the war by transforming the ugly, horrifying realities of war into something beautiful and magical. But midnight tolls, and Billy once again sees the real picture of warfare when he goes outside to move his bowels. He finds all his fellow Americans terribly sick with diarrhea and suddenly becomes snagged to a barbwire fence.

Vonnegut suggests that the United States Air Force tried to transform the Dresden fire-bombing from an atrocity to something almost heroic. While in a hospital recovering from an accident, Billy Pilgrim meets Bertram Copeland Rumfoord, a retired brigadier general in the Air Force Reserve and the official Air Force Historian. Rumfoord examines David Irving's *The Destruction of Dresden* because he is interested in the forewords by retired Lieutenant General Ira C. Eaker and by British Air Marshall Sir Robert Saundby. Eaker concludes his foreword by pointing out that, while he regrets that 135,0-00 people were killed in the fire-bombing of Dresden, he feels far worse about the five million Allies killed in the effort to destroy Nazism. As Donald J. Greiner has noted, Vonnegut despises Eaker's reasoning since the general apparently believed that the balancing of one atrocity with another by the other side neutralizes both and expiates all guilt.[11]

Saundby's foreword, on the other hand, points out that the Dresden attack was not a military necessity; it was merely an unfortunate incident caused by circumstances. The men who approved the attack were not evil or cruel, but they may have been too remote from the reality of the war to understand the destruction such an attack would bring. Such a point of view is much closer to Vonnegut's reaction to the atrocity. Rumfoord reveals that the Dresden bombing has not heretofore been a part of the official Air Force history of World War II "for fear that a lot of bleeding hearts . . . might not think it was such a wonderful thing to do" (165). Vonnegut finds such reasoning reprehensible.

While *Slaughterhouse-Five* is about the Dresden air attack and about World War II, its major focus is on death. Many deaths in the novel are ironic, especially that of unfortunate school teacher Edgar Derby who survives the Battle of the Bulge only to be shot for plundering a teapot from the ruins of the smoldering city. Vonnegut offers another view of death when he describes the Tralfamadorian view that all moments always have and always will exist and that death is just one moment in anyone's life. The Tralfamadorians enjoy the good moments and ignore the bad moments, but this solution is unsatisfactory to Vonnegut who believes that death is far too important to ignore.

Vonnegut's view of death becomes clear in the final chapter of *Slaughterhouse-Five* in which he describes not his visit to Dresden in 1968 but Billy Pilgrim's efforts to dig up the bodies buried beneath the rubble of the fire-bombed city. When Billy is released from captivity, Vonnegut describes the scene as follows:

And somewhere in there was springtime. The corpse mines were closed
down. The soldiers all left to fight the Russians. . . . And then one morning,
they got up to discover that the door was unlocked. World War Two in
Europe was over.

Billy and the rest wandered out onto the shady street. The trees were leafing out. There was nothing going on out there, no traffic of any kind. There
was only one vehicle, an abandoned wagon drawn by two horses. The wagon
was green and coffin shaped.

Birds were talking.

One bird said to Billy Pilgrim, "Poo-tee-weet?" (186).

Billy's world is filled with both life and death. Though it is spring
and the trees are leafing out, the coffin-shape of the abandoned
wagon serves as a reminder of the death surrounding him. The last
word in the novel is the bird's message to Billy Pilgrim, and it is the
same message Eliot Rosewater received as *God Bless You, Mr.
Rosewater* concluded. As Raymond Olderman has pointed out in
Beyond the Wasteland, "Poo-tee-weet represents a 'cosmic cool,' a
way of viewing life with the distance necessary to cope with the horrors that both Billy Pilgrim and Eliot Rosewater experience."[12] It is
not callousness or indifference but merely a defense mechanism that
allows Vonnegut to smile through his tears and to continue to live
and to write.

Slaughterhouse-Five concludes with Vonnegut himself describing
among other things the latest casualty lists in Vietnam, the death of
his father, the assassination of Robert Kennedy, the execution of
kindly Edgar Derby, and the end of World War II. Though Vonnegut sees the Dresden fire-bombing in the context of the political
assassinations and of the unpopular war that overshadowed almost
all other issues in the 1960's, he is able to smile through his tears and
provide an affirmation of life. The message of *Slaughterhouse-Five* is
the need for compassion; Malachi Constant *(The Sirens of Titan)*
and Billy Pilgrim both learn that the purpose of life, no matter
whether there is free will or not, is to love whomever is around to be
loved.

CHAPTER 5

Breakfast of Champions

I *The Anti-novel Tradition*

Slaughterhouse-Five and *Breakfast of Champions* (1973) "used to be one book," Vonnegut has revealed; but they "just separated completely . . . they simply were not mixable."[1] The two books were not mixable because while they both deal with many of the same subjects, the tone in *Breakfast of Champions* is much bleaker with, as Vonnegut has confessed, "suicide at the heart of the book."[2] Vonnegut's fiftieth-birthday present to himself, this book contains a reluctant confession that the artist cannot create order out of chaos, particularly in an America which has no well-defined culture. The novel's plot revolves around the wealthy, Midwest Pontiac dealer named Dwayne Hoover and the science-fiction writer Kilgore Trout. Life has lost all meaning for Hoover, and he hopes that at least one artist at the coming Festival of Arts will give him a key to the meaning of life. Since Trout is invited to the Festival at the recommendation of Eliot Rosewater, Vonnegut describes the movement of both Trout and Hoover to the Festival in alternating chapters. There is very little suspense since Vonnegut reveals in his first chapter that Hoover will learn from a Trout science-fiction novel that he is the only person on Earth with free will and that he will go temporarily insane, maim some people, and lose all his money through law suits. Trout, on the other hand, will become famous and even win the Nobel Prize for medicine.

In the novel's Epilogue, Vonnegut confronts Trout and confesses to him that he is his creator; and, for Trout to symbolize this new knowledge, Vonnegut offers the science-fiction writer an apple and indicates that ". . . Americans require symbols which are richly colored and three-dimensional and juicy. Most of all, we hunger for symbols which have not been poisoned by great sins our nation has committed, such as slavery and genocide and criminal neglect, or by tinhorn commercial greed and cunning" (293). Just as W. B. Yeats describes a poet stripped of his creations in "The Circus Animals Desertion," Vonnegut sets "at liberty all the characters who have served me so loyally during my writing career" (293); and he will not need Trout anymore because he has changed many of his ideas about what fiction should be. Among the major influences found in this novel are Alain Robbe-Grillet's theories of experimental fiction and the work of contemporary American artists, particularly the Pop artists.

In many ways *Breakfast of Champions* is an anti-novel, a reaction to the fictional theories of Henry James that have dominated American fiction for almost a century. Vonnegut does not restrict himself to a conventional third-person point of view for he frequently speaks directly to his reader; his comments vary from determinations of a character's reliability ("This was true") to statements about the size of a Mexican beetle and about the theory of floating continents. Vonnegut ridicules the Aristotelian concern with the unity of time and the New Critical concern with the tightly plotted novel by stating "Let's see: I have already explained Dwayne's uncharacteristic ability to read so fast. Kilgore Trout probably couldn't have made his trip from New York City in the time I allotted, but it's too late to bugger around with that. Let it stand, let it stand!" (249).

In *For a New Novel: Essays on Fiction* the French experimental novelist Alain Robbe-Grillet points out that the "novel of characters belongs entirely to the past, it describes a period: that which marked the apogee of the individual."[3] The characters in *Breakfast of Champions* are puppets, and Vonnegut makes it clear that he is the puppet-master, that both Dwayne Hoover and Kilgore Trout are his creations, and that they must do whatever he wants them to do. He then destroys any suspense the novel might contain by revealing his plot in the first two chapters, and at one point he stops describing his characters and says with some resignation: "I could go on and on with intimate details about the various lives of people on the superambulance, but what good is more information . . . accumulations of nit-picking details" (278). Vonnegut wants his audience to concentrate on his ideas and not become too occupied with the characters' destinies.

One reason Vonnegut has written an anti-novel is his feeling that people read conventional fiction and then try to "live like people invented in story books. This was the reason Americans shot each other so often: It was a convenient literary device for ending short stories and books" (210). After Vonnegut understood this fact, he "resolved to shun storytelling. I would write about life. Every person would be exactly as important as any other. All facts would also be given equal weightiness. Nothing would be left out. Let others bring order to chaos. I would bring chaos to order, instead, which I think I have done" (210). When Vonnegut views his contemporary Vanity Fair, he sees no pattern of good that is triumphing over evil; in fact, life is so complex and so confused that Vonnegut is unable to discern any meaningful patterns in the chaos.

When Vonnegut was working on his play, *Happy Birthday, Wanda June,* he expressed his unhappiness about the necessity of writing an ending for it. He has always disliked the artificiality of the old-fashioned ending that neatly ties together everything and everybody. In *Breakfast of Champions* he points out that, since life is like a polymer, the proper ending for any story about people should be the abbreviation *etc.* He confesses that it is to "acknowledge the continuity of this polymer that I begin so many sentences with *And* and *So* and end so many paragraphs with . . . *and so on*" (228). Vonnegut has also expressed his dislike for the inherent morality of the conventional plot which unrealistically meted out rewards to the good and punishments to the wicked. He points out that *Breakfast of Champions* "isn't the kind of book where people get what is coming to them at the end. Dwayne hurt only one person who deserved to be hurt for being so wicked: That was Don Breedlove" (274). Kilgore Trout is innocent yet suffers a bitten finger while Vonnegut himself comes too close to the action and suffers a broken watch crystal and a broken toe.

Perhaps Vonnegut's broken watch is well deserved because he repeatedly interrupts the narrative flow of his story to intrude with seemingly irrelevant details. When a young waitress named Patty Keene meets Dwayne Hoover, Vonnegut interrupts to state that he has just read that the theory of floating continents was more than a mere theory. He then casually gives the exact measurements of all his male characters' penises and the bust and hip measurements of all his female characters. While these details seem entirely irrelevant, they do serve a purpose; they point out a very common Black Humor theme, the inadequacy of science to deal with human problems. Knowing that San Francisco and Japan are in hideous danger because they are undergoing tremendous geological stress and knowing the exact physical measurements of Dwayne Hoover do not help either the two cities or the Pontiac salesman.

II   *The Problem of Communication*

In many ways Vonnegut's anti-novel is composed of a series of nonconversations. Just as plays by Eugene Ionesco and Harold Pinter contain conversations sprinkled with clichés and trite conversations, Vonnegut's conversations illustrate the hopelessness of communication. Here is a typical conversation between Kilgore Trout and a truck driver who has picked up the hitchhiking science-fiction writer:

> The driver mentioned that the day before had been Veteran's Day.
> "Um," said Trout.
> "You a veteran?" said the driver.
> "No," said Trout. "Are you?"
> "No," said the driver.
> Neither one of them was a veteran (103).

Veteran's Day is not important either to the truck driver or to Kilgore Trout, but it is significant to Vonnegut since it is his birthday and he manages to work it into many of his novels. Just as Alfred Hitchcock makes an appearance in each of his movies, Vonnegut appears in each of his novels. Both the truck driver and Kilgore Trout are merely going through the ritualistic responses that pass for polite conversation, and Vonnegut's flat statement that neither man was a veteran is totally unnecessary since his readers already know this fact, but it helps to point out the difficulty his characters have in communicating any meaningful messages to each other.

Vonnegut provides another example of a futile conversation when Dwayne Hoover develops a case of echolalia and finds himself echoing everything he hears on his radio and everything people say to him. When the young waitress talks to him in the restaurant, she is not even aware of his echolalia:

> "Anyway," she said, "it certainly is an honor to have you visit us and those aren't the right words, either, but I hope you know what I mean."
> "Mean," said Dwayne.
> "Is the food all right?" she said.
> "All right," said Dwayne.

"It's just what everybody else gets," she said. "We didn't do anything special for you."
"You," said Dwayne (142).

Vonnegut points out that it does not matter what anyone says in Midland City because people do not listen; they merely assume that they know what they will hear. When language is not composed of meaningless clichés in *Breakfast of Champions*, it consists of ritualistic responses that serve to block out the unpleasant real world. Dwayne Hoover's son Bunny was sent to a military school because he told his parents "he wished he was a woman instead of a man, because what men did was often cruel and ugly" (180). As a result of years of sports, buggery, and fascism at the school, Bunny returns to Midland City as a homosexual who forces himself through the day by mumbling "the motto of the school, a motto he used to have to shout about a hundred times a day" (184). When Bunny is not muttering the motto "can do," he is chanting "Aye-eeem, aye-eeem" which the Maharishi Mahesh Yogi taught him. When practicing this form of Transcendental Meditation, Bunny believes he is able to leave the cocktail lounge and also the planet Earth. Language serves, therefore, as a ritualistic mode of escape.

III *Pop Art and American Culture*

Breakfast of Champions is profusely illustrated by Vonnegut; and the drawings include sketches of Volkswagens, sheep, chickens, snakes, trucks, and light switches. The cover of the novel resembles a Wheaties cereal box, and the book opens with the disclaimer that "the identical expression as the title of this book is not intended to indicate an association with or sponsorship by General Mills, nor is it intended to disparage their fine products" (1). Despite the disclaimer that is obviously a legal necessity, Vonnegut's decision to package his product to resemble a box of cereal does represent a criticism of contemporary American values. Through skillful use of advertisements, General Mills has established an American myth concerning physical prowess and its breakfast cereal. Vonnegut reveals in his Preface why his novel contains so many references to commercial products:

I think I am trying to clear my head of all the junk in there — the assholes, the flags, the underpants. Yes — there is a picture in this book of underpants. I'm throwing out characters from my other books, too. I'm not going to put on any more puppet shows. I think I am trying to make my head as empty as it was when I was born onto this damaged planet fifty years ago.

I suspect this is something most white Americans and nonwhite Americans who imitate white Americans, should do. The things other people have put into *my* head, at any rate, do not fit together nicely, are often useless and ugly, are out of proportion with life as it really is outside my head.

I have no culture, no humane harmony in my brains. I can't live without a culture anymore (5).

Pop artists such as Claes Oldenburg, Andy Warhol, and Roy Lichtenstein dominated the past decade with their pictures of coke bottles, automobiles, and light switches. Many of Vonnegut's drawings resemble work by these Pop artists; in fact, Vonnegut's portrait of a light switch is virtually identical with Claes Oldenburg's "Switches Sketch 1964." An art critic has explained the Pop Art movement as an attempt by these artists to grasp "some understanding of the present, and in the commonplace of everyday existence their own *raison d'etre* is that they hope to make ordinary banalities take on a new, mysterious, totemic meaning."[4]

Vonnegut appears to believe that Americans have substituted material goods and the commercial myths behind these for a meaningful culture. His childlike drawings of cars, trucks, and light switches illustrate what Americans have substituted for a meaningful culture at the same time they provide Vonnegut with a great deal of amusement. Vonnegut has expressed his contempt on a number of occasions for what he calls High Art critics,[5] and to some extent his drawings represent a personal Declaration of Independence — proof that he can do anything he wants to in his fictive universe, including drawing pornographic pictures.

At one point in *Breakfast of Champions* Kilgore Trout looks into a gully and sees what amounts to a Sargasso Sea of a nation obsessed with conspicuous consumption. He sees a "1968 Cadillac El Dorado and several old home appliances — stoves, a washing machine, a couple of refrigerators" (120). He also sees a child who "clasped an eighteen-ounce bottle of Pepsi Cola to her breast" (120). When Vonnegut looks beneath the comforting illusions that materialism provides, he sees only chaos, a world becoming more and more polluted and overpopulated. He sees a world where the largest tombstone in Calvary Cemetery is a sixty-two-foot marble football immortalizing a seventeen-year-old boy who was killed while playing high school football. The citizens of Midland City fail to see anything inappropriate about placing such a monument in a cemetery named after the site of Christ's crucifixion.

IV *Prose Style*

In many ways *Breakfast of Champions* is Kurt Vonnegut's nonfictional novel since he deliberately abandons many of the novelist's traditional techniques to narrate his story in a prose style that is unusually succinct and stark. The novel's nostalgic yet bitter tone is set by Vonnegut's dedication to the woman who, when he was in high school, taught him how to write copy for advertisements about teenage clothes; he even remembers how she "taught us to be impolite in conversation not only about sexual matters, but about American history and famous heroes. . ." (2). His book debunks many of America's sexual mores and many of her traditional heroes, but its real concern is with the effect advertising has had on the American imagination. Much the same way Samuel Coleridge expressed himself in "Dejection: An Ode," Vonnegut bitterly laments the loss of his imagination and artistic ability.

Because Vonnegut feels so strongly about his subject, he speaks directly to his reader without the masks that have characterized his earlier novels. He matter-of-factly describes the most personal details of his life, including his mother's suicide and his relationship with his psychiatrist. The result is a book that is very much in the American colloquial-style tradition that can be traced back to Mark Twain's *The Adventures of Huckleberry Finn*. American colloquial style can be characterized by its emphasis on shorter sentences, the removal of references to the historical and cultural past, and the extensive use of repetition.[6] In *The Colloquial Style in America*, Richard Bridgeman has pointed out that Jamesian characters "repeat to define themselves, Twainians to keep a grip on reality."[7] Vonnegut's characters in *Breakfast of Champions* try desperately to keep their grip on reality, and Dwayne Hoover even develops echolalia just before he goes berserk.

Furthermore, the repetitive use of "and so on" in *Breakfast of Champions* links the book even more closely to American colloquial style; for, as Bridgeman has pointed out, "Because the speaker lacks the time to distribute the events in synthetic categories, he parodies a linear sequence, moving from event to event, observing democratic equality in the arrangement of his clauses. The most repeated phrase in *Huckleberry Finn* is 'by-and-by' which is no more than a vernacular alternative to 'and then . . .' Actions enumerated but barely related constitute the basic sentence of the colloquial style."[8]

Breakfast of Champions moves to a linear sequence with almost no emphasis on details, but Vonnegut has stated that, though he could be more specific, he prefers to move ahead with his story. In defending a prose style identified with both his novels and those of Joseph Heller, Vonnegut has explained that he does not think that either writer really sacrificed characters or setting by using a readable style. He also noted that "What we have done is write shorter sentences and we could easily mask what we've done and substitute semicolons and dashes for periods and get wonderfully intricate sentences and also pages that would be much more tiring to the eye."[9] Vonnegut's technique can be illustrated by examining a few key paragraphs in the section of his novel in which he summarizes his feelings just before he realizes the value of all human life:

> As I approached my fiftieth birthday, I had become more and more enraged and mystified by the idiot decisions made by my countrymen. And then I had come to pity them, for I understood how innocent and natural it was for them to behave so abominably, and with such abominable results: They were doing their best to live like people invented in story books. This was the reason Americans shot each other so often: It was a convenient literary device for ending short stories and books.
>
> Why were so many Americans treated by their government as though their lives were as disposable as paper facial tissues? Because that was the way authors customarily treated bit-part players in their made-up tales.
>
> And so on (209 - 210).

To make reading his prose as easy as possible for his readers, Vonnegut uses simple sentences almost exclusively; and he avoids words in "self-embedding" positions where they might lower reader comprehension. His diction is so unpretentious that it even contains some slang expressions such as "bit-part players."

It should be apparent that Kurt Vonnegut's prose style in *Breakfast of Champions* is highly rhetorical; he continually seeks to manipulate his audience through parenthetical expressions and political allusions. Very early in his novel he points out to his readers that he controls his fictive world although he admits that he occasionally loses control of it. Having thus established his expertise, he announces that, while he could go into much greater detail about certain characters, his audience should take his word about them and allow him to move ahead with his story. At one point, he stops his story to declare:

This book is made up, of course, but the story I had Bonny tell actually happened in real life — in the death house of a penitentiary in Arkansas. As for Dwayne Hoover's dog Sparky, who couldn't wag his tail: Sparky is modeled after a dog my brother owns, who has to fight all the time, because he can't wag his tail. There really is such a dog (216 - 17).

The protagonist in *Breakfast of Champions* is Vonnegut himself, not Dwayne Hoover or Kilgore Trout. Vonnegut consistently destroys any illusion that Hoover's story is real or even important since the real story in this novel is the author's movement from deep depression to a renewed faith in mankind. Stripped of the Dwayne Hoover and Kilgore Trout subplots, the novel can be regarded as a confessional novel in which Vonnegut reveals his problems, discovers a possible solution, and then declares publicly that he is abandoning the old way he used to write for a nonfictional style stripped of all symbols, metaphors, and similes.

V   *The Kilgore Trout Stories*

Kilgore Trout plays a larger role in *Breakfast of Champions* than he has in any previous Vonnegut novel, and he is still the pessimistic science-fiction writer whose misfortune is to write books about ideas that are seized upon by greedy publishers who issue them as pornography. Trout's stories serve much the same function that they did in Vonnegut's previous novels — they comment on the major themes in *Breakfast of Champions* and thereby tighten the novel's structure. "Plague on Wheels," for example, describes life on a dying planet named Lingo-Three where all the inhabitants, who resemble American automobiles, have destroyed their planet's resources and hopelessly await death. A friendly group of space travelers preserve their memory by telling Earthlings about the automobiles. It is appropriate then that Dwayne Hoover is a successful Pontiac dealer whose every sale brings mankind that much closer to ecological suicide.

Vonnegut's concern with the devasting effects of Madison Avenue's style of advertising is echoed in the Kilgore Trout novel *How You Doin'?* which describes a planet where an advertising agency promoting Shazzbutter interests the entire populace in statistical averages. Everyone on the planet becomes very much concerned with whether or not he or she measures up to the agency's statistics. When peanut butter-eaters on Earth prepare to invade this planet, they discover that it is too proud and resourceful to conquer militarily so they turn to subterfuge. An Earthling infiltrates the

advertising agency agency and alters the statistics so that everyone
on that planet feels inferior. Vonnegut then describes how " . . . then
the Earthlings armored space ships came in and discovered the
planet. Only token resistance was offered here and there, because
the natives felt so below average" (171). Much of the "junk" that
Vonnegut wants to erase from his mind is composed of advertising
jingles and phony claims for substandard products, and he suggests
that the advertising agencies on this planet manipulate people as effectively as the agencies in Kilgore Trout's story.

Another major theme found in Trout's stories is the tragic results
of a lack of communication, and one Trout story effectively counterpoints the many conversations in *Breakfast of Champions* that are
almost completely devoid of content:

It was about a planet where the language kept turning into pure music,
because the creatures there were so enchanted by sounds. Words became
musical notes. Sentences became melodies. They were useless as conveyors
of information, because nobody knew or cared about what the meanings of
words were anymore.

So leaders in government and commerce, in order to function, had to invent new and uglier vocabularies and sentence structures all the time, which
would resist being transmuted to music (110).

Trout's story may explain why Vonnegut's style in *Breakfast of
Champions* is even starker than usual; he eliminates virtually all
imagery; and, rather than describe many situations in detail, he dismisses them, as already noted, with "and so on." His concern with
the pressing problems of pollution, racism, and conspicuous consumption drives Vonnegut to court his reader more than usual. The
result in *Breakfast of Champions* is a prose style that is serviceable
but not flashy, a more effective vehicle for facts than for fiction.

In addition to a concern with the problems of communication,
Kilgore Trout also writes some stories that illustrate his interest in
American economics. Since Vonnegut carefully contrasts Dwayne
Hoover's enormous wealth with Trout's poverty, it is not surprising
that the science-fiction writer would write a story entitled "This
Means You" which is set in the Hawaiian Islands at a time when all
the land is owned by forty people who decide to put up "no tres-
passing" signs. The government solves this problem by providing
everybody else with balloons so that "Hawaiians could go on in-
habiting the islands without always sticking to things other people
owned" (73). Trout's viewpoint is not different from his numerous

statements in *God Bless You, Mr. Rosewater* where he advocated a mild form of socialism. At one point in *Breakfast of Champions*, a retired coal miner tells Trout how unfair it is that Eliot Rosewater can own so much land while other people own absolutely nothing. Vonnegut ends his novel with the ironic Horatio Alger twist that Dwayne Hoover eventually will lose his entire fortune while Kilgore Trout eventually will become fabulously wealthy.

While Trout's stories do illustrate Vonnegut's concern with communication and economics, the key Trout story in *Breakfast of Champions* is *Now It Can Be Told*. The book drives Dwayne Hoover to madness and violence because of its startling thesis from which Hoover learns that he is the only creature in the entire universe with free will. Just as Winston Niles Rumfoord learns in *The Sirens of Titan* that all human history has taken place for the sole purpose of helping a robot obtain a spare part for his rocket ship, Dwayne Hoover reads *Now It Can Be Told* and realizes that only he matters because of his freedom.

Perhaps to some extent Vonnegut is parodying the literary world's concern during the 1950's and 1960's with the malady known as "existential despair," for Hoover's burden of freedom is overwhelming since his decisions are in effect made for all mankind. There is no loving God in such a universe to comfort Dwayne, for Trout reveals that God is only a machine. While Dwayne was despondent when he believed that life had no meaning, he becomes psychotic when he discovers that he is the meaning of life. Dwayne goes mad much the same way Eliot Rosewater did in *God Bless You, Mr. Rosewater;* and both men are overwhelmed by the realization that other people do not matter and that they themselves have godlike power and responsibilities.

Vonnegut's belief that people are important and should control their own destinies results in his severing of the puppet strings of his own literary creations. When Vonnegut symbolically gives Trout the fruit of knowledge and looses him from his puppet strings, the old writer cries out "'Make me young, make me young, make me young!'" (295). He may be free now, but he is also mortal; and now, like Vonnegut, he must face the prospect of death without the comfort of either religious faith or a culture to sustain himself.

VI   *The End of Cosmic Detachment*

Breakfast of Champions appears to mark a transition in Vonnegut's career. While *Slaughterhouse-Five* was constructed around the tension between Vonnegut's personal anguish over the fire-

bombing of Dresden and the cool, detached narrative voice he chose
to tell his story, he drops all pretense of objectivity in *Breakfast of
Champions*. Again and again he expresses his feelings on such subjects as pollution, crass commercialism, and overpopulation. While
he takes the same Humanistic position reflected in his fiction for the
past twenty years, there is a new note of urgency and a stridency not
found in his past novels.

Considering Vonnegut's movement toward an autobiographical
mode of writing, it is not surprising that he returns to the theme that
has haunted him since childhood — the unsatisfactory relationship
between fathers and sons. The novel's two main characters, Dwayne
Hoover and Kilgore Trout, are both unable to establish healthy
relationships with their sons. Hoover's son is a homosexual whom he
assaults during his madness, and Trout's son denounces his father's
unbearable pessimism and enlists in the army only to desert and join
the Viet Cong. Recently, when questioned about the possible appeal
of a man like Charles Manson who ruled his strange "family" with a
firm hand, Vonnegut replied that "It's one of the weaknesses of our
society that so few people are willing to be a father, to be responsible."[10] His treatment of parents who abrogate their responsibilities
is not limited to fathers who remind Vonnegut of his own father, for
he has Dwayne Hoover's wife commit suicide in much the same way
his own mother took her life. Vonnegut links his own suicidal
tendencies to his mother at one point in his novel, and then stops his
book to remark on how much he enjoys his psychiatrist and her
group-therapy sessions.

While Vonnegut's revelations about his parents and his comments
about his psychiatrist are tangentially related to Dwayne Hoover's
pressing problems, they reflect not only his new concept that a novel
should be about real people and real problems but also his decision
to "shun storytelling" and "write about life" (210). In *Slaughterhouse-Five*, Vonnegut exorcised his feelings of guilt for the Dresden
holocaust; in *Breakfast of Champions*, he exorcises his attraction to
suicide. Vonnegut recently revealed to an interviewer that his new
novel "isn't a threat to commit suicide, incidentally. It's my promise
that I'm beyond that now. Which is something for me. I used to
think of it as a perfectly reasonable way to avoid delivering a lecture,
to avoid a deadline, to not pay a bill, to not go to a cocktail party."[11]
His new novel is really an attempt to find a good reason for not committing suicide.

Writing about the possibility that there is no such thing as free will, Vonnegut finds himself believing it himself and becoming more and more depressed. He confesses that "I had come to the conclusion that there was nothing sacred about myself or about any human being, that we were all machines, doomed to collide and collide and collide" (219). Vonnegut finds himself surprised by the words of his own characters, particularly by the philosophy of a very unpleasant minimalist painter named Rabo Karabekian. The painter defends his painting by indicating "the sacred immaterial core of every material, the 'I am' to which all messages are sent. It is all that is alive in any of us. . . . It is unwavering and pure, no matter what preposterous adventure may befall us" (221). These words renew Vonnegut, and he suddenly feels that he is reborn. Karabekian actually mouths many of the same sentiments as Paul Proteus in *Player Piano*, but the painter's words are couched in a form the novelist can now accept.

Ironically, both *The Sirens of Titan* and *Breakfast of Champions* were originally conceived as playful books that would be fun for Vonnegut to write and that both deal with the same subject that haunts him — the question of free will. Just as Malachi Constant retains his humanity even when turned into a killing machine named Unk, Vonnegut realizes that all people have a spark of divinity — what he calls an unwavering band of light. Unlike many of his earlier novels that are shrouded in ambivalence, Vonnegut provides a self-portrait at the end of *Breakfast of Champions* that illustrates the tears in his eyes. On his fiftieth birthday he is weeping not only about America's loss of values but also about the approach of his own old age. The last words he hears from Kilgore Trout are shouted in the voice of Vonnegut's father: "Make me young, make me young, make me young!" (295), but not even a breakfast of champions can do that.

CHAPTER 6

Slapstick

I *Plot and Structure*

IN *Breakfast of Champions,* Kurt Vonnegut, Jr., cut the strings from his puppets and spoke straightforwardly about his depression, his relationship with his psychiatrist, and his views about the destruction of American cultural values. *Slapstick* (1976) opens with Vonnegut's confession that this novel is as close as he will ever come to writing an autobiography. In 1974, he flew to Indianapolis with his brother to attend the funeral of his Uncle Alex Vonnegut; and this novel is a result of the recollections stirred by this trip. As Vonnegut admits, ". . . the mind I was given daydreamed the story in this book. It is about desolated cities and spiritual cannibalism and incest and loneliness and lovelessness and death, and so on. It depicts myself and my beautiful sister as monsters and so on. This is only natural, since I dreamed it on the way to a funeral" (17).

Vonnegut's fictional autobiography professes to tell the story of seven-foot Dr. Wilbur Daffodil-ll Swain, the final President of the United States. At the time Swain writes this autobiography, he is a hundred years old and lives in the ruins of the Empire State Building; for the entire country has been destroyed by the mysterious Albanian flu and by the Green Death. The flu germs were Martian ones whose invasion had finally been repelled by antibodies in the systems of the survivors, but the Green Death was the result of microscopic Chinese microorganisms that caused death when inhaled or ingested.

Swain and his twin sister Eliza were born "neanderthaloids"; for they were burdened with massive brow-ridges, sloping foreheads, and "steamshovel jaws." In addition, they have twelve fingers, twelve toes, and supernumerary nipples. Although their doctors were convinced that they would not survive childhood, their parents prepared a splendid retreat for them in Vermont where they were reared by practical nurses. Upon discovering that the mansion — the home of the founder of the family fortune, Professor Elihu Roosevelt Swain — contained trap doors and secret passages leading to a secret mansion within the larger building, the two children led a double life. They played the roles of idiots to please their nurses whose livelihood depended upon having helpless children to serve, but in the privacy of their secret world Wilbur taught himself French, German, Italian, Latin, and Greek by the time he was seven.

Eliza could not read or write, but she possessed an uncanny intuitive ability which, when combined with Wilbur's knowledge, made them creative geniuses; in other words, they were specialized halves of a single brain. Just as Howard W. Campbell, Jr., and his wife Helga created a "world of two" in *Mother Night* and found the outside world irrelevant to their needs, Eliza and Wilbur functioned as one individual and were completely happy until they became fifteen. Then, sensing that their parents desired more than anything else to have normal children, the two dropped any pretense of idiocy and announced that they were ready to make their parents proud of them. Unfortunately, the result of this confession was the destruction of their secret world and, more important, the beginning of their separation. Wilbur went to school while his sister was confined in a hospital and was labeled mentally retarded.

A few years later, they were reunited both physically and spiritually in a frenzied orgy that lasted five days. After their second forced separation, they were able to communicate again only after Eliza's death through an electronic device. Swain became not only a pediatrician, but eventually the President of the United States whose platform was "Lonesome No More!" Because Swain died before completing his autobiography, Vonnegut closes the novel by revealing not only the final meeting between the brother and the sister but their revelation that life after death is boring. The novel concludes with a brief description by Vonnegut of how Melody Oriole-2 von Peterswald, Swain's teenage granddaughter, manages to cross the wilderness in order to live with him.

At the center of *Slapstick* is Alice Vonnegut, Vonnegut's sister who died of cancer at forty-one only two days after her husband had been killed in a train accident. Vonnegut confesses in his first chapter that he has always written for her and that she is the secret of any artistic unity his fiction possesses. It is a fitting tribute to her that the synergistic brother and sister in *Slapstick* are able to form a secret, harmonious world that completely ignores the ugliness of the real world. Alice Vonnegut's final commentary about a world that would kill both her and her husband and leave their four small children parentless is "slapstick," but her view is also Vonnegut's judgment.

Slapstick is composed of the series of short comments separated by three small diamonds that Vonnegut presents in much the same way in *Breakfast of Champions*. In this latest novel, the medium is a significant expression of the message; for the book is really a collection of slapstick routines that reinforces a commentary about the slapstick nature of life. The book opens with Vonnegut's admission that "I have called it 'Slapstick' because it is grotesque, situational poetry — like the slapstick film comedies, especially those of Laurel and Hardy, of long ago. It is about what life *feels* like to me. There are all these tests of my limited ability and intelligence. They go on and on. The fundamental joke with Laurel and Hardy, it seems to me, was they did their best with every test. They never failed to bargain in good faith with their destinies, and were screamingly adorable and funny on that account . . . what does seem important? Bargaining in good faith with destiny" (1-2). Vonnegut's novel is also grotesque, situational poetry. Years earlier, critics described *Cat's Cradle* as Black Humor — humor so savage that the reader could only laugh with tears in his eyes. Conceived while Vonnegut was flying to the funeral of a loved one, *Slapstick* is savage; but it also exalts the good faith with which helpless humans struggle to pass every test of endurance and faith. Wilbur Swain's life is tragic, pathetic, but laudable because he constantly tried to make the right decision from a Humanistic position.

A critic has commented that a slapstick comic is not a mere funny man or buffoon; he "must often be an acrobat, a stunt man, and something of a magician — a master of uninhabited action and perfect timing . . . The best of slapstick comedians may be said to have turned low humor into high art."[1] Wilbur and Eliza Swain's efforts to please their parents by suddenly transforming themselves into intelligent teenagers is laudable, and their puzzled reaction to their parents' guilt feelings for having treated them as idiots for fifteen years is perfectly human and very appropriate. But what perfectly captures the slapstick quality of Laurel and Hardy at their very best is the naïve decision by the brother and the sister to make everyone once again happy by reverting to their idiotic behavior and by beginning to throw food while drooling. Their motivation is laudable, it is certainly an attempt to bargain in good faith with their destiny, but it is also ludicrous and hilarious.

Moreover, Vonnegut's ironic tone and use of understatement effectively complements the slapstick routines. Just before Swain's death, he visits the King of Michigan in order to sell him the Louisiana Purchase for one dollar. The King, who is pompous and psychopathic, lacks any sense of humor; he proudly informs Swain that he is reading Thucyidides since those who fail to learn from history are condemned to repeat it. Swain replies that, "If our descendants don't study our times closely, they will find that they have again exhausted the planet of fossil fuels, that they have died by the millions of influenza and the Green Death, that the sky has again been turned yellow by the propellants for under-arm-deodorants, that they have a senile President seven feet tall, and that they are clearly the intellectual inferiors of teeny-weeny Chinese.' He did not join my laughter" (21 - 11). Although scribes recorded these words for posterity, there is reason to doubt that there will be any future for a world so decimated.

II *Loneliness and the Extended Family*

One of the major themes in *Slapstick* is the pervading loneliness of contemporary American life. To Vonnegut, the underlying cause of loneliness is the American melting pot that destroys cultural and regional differences and that creates homogenized Americans that look alike, dress alike, and even think alike. He laments the loss of the earlier Vonnegut family life in Indianapolis which had retained its German language and heritage and which had also given its progeny a thorough background in European culture. Although the children matured and traveled, they ultimately returned to Indianapolis to live since "There were good things to inherit, too . . . sane businesses, comfortable homes and faithful servants, growing mountains of china and crystal and silverware, reputations for honest dealing. . ." (6). Because this type of life was lost because of the anti-German sentiment that swept America during World War I, Vonnegut sees today no reason why any Vonneguts should return to Indianapolis since it is only distinguished by its race track from any other American cities.

When Wilbur and Eliza Swain were born, their father supervised the preparation of the mansion in Vermont that included the construction of a barbed-wire fence that surrounded the grounds. He told his wife that he had constructed a delightful "asteroid" for his children — and then he accompanied her back to their own "asteroid" in Turtle Bay. The lack of communication between parents and children is apparent, but what is surprising is that the parents themselves find it difficult to communicate with each other because of their strongly desired but unstated wish that their idiots would die. Eliza and Wilbur, on the other hand, possess telepathic communication with each other within a range of ten feet.

When Wilbur and Eliza have revealed their true intelligence, they not only find themselves separated from each other but forced to face almost unbearable loneliness. To survive, each assumes a different personality, one more appropriate for facing a hostile world; and they become Betty and Bobby Brown, their code names for the vacuous selfish children that the world understands and even loves. They become the stereotyped children that appear in first grade readers and that are replete with happy smiles and with eagerness to please their parents. Only when Eliza and Wilbur are united can they once again become themselves, complete and unalone.

When Wilbur lost his sister Eliza, just as Vonnegut lost his sister Alice, both individuals had to look elsewhere to ameliorate their loneliness. Vonnegut has always believed that he is part of a larger family of writers and that his brother, an atmospheric scientist, is part of a family of scientists. It is appropriate, then, that President Wilbur Swain, elected on a platform of "Lonesome no more!", decides to eliminate loneliness for Americans by making them part of larger extended families. Using a computer, Swain gives all Americans new middle names that consist of a noun — the name of a flower, fruit, or vegetable — that is connected by a hyphen to a number between one and twenty. When the Green Death and the Albanian flu destroy the American infrastructure, the country becomes nothing more than a series of large families. When President Swain attends a family meeting of Daffodils in Indianapolis, he suddenly realizes that a major advantage of his system of extended families is that wars have become less vicious; they are more like family affairs that frequently end with the soldiers' embracing one another and deserting the battlefield.

III   Slapstick as a Coda to Vonnegut's Fiction

Thematically and technically, *Slapstick* functions as a coda to Vonnegut's fiction. It is not surprising that this novel is concerned with harmony and loneliness since its inspiration, Alice Vonnegut, gave

Vonnegut's fiction its harmony and direction. The thrust of Vonnegut's fiction has moved from detached, ironic observation to impassioned participation. His early works, *Player Piano* and *The Sirens of Titan*, were concerned with the external environment — the dangers of technology and the glorification of the machine. He also evinced a marked concern with the relationship between destiny and fate, but the detached tone of his novels made it difficult to penetrate the layers of ambivalence. In *Mother Night*, Vonnegut began to concern himself more with the internal state of consciousness and with the problem of schizophrenia, as well as with the epistomological question of what can be perceived as real and what is simply illusory. *Cat's Cradle* and *God Bless You, Mr. Rosewater* express Vonnegut's feelings about institutionalized religion, about the destructive nature of a social system that values money much more highly than love, and about the loneliness of the thousands of unloved that Eliot Rosewater wants to help but cannot without destroying himself. In *Slaughterhouse-Five* and in *Breakfast of Champions*, Vonnegut began to speak much more confidently with his own voice about himself and his views of society; and he culminated *Breakfast of Champions* by cutting his ties to Kilgore Trout, his erstwhile spokesman. Perhaps Vonnegut had outgrown his idealistic and very naïve *alter ego*.

Explicit in both *Breakfast of Champions* and *Slapstick* is Vonnegut's search for a philosophy of life that would explain its cruelties and injustices — for some code that would make life meaningful and understandable. In *Breakfast of Champions*, he wrote of a moment of illumination when suddenly he saw life as harmonious; but, by the time Vonnegut began writing *Slapstick*, his perception of life had changed to that of a slapstick comedy in which he again and again confides that he and his sister never achieved successful harmonious living. With the possible exception of Kilgore Trout, none of Vonnegut's characters are successful; in fact, the effort to create a harmonious world destroys Paul Proteus *(Player Piano)* and Howard W. Campbell, Jr. *(Mother Night);* and the attempt drives Bokonon *(Cat's Cradle)* and Eliot Rosewater *(God Bless You, Mr. Rosewater)* insane.

While Vonnegut's protagonists strive to create an harmonious world filled with love, the price they pay is their loss of any personal happiness and their abrogation of any love relationship with their spouses. A psychiatrist in *God Bless You, Mr. Rosewater* suggests that Eliot Rosewater has channeled his sexual energies into a utopic vision and thus is impotent with his wife. At the beginning of *Slapstick*, Vonnegut likens his attitude toward love to that found in the films of Laurel and Hardy:

> There was very little love in their films. There was often the situational poetry of marriage, which was something else again. It was yet another test — with comical possibilities, provided that everybody submitted to it in good faith.
>
> Love was never at issue. And, perhaps because I was so perpetually intoxicated and instructed by Laurel and Hardy during my childhood in the Great Depression, I find it natural to discuss life without ever mentioning love.
>
> It does not seem important to me.
>
> What does seem important? Bargaining in good fate with destiny (2).

Wilbur Swain, in much the same way as Eliot Rosewater and Paul Proteus, discovers that his wife will leave him unless he abandons his utopic dream; for the choice of Vonnegut's fictional characters is always the greater good for all humanity rather than personal happiness.

Inevitably, despite the best efforts of Vonnegut protagonists who "bargain in good faith with their destinies," the world is destroyed or is so unpleasant that destruction would be a relief. Usually lurking behind the destruction is Vonnegut's favorite target — unbridled technology that is divorced from any concern for Humanistic values. Vonnegut's scientific grotesques read like a lexicon of Halloween horrors: ethical birth-control pills ("Welcome to the Monkey House"), anti-gerasone ("Tomorrow and Tomorrow and Tomorrow"), ice-nine *(Cat's Cradle)*, and fire bombs *(Slaughterhouse-Five)*. In *Slapstick*, the Chinese Communist scientists observe that America and its allies produced their greatest weapon, the atomic bomb, by cooperating with each other. By following this example of cooperation, the Chinese miniaturize themselves and join together psychically to form the most powerful cosmic force in the universe. The result is the destabilization of the Earth's gravity and the destruction of the entire Western world by the Green Death, the ingestion of microscopic Chinese. Vonnegut stresses the innocence of the Chinese who did not specifically try to destroy the world; their effort was simply the natural one of tinkering with forces far too powerful for mankind. To Vonnegut, it is appropriately ironic that America's greatest scientific achievement (the atomic bomb) ultimately leads to its destruction by microscopic Chinese who are almost as small as the atoms American scientists had unleashed.

The strong eschatological thread that runs through all of Vonnegut's fiction seems to be linked closely to his continued preoccupation over the question of man's ability to control his own destiny. Skeptical of institutionalized religion, Vonnegut has long pondered whether life has any intrinsic meaning or is simply haphazard. This question is the more fundamental one behind Vonnegut's consideration of the fire-bombing of Dresden in *Slaughterhouse-Five*, of the lack of American culture in *Breakfast of Champions*, and of the loss of his sister in *Slapstick*. The autobiography he writes in *Slapstick* is simply his acceptance of the impossibility of ever discovering life's inherent meaning and his realization that the key to humanity's survival and happiness is its embracement of life with the good natured earnestness and sincerity of Laurel and Hardy. In cinematic terms such as those Vonnegut uses in *Slapstick*, man is part of a Laurel and Hardy comedy and is not detached enough to see the entire film; he can only play one scene at a time, bargain good naturedly with his destiny, and be aware that he is not good at life and will often fail.

Vonnegut's tone in *Slapstick* lies somewhere between his cosmic detachment in *Cat's Cradle* and his frenzied involvement in *Breakfast of Champions*. His acceptance of the slapstick quality of life permits him to introduce his autobiography in the first chapter of *Slapstick* and then to step aside until the final chapter without the numerous interruptions found in *Breakfast of Champions*. Swain's autobiography remains unfinished just as Vonnegut's own story is still in progress, and *Slapstick's* last line, "Das Ende," reflects the efforts of both Vonnegut and Swain to retain their cultural individuality in a country that obliterates all differences in favor of "Bobby and Betty Brown."

IV   *The Ending of* Slapstick

Kurt Vonnegut's hatred of endings is not simply a technical flaw in his novels; it is a reflection of his belief that art should emulate life and that the artist should not feel compelled to stop his story in order to satisfy a New Critic's conception of what is appropriate. Endings in real life seldom match the precision and neatness of E. M. Forster's *A Passage to India*. In *Slapstick*, Wilbur Swain dies while recounting his trip to see the King of Michigan and his subsequent birthday party. The owner of a thousand candlesticks without a single candle, Swain is delighted when presented with a gift of a thousand candles. Lonely and without his sister, Swain has been as incomplete as his candlesticks without candles; but he dies with a sense of harmony and oneness with all creation.

Just as Vonnegut wrote for an audience of one — his now deceased

sister — no one reads Swain's autobiography after his death. Vonnegut concludes by narrating the heroic adventure of Melody Oriole-
2 von Peterswald, Swain's granddaughter, who escaped slavery and
rowed across the Harlem River to live with him. Vonnegut's "and so
on" is followed by "Das Ende." Swain's life is over, but Melody's
story will continue though the reader will never know if her heroic
efforts have been worthwhile. Vonnegut's "and so on" refocuses attention on the autobiographical elements of *Slapstick* and away from
Melody's story.

When Swain dies, he leaves a poem that Vonnegut presumes
might make a good epitaph for the lonely giant:

> And how did we then face the odds,
> Of Man's rude slapstick, yes, and God's?
> Quite at home and unafraid,
> In a game our dreams remade. (215 - 16).

Slapstick has much of the dream-like quality of *Slaughterhouse-
Five;* and both novels are fantastical responses to bleak situations —
to the destruction of American culture and of Vonnegut's ancestral
home. In fact, the slapstick quality of his own life is at last sufficiently bearable for Vonnegut to reshape it into such a dream-like fantasy.
Because of the gravitational instability in Swain's world, the
characters occasionally walk like Charley Chaplin in one of his films
where the camera has speeded up in order to emphasize the absurdity of Chaplin's situation. In *Slapstick,* Vonnegut has fashioned a
new medium of fantasy juxtaposed with very sincere, confessional
journalism. In this new element, Vonnegut, like Swain, appears to be
"quite at home and unafraid."

CHAPTER 7

The Short Stories

I The Apprenticeship

KURT Vonnegut, Jr., will probably be remembered for his novels and not for his short stories though some are certainly memorable. He published his first collection of short fiction in *Canary in a Cat House* which appeared in 1961. Though the book is now long out of print, Vonnegut incorporated most of the stories in *Welcome to the Monkey House* which appeared in 1968. Vonnegut has confessed that the "short stories in *Welcome to the Monkey House* supported me through the lean years. They are sunny because the magazines (paying up to $3000 a shot) wanted them to be that way. Stories were often rejected with the comment that they were 'too downbeat.' I learned how to be more upbeat. Business is business."[1]

While these stories were written expressly for the popular market, many of them are somewhat superior to the usual stories found during the 1950's in such periodicals as *Saturday Evening Post, Colliers,* and *Ladies' Home Journal.* Vonnegut has pointed out that, when he quit General Electric in 1951, there was a flourishing short-story industry in the United States. He has admitted that from this experience he did "learn how to tell a story, how to make a story work, so that the thing has a certain flow and suspense and so forth. It is mechanical and it's somewhat worth knowing. Because I went through that apprenticeship I did learn how to tell a story."[2] While Vonnegut has denied even contemplating the creation of a fictional Rosewater County with a consistent history and a set of characters much like those of William Faulkner's Yapnapatawpha County, he does use in his short fiction many of the same characters and settings that are found in his novels. Moreover, he focuses in his short stories on many of the same themes that dominate his fiction: the dangers of unchecked technology, the evils of egotism, and the need for love and compassion.

II *Science and Technology*

Vonnegut's scientists frequently discover that they have unwittingly opened a modern version of Pandora's box, and the question becomes whether or not mankind has the emotional, spiritual, and moral strength to match its technological progress. "Thanasphere" (1950) deals with the relationship between science and religion in much the same way as *Cat's Cradle*. In this story American military officials send a secret rocket ship orbiting around the earth; and the stoic pilot aboard is assigned the job of observing weather conditions over enemy territory and the accuracy of guided atomic missiles in the event of war. Doctor Bernard Groszinger, the youthful rocket consultant for the Air Force, cares nothing about the military purpose of the mission. Like Felix Hoenikker *(Cat's Cradle)*, Groszinger cares nothing about politics and muses to himself that the "threat of war was an incident, the military men about him an irritating condition of work — the experiment was the heart of the matter" (19).

The pilot discovers that the dead space, the thanasphere, is not empty but filled with ghosts who keep whispering messages to him that vary from a murder victim's indictment of his own brother to an invitation from his own deceased wife to join her. The pilot crashes the rocket ship into the ocean, and young Groszinger is left to ponder the implications of a world "in constant touch with the spirits, the living inseparable from the dead . . . Would it make life heaven or hell? Every bum and genius, criminal and hero, average man and madman, now and forever part of humanity — advising, squabbling, conniving, placating. . ." (62).

"Report on the Barnhouse Effect" (1950) describes the pressures applied to a scientist who courageously chooses to face real problems rather than to accept the comforting illusions that military men offer him. He dares to question the morality of using an invention with potentially enormous beneficial humanitarian effect as a strictly destructive military weapon. When Professor Barnhouse first discovers the power of dynamopschism, he looks upon it as only a toy, as a way to amuse himself by causing dice to produce the combinations he requests. Gradually the absent-minded psychology professor practices and perfects this power to the point where he can destroy individuals, houses, even mountains. While he would have preferred to use this power to run generators "where there isn't any coal or waterpower" and to irrigate deserts, the United States Army feels that this priceless gift should be used as a weapon since "Eternal vigilance is the price of freedom" (165). Since this time-worn cliché is so much patriotic bilge as far as Vonnegut is concerned, it becomes clear that Barnhouse eventually must oppose the military establishment.

When Barnhouse turns to his graduate research assistant for advice, he repeatedly asks him such questions as "Think we should have dropped the atomic bomb on Hiroshima?" and "Think every new piece of scientific information is a good thing for humanity?" (161). When Paul Proteus is asked in *Player Piano* to tell a lie during his trial so that his lie detector can be calibrated, he replies that "every new piece of scientific knowledge is a good thing for humanity" (297). The turning point for Barnhouse comes when military officials request him to prove how powerful his gift is by destroying a number of missiles and ships during "Operation Barnhouse," for the scientist reacts by declaring that he finds the idea "childish and insanely expensive" (164). While the military officials are exulting over Barnhouse's successful destruction of the weapons, he quietly makes his escape. The scientist, from his secluded sanctuary, spends the next few years destroying all military stockpiles despite the outraged cries of "stouthearted patriots" (168). Vonnegut concludes his story by revealing that the narrator, Barnhouse's former research assistant, is planning to flee and assume his former mentor's antiwar activities so that the elderly scientist's death will not result in the resumption of hostilities.

"Report on the Barnhouse Effect" provides a rather unsatisfactory answer to the question of how man is to control his scientific and technological advances. Barnhouse is a godlike figure who, when asked by the military establishment to do what he feels is morally wrong, personally guarantees the safety of the world by destroying all weapons; suh a re, a scientist who values human life over research in pure science, does not appear either in *Cat's Cradle* or in *Player Piano* to help Paul Proteus or John. If Vonnegut means to imply that the world is in such dire straits that no mere mortal, but only a man with superhuman power like Barnhouse, can solve its problems, then his cosmic view is a pessimistic one indeed. He seems to modify this view, however, in his short story "EPICAC" (1950).

In *Player Piano* EPICAC is the giant computer that helps to govern men in an automated society. Its decisions result in the elimination of Bud Calhoun's job classification and in his subsequent relegation to the rank virtually of a nonperson. EPICAC is the heart of such a society, and perhaps it does represent the progressive decline of man, the epic of man since Christ's crucifixion. It is little wonder in *Player Piano* that when the Shah of Bratpuhr, the religious potentate of millions, visits the computer center, he addresses the machine directly, not bothering to deal with the humans who are obviously merely middle men. In his short story "EPICAC" Vonnegut shifts the emphasis from the omnipotence of EPICAC to the relationship between it and its human operator.

EPICAC was designed to be a "super computing machine that [who] could plot the course of a rocket from anywhere on earth to the second button from the bottom of Joe Stalin's overcoat" (269). For some reason, the computer appears to be sluggish, almost reluctant to do its job. One day, when its operator playfully feeds a simple code that will enable it to converse with him, the result is a dialogue of sorts. The technician describes his girl friend Pat Kilgallen in such attractive terms that the computer quite logically falls in love with her; it writes beautiful love poems for the girl; and the human shamelessly pirates these as his own. When the machine questions the justice of its operator's contention that "Machines are built to serve men" (272), the technician replies that men are superior since they are composed of protoplasm which is indestructible. He also points out that "Women can't love machines" because of fate which is "Predetermined and inevitable destiny." EPICAC responds by destroying itself, and it leaves a final suicide note saying that it does not "want to be a machine and think about war"; it wants to "be made out of protoplasm and last forever" so Pat can love it. The human victor in this struggle between man and machine declares that "Epicac loved and lost, but he bore me no grudge. I shall always remember him as a sportsman and a gentleman. Before he departed this vale of tears, he did all he could to make our marriage a happy one. Epicac gave me anniversary poems for Pat — enough for 500 years" (275).

"EPICAC" is the only Vonnegut tale in which a man manages successfully to outwit a machine, and even here a certain amount of ambivalence is evident. The computer professes the very values that Vonnegut himself seems to hold sacred — a dislike for war and a strong feeling for the importance of love. The human technician manages to outwit EPICAC by deceit, something it obviously was not programmed to handle. The computer operator manages to redeem himself in his readers' estimation by candidly confessing to

EPICAC and by admitting that he is ashamed of his actions. The story contains an additional twist that distinguishes it from Vonnegut's other tales; for instead of illustrating the dehumanizing effect that machines have on man, "EPICAC" illustrates the humanizing effect man can have on machines.

Unlike the bemused tone of EPICAC's operator, both "Welcome to the Monkey House" (1968), the title story of Vonnegut's collection of short stories, and "Tomorrow and Tomorrow and Tomorrow" (1954), its concluding selection, demonstrate on a more somber note how the irresponsibility of the scientific community and the American government, combined with a lack of respect for man's individuality and personal dignity, can create an intolerable situation. In "Welcome to the Monkey House," Vonnegut describes a future America in which a scientist has invented an ethical birth-control pill that removes all pleasure from the sexual act, and in which the government requires all men and women to take them. The narrator points out that

The pills are ethical because they didn't interfere with a person's ability to reproduce, which would have been unnatural and immoral. All the pills did was take every bit of pleasure out of sex.

Thus did science and morals go hand in hand (28).

The hero who works to alter this situation is not a Barnhouse with superhuman power, but a very short, funny looking man named Billy the Poet. He spends his time seducing Suicide Parlor Hostesses at gun point and then forcing them to abandon their ethical birth-control pills. The young poet also repudiates the scientist who invented the pills and rebels against a government that forces its citizens to use them.

Billy describes how after a scientist had brought his family to a zoo and had been shocked because a monkey was playing with his private parts, he had gone home and invented an ethical birth-control pill that would make monkeys insensible below their waists. Vonnegut describes the results of this scientist's actions quite succinctly: "When he got through with the monkey house, you couldn't tell it from the Michigan Supreme Court. Meanwhile there was this crisis going on in the United Nations. The people who understood science said people had to quit reproducing so much, and the people who understood morals said society would collapse if people used sex for nothing but pleasure" (32). Billy's avowed purpose is to "restore a certain amount of innocent pleasure to the world which is poorer in pleasure than it needs to be" (45). He appears to find absolutely no pleasure in his role as a human rape machine, but he is driven by his altruistic desire to bring sexual pleasure back to the American people.

While this story is not so pessimistic as many of Vonnegut's novels, it certainly is not optimistic and it has an ambivalent note. The government obviously felt that something had to be done to prevent Americans from overpopulating themselves out of existence, especially since it is quite clear that citizens have a strong desire to live. Yet, does this fact make the government and the scientific community villains for marketing ethical birth-control pills and for requiring citizens to take them — and does it make Billy the Poet a hero for rebelling against such an edict and for trying to spread his philosophy of pleasure through sexual intercourse? Since the story was written for *Playboy,* it is easy to assume that the sympathy of the reader will probably be with Billy the Poet rather than with J. Edgar Nation, the scientist who invented the pill, or with the government that required it.

Vonnegut's tone is ambivalent, however, particularly in the story's final lines. After Billy rapes Nancy and removes her ethical birth-control pills, he leaves her with a poem and with a bottle of birth-control pills that has a label on it. The poem, Elizabeth Barrett Browning's "How Do I Love Thee? Let Me Count the Ways," is ironic since Billy has shown no love for Nancy, only a certain degree of missionary zeal to convert her to a "nothinghead." Yet, the now trite lines are also appropriate because Nancy's feelings about sex were shared by many Victorian ladies and because her numbness below her hips is much like that experienced by Elizabeth Barrett Browning after she fell from her horse. Many scholars now believe her injuries were psychosomatic, the result of her domineering father; for, during her honeymoon, her injury miraculously healed. The label on Nancy's birth-control pills reads "Welcome to the Monkey House." Billy the Poet points out that the legislation for ethical birth-control pills was forced upon the people by misguided moralists who did not realize that the world can afford sex, but that what "it can't afford anymore is reproduction" (44). His birth-control pills provide a possible answer to this problem: Nancy can now be herself, another monkey in the human zoo that Vonnegut both satirizes and loves.

In "Tomorrow and Tomorrow and Tomorrow" (1954), Vonnegut

once again deals with the major themes of "Welcome to the Monkey House" — the problem of overpopulation and the irresponsibility of the scientific community which constantly produces new inventions but which fails to deal with the moral problems that each new product brings. These sentiments are well expressed by a college president who is quoted by a newscaster as saying that "most of the world's ills can be traced to the fact that Man's knowledge of himself has not kept pace with his knowledge of the physical world" (290). In the story, the example of such views is the Schwartz clan, all eleven couples, which lives in a four-room apartment in New York in 2158 A.D. Medical science has invented anti-gerasone which prevents humans from aging; unfortunately, it has ignored the question of how the ever-increasing population could live together in cramped conditions without any privacy.

Perhaps the resulting loss of human dignity is best illustrated in the indignant complaint of the newest member of the Schwartz clan, a great grand-nephew Mortimer, and his new wife who have arrived for a honeymoon. Mortimer advises anybody who thinks he has it rough to "try honeymooning in the hall for a real kick" (296). The conclusion of the story finds Vonnegut again refusing to provide a workable solution to the problems he recognizes. Grandfather Schwartz gains suitable revenge on his clan for what he feels is an attempt to dilute his anti-gerasone by disappearing after leaving a will which requests that his apartment and fortune be divided equally among all his family. As a result of the subsequent riot among the Schwartzes, the police arrest all of them and place them in jail cells. The tale ends with the contentment of Lou and Emerald Schwartz who are amazed about how wonderful it is to have a jail cell of their own. A turnkey admonishes them to "pipe down . . . or I'll toss the whole kit and caboodle of you right out. And first one who lets on to anybody outside how good jail is ain't never getting back in!" (296).

Since obviously all humans cannot crowd themselves into their nations' prisons, the Schwartzes' solution is amusing but impractical. The story concludes with a television advertisement for the new super anti-gerasone which will make all senior citizens look years younger. Gramps Schwartz writes his name on a postcard; sends for a free sample; and, looking like a man in his early thirties, apparently no longer has any reason to contemplate suicide. Vonnegut is astute enough to realize, however, that the desire for longevity is a very human wish; it is not merely a goal of the scientific community. What science has achieved in "Tomorrow and Tomorrow and

Tomorrow" is, therefore, the fulfillment of one of man's most basic desires, his will to live.

Ironically, the price man must pay for longevity is the loss of his dignity and his privacy, without which long life becomes a mere prison sentence rather than a blessing. Perhaps this price is too high to pay, as Vonnegut implies by the bleak despair associated with Macbeth's "Tomorrow and Tomorrow and Tomorrow" speech. The Schwartz clan feels as trapped and as resigned to its collective fate as Shakespeare's tragic hero. Just as Macbeth must shoulder responsibility for his actions, so too must the members of the Schwartz clan because they cannot blame science for their plight since scientific institutions are man-made and are mere reflections of man's ever-increasing knowledge and curiosity. This Faust-like quality of mankind is what Vonnegut blames for the creation of Ilium, New York; ice-nine; ethical birth-control pills; and anti-gerasone. Perhaps because of his anthropological training, Vonnegut appears to believe that man may be fatally flawed, an idea developed more fully in such popular anthropological studies as Arthur Koestler's *The Ghost in the Machine* and Robin Fox and Lionel Tiger's *The Imperial Animal*. If Frank Hoenikker in *Cat's Cradle* learns anything at all from the ants that survived ice-nine, it is that, although man might survive even that holocaust by clinging at all costs to the will to live, he will eventually reach a state of development where he will once again attempt annihilation of the entire human race.

The answer to man's dilemma, however, is not to seek a separate peace. There is no place for Paul Proteus (*Player Piano*) or John (*Cat's Cradle*) to flee. On the other hand, it is impractical for man to await the arrival of a superman figure such as Professor Barnhouse to save him. What man can do, Vonnegut suggests in his fiction, is to realize his own limitations. He should consciously shun anything, no matter how appealing, if it will dehumanize him. Scientists as men, rather than machines, should be morally responsible for their inventions. Any invention that would treat men as mere numbers, rather than as individuals, or that would at all limit their personal dignity and privacy should be discarded since the human animal's proclivity for destruction is enhanced when he is able to think of his carnage in terms of abstract casualty lists rather than in terms of flesh and blood people he has destroyed. The alternative to such measures is either total annihilation or the world of "Tomorrow and Tomorrow and Tomorrow" in which life becomes "a tale/told by an idiot, full of sound and fury,/ signifying nothing."

III *The George M. Helmholz Stories*

Several Vonnegut stories written for *Saturday Evening Post* feature George M. Helmholtz, the fat, jovial head of the music department and the director of the Lincoln High School Band. Good-hearted, sincere, and completely devoted to his band, Helmholtz dreams of winning first place every year in the state's high-school-band competition. His obsessive devotion to this dream makes him a comical yet strangely moving character. Helmholtz has much in common with the traditional Jewish *Das Kleine Menschele* figure, the little man of Eastern European Jewish folklore who is physically helpless to control his own destiny and who constantly lives in fear of the outside world entering his *shtetl* community. The band director lives in his own private world of music, and he dreads the frequent invasions by the Principal who is constantly shaken by Helmholtz's budget requests. In virtually every Helmholtz story Vonnegut focuses on the relationship between the harassed band director and a very unhappy boy with whom he frequently tries to share his dream about music in order to open a new world for him.

"The No Talent Kid" (1952) is the story of Helmholtz's confrontation with Plummer, a boy who has no musical talent but who has an all-consuming desire to make the "A" band. Each challenge day Plummer challenges the first clarinetist in the elite "A" band even though he barely holds down the last chair in the remedial "C" band. He is convinced that he loses each week only because Helmholtz is prejudiced. Meanwhile, Helmholtz has serious problems of his own. His band was defeated the previous spring because the enemy band had a seven-foot drum, and he longs for a bigger drum. Plummer buys the biggest drum in town, demands to be made the first drummer in the "A" band, and then wounds Helmholtz by informing him that he will give the drum to his mother to use as a coffee table. The compromise Vonnegut conceives to obtain the instrument is a typical *Saturday Evening Post* formula ending: Plummer agrees to provide his drum and to contribute to the band by carrying the drum during parades. Thus the boy becomes part of the band he loves, and the music teacher gets the drum he needs without having to compromise his ideals.

"The Ambitious Sophomore" (1954) is the story of Helmholtz's efforts to understand why his brilliant piccoloist LeRoi Duggan suddenly forgets how to march and stumbles whenever people watch. Helmholtz buys a special and incredibly ornate uniform that is specially padded to make LeRoi look like a professional football player. The uniform gives LeRoi confidence in himself; and, when a rival suitor rips the uniform to shreds, he floors the bully and then performs a magnificent piccolo solo that wins the band first place in the competition. Helmholtz sells his spare tire to help pay for the uniform and then has to take a streetcar home when he has a flat tire, but these seem minor inconveniences compared to the trophy awarded his band for first place.

"The Boy Who Hated Girls" (1956) reveals Helmholtz's naïveté. He is so devoted to his boys and to his band that he does not realize that the fatherless boy Bert feels rejected when Helmholtz sends him to a different music teacher for final polishing. Bert has limited musical ability but apparently practices constantly to please Helmholtz. Bert does not really hate girls, but he does ignore them. The story ends with Bert's returning a beautiful coed's interest in him. A school nurse scolds Helmholtz for playing with human life and then ignoring the results. Unlike Vonnegut's cold father figures who tend to ignore their sons because of their own egotism, Helmholtz is so shocked by the nurse's revelation that he presumably reforms and assumes his responsibility.

In "The Kid Nobody Could Handle" (1955), the most revealing of the George Helmholtz stories, Helmholtz echoes some of the despair that years later permeates *Breakfast of Champions*. The music teacher is appalled to discover that Jim Donnini, a juvenile delinquent from the streets of Chicago, has been vandalizing Lincoln High School. Filled with compassion and desperation, Helmholtz offers him his most precious possession, John Philip Sousa's trumpet. When the boy initially shows no interest, Helmholtz hammers the instrument against a coat tree and mutters that "Life is no damn good" (255); and only then does Donnini show any interest in Helmholtz. With the start of the new school semester, Jim Donnini takes his seat in the last seat of the worst trumpet section of the "C" band. As Helmholtz tells him and the rest of the band, "Our aim is to make the world more beautiful than it was when we came into it. . . . Love yourself . . . and make your instrument sing about it" (255). Without a sense of self-worth, Vonnegut thinks it is impossible for anyone to achieve anything.

IV *Fathers and Sons*

One of Vonnegut's major subjects has always been the relationship between fathers and sons, and his fathers are often driven men who either are indifferent to their sons or seek actively to transform their children into carbon copies of themselves. "This Son of Mine" (1956) is a very early short story that deals with the conflict between a father's expectations for his son and his child's responsibilities both to his father and to himself. Merle Waggoner, a fifty-one-year-old widower, owns a centrifugal pump factory and longs for his son Franklin to inherit the business. When he observes the relationship between his lathe operator Rudy Linbert and his son Karl, he wonders why Franklin could even think of becoming an actor instead of following in his footsteps.

Franklin sees that his career decision has wounded his father deeply, and he does not feel like attending a country club dance where he would see his friends who also had rejected their fathers' business and thus become "the killers of their fathers' dreams" (76). The Waggoners and Linberts take a short hunting trip together, and Franklin is shocked when Karl tells him "get out from under your old man . . . that's the thing to do" (78). He then goes on to point out "Your father doesn't just have you. He's got his big success . . . All my old man's got is me" (78). Listening to Rudy and Karl play a duet, the two Waggoner men feel very close; and Franklin listens to the music and realizes that

It was speaking of all fathers and sons. It was saying hauntingly what they had all been saying haltingly, what they had all been saying, sometimes with pain and sometimes with love — that fathers and sons were one.
It was saying too, that a time for a parting in spirit was near — no matter how close anyone held anyone, no matter what anyone tried (78).

Rarely has Vonnegut come closer to articulating the complex relationship he sees between fathers and sons — the bond between Paul Proteus and his father *(Player Piano)* and between Eliot Rosewater and Senator Rosewater *(God Bless You, Mr. Rosewater)*. The son must rebel against his father despite his subsequent guilt feelings because, if he does not, he will not be an individual but only a carbon copy of his parent.

In "The Foster Portfolio" (1951), another Vonnegut story about the relationship between fathers and sons, Herbert Foster works as a bookkeeper to support his wife and child by moonlighting. He has inherited almost a million-dollar stock portfolio, but he feels the money is tainted because it came from his father, a man who abandoned wife and child to devote his life to playing music in dives and to drinking gin. Three nights a week Herbert goes to a cheap bar for, as Vonnegut points out, Herbert "had the respectability his mother had hammered into him. But just as priceless as that was an income not quite big enough to go around. It left him no alternative but — in the holy names of wife, child, and home — to play piano in a dive, and breathe smoke, and drink gin, to be Firehouse Harris, his father's son, three nights out of seven" (66). Foster's split personality links him to many Vonnegut protagonists including Paul Proteus, Eliot Rosewater, and Billy Pilgrim; for all find it necessary to create roles that help them to cope with what appears to be unbearable problems.

V   *Roles People Play*

Vonnegut's stories often focus on characters' attempts to play roles that appear to be more exciting than their real lives, but these roles are frequently linked to unrealistic dreams that tend to stultify the dreamers. "Custom-Made Bride" (1954) is the story of Otto Krummbein, an eccentric inventor who tries to redesign everything and everyone to fit his specifications. The story is narrated by an investment counselor who tries to straighten out Krummbein's tangled finances; for, brilliant as an inventor but incredibly naïve as a businessman, Krummbein has never paid income tax because he has never received a bill. He introduces his wife Falloleen whose hair is bleached silver with a touch of blue and who wears zebra-striped leotards and one large earring. Falloleen is really Otto's former secretary, Kitty Calhoun, who has allowed her husband to redesign her. Otto confesses though that, when Falloleen is not striking a pose or making a dramatic entrance or exit, she is a "crashing bore." The story concludes with her reassumption of her original identity. This conclusion is consistent with other Vonnegut stories and novels since his personal version of Nathaniel Hawthorne's "unpardonable sin" is the distortion or elimination of an individual's personality.

In "The Powder Blue Dragon" (1954) Vonnegut describes the plight of Higgins, a twenty-one-year-old boy who has worked at three jobs for four years in order to save the $5651 necessary to buy a Marittima Frascati. A native living in a seacoast resort city, he resents the way tourists seem to lord it over him. When he takes his new car for a trial run, he sees a beautiful girl driving a Cadillac. He follows her into the cocktail lobby of a resort hotel where he feels "he'd been dumped in a strange, hostile world" (50). Lacking the sophistication or money of the girl's fiancé, he races him even though his car has not been properly broken in. The car's engine burns out, and young Higgins sobs "I'm glad it's dead . . . I'm glad I killed it" (53). Like the poor creature in the song "Puff the Magic Dragon," Higgins' powder-blue dragon cannot survive in the adult world. The lesson he learns is a common Vonnegut bromide, for a kindly old druggist tells the boy that expensive cars are part of a "phony world, a toy world, full of useless trinkets. . ." (47). In Vonnegut's fictive universe, anyone who places a higher value on things than on people inevitably suffers.

In "More Stately Mansions" (1951), which is built around much the same theme as "The Powder Blue Dragon," the dream is always more precious and satisfying than the reality. A couple moves into a suburban home and discovers that their neighbor Grace has an obsessive interest in home decoration. She collects dozens of home magazines and files the best ideas for the dream home she will have when she has enough money to redecorate her home. When she is stricken with virus and hospitalized, her husband inherits enough money to redecorate secretly according to her plans. He surprises her with the newly decorated home, but he destroys in the process the hobby that has given her so much pleasure for years. When he points out that a new *House Beautiful* has just arrived, Grace's response is "Read one and you've read them all" (132).

In "Bagombo Snuff Box" (1954) Eddie Laird, a traveling salesman, decides to visit his ex-wife whom he has not seen in eleven years. Like so many Vonnegut characters, he feels compelled to play a role, that of the adventurous man of the world; and he gives a Bagombo snuff box to Amy and her husband that he says he purchased in Ceylon. As he describes his adventures in France, Ceylon, and the Klondike, his former wife and her department-store-manager husband begin to wince at the lack of adventure in their own lives. However, their nine-year-old-boy Stevie punctures Eddie's facade by revealing that the snuff box was actually made in Japan and that Eddie does not even know where Ceylon is. The story ends with Amy's family united in its common amusement while it watches Eddie flee; later, he calls his second wife long distance and discusses his son's reading problem and his daughter's need for braces. His adventurous tales are mere fantasies and are as unrealistic as Higgins' dream of owning a Marittima Frascati.

"Who Am I This Time?" (originally published in 1961 as "My Name is Everyone") is another example of Vonnegut's concern with role playing. The shy clerk Harry is only alive when he becomes the character he plays for the local drama group in North Crawford. When the director decides to do Tennessee Williams' A Streetcar Named Desire for the spring play, Harry is chosen to play the role Marlon Brando made famous. He becomes Marlon Brando, and a young girl named Helene who plays Stella falls in love with him. Because Harry was left at the doorstep of a church and never knew his real parents, he has no concept of self; and Helene has moved around so much as a child that she never has been able to develop a personality of her own. As a result, both are chameleons who yearn to blend into any environment so that they can feel that they have identity. They marry and make their marriage work by playing different roles each week that range from those of Romeo and Juliet to those of Othello and Desdemona.

When writing for magazines with essentially middle-class audiences, Vonnegut often twists the role-playing theme to imply that his readers should be content with their lives since the very wealthy are really unhappy role players who long for a middle-class life style. "A Night for Love" (1957), which first appeared in Saturday Evening Post, is a good example of just such a Vonnegut formula story. Turley Whitman and his wife lie in bed awaiting their daughter's return from a date with the son of the wealthy L. C. Reinbeck. Turley had once dreamed of being wealthy, but he is now merely working as a policeman in Reinbeck's factory. Because Turley's wife was once the town beauty who had dated Reinbeck, Turley has never really forgiven his wife for those dates because he is convinced that she constantly compares the two men and regrets her decision to marry him.

The tension between the Whitmans is matched by the Reinbecks; for, when Turley calls them to complain that his daughter is still not home, he mentions that surely Reinbeck must remember his wife. Both couples anguish over what might have been, both decide that their marriages have been the result of a lover's moon in the sky, and both learn that their children have just been married. Vonnegut concludes by pointing out that now there is a new household: "Whether everything was all right here, remained to be seen. The moon went down" (84). The story is competently plotted but shallow. Reinbeck and his wife are conventionally rich; the Whitmans are conventionally middle class. Whitman is poor but capable of love; Reinbeck is shown to be married to his factory. As is made clear, in Vonnegut's personal hierarchy, love is valued far more than money or personal possessions as long as it is real love and not mere infatuation.

In "Runaways" (1961), a variation on "A Night For Love," the daughter of the governor of Indiana flees with the son of a clerk. When the two families express common grief and outrage, both are convinced that mere children cannot really know what true love is. After the teenagers are captured, returned to their parents, and flee again, the parents decide this time that the two youngsters should be allowed to be married. Both now agree that they are too young — not too young to love, but too young "for about everything else there is that goes with love" (56). Significantly, the boy and girl are merely role playing; they never really talk to each other; instead, they mouth platitudes they have heard expressed in the popular music of the time. If the two had really listened to each other's conversation, Vonnegut concludes that they would have bored each other. Years later, in *Breakfast of Champions*, Vonnegut once again expresses his feelings about an American culture composed almost entirely of commercials, sports, and popular music.

Perhaps Vonnegut's lightest treatment of role playing is "Any Reasonable Offer" (1952) in which a real-estate salesman learns that a Colonel and Mrs. Peckham wish to see an estate. After they have stayed for cocktails and have swum and walked in the gardens, the salesman eventually learns that the Colonel is really a draftsman who manages to enjoy free vacations each year by pretending he is interested in expensive homes and by enjoying the hospitality offered him by the anxious-to-sell owners. The salesman concludes that maybe such role playing is not a bad idea for other middle-class Americans — considering the price of vacations.

VI *The Political Fables*

Many Vonnegut stories are political fables that satirize the American political system and this country's relationship with both China and the Soviet Union. "Harrison Bergeron" (1961) is a fable about what ultimately could happen in America if all people are forced to be equal. A Handicapper General, the same Diane Moon Glompers who appears in *God Bless You, Mr. Rosewater*, places weights on strong people and hideous masks on beautiful girls to insure that everyone is equally mediocre. When seven-foot Harrison Bergeron strips himself of his handicaps and dances with a beautiful ballerina over national television, he shows Americans how beautiful life could be with individual differences. Since such flagrant abuse of the law cannot be tolerated, Miss Glompers kills the two dancers. In any leveling process, what really is lost, according to Vonnegut, is beauty, grace, and wisdom.

"All the King's Horses" (1951) is a product of the Cold War of the early 1950's when Americans were becoming more and more suspicious of the Soviet Union and China, and the story describes the battle between Colonel Kelley and Pi Ying, a Chinese guerilla leader. Ying brings Kelley, his wife, his sons, and twelve American soldiers to a hideout where he offers the Colonel one chance to save their lives: he must use the Americans as chess pieces in a game against Pi Ying while the Russian advisor observes. If Kelley wins, the Americans will go free. Ying is described as inscrutable and evil, and his Russian advisor Barzov is presented as a military man eager for a confrontation between Russia and the United States as soon as the time is ripe. After Ying is assassinated by his mistress, Kelley wins; and the Russian is outraged. He lets the Americans go, but he indicates that he will look forward to the war that ultimately will come. While the story now seems very dated, it does reflect accurately American sentiment during the early Cold War period.

"Unready to Wear" (1953) is a Vonnegut story that suggests a way of eliminating wars between nations. A scientist with an ugly, highly ineffective body discovers how to leave his body and become "amphibious." He soon is joined by thousands of people, and one of them is a pay-toilet businessman who describes how enjoyable it is to be free of material goods. Amphibians choose among several bodies whenever they wish to march in parades or read books. The real reason nations fight each other, suggests the businessman, is a Darwinian drive toward self-preservation. With no bodies to preserve, the amphibians represent the ultimate in counterculture values since they have no desire for commercial products.

VII   *The Man Behind the Stories*

Because Vonnegut's short stories were written to meet the formulaic requirements of mass-circulation magazines, they tend to be rather conventional both technically and thematically. They do reveal, however, a good deal of information about Vonnegut himself, particularly that he is the product of an Indianapolis middle-class family. Since most of these short stories were written in the interval between *Player Piano* and *The Sirens of Titan*, they reflect the preoccupation of both Vonnegut and Middle America with the Cold War, love, status, and identity. In many ways they reflect a childhood during which Vonnegut was nurtured on an anthology of sentimental poetry "about love which would not die, about faithful dogs and humble cottages where happiness was, about people growing old, about visits to cemeteries, about babies who died."[3] Vonnegut, remembering this anthology, confesses he wished he had a copy now since "it has so much to do with what I am."[4]

In his novels Vonnegut continues to treat the same themes found in his short fiction. Years later he utilizes the lessons he learned while writing for the readers of *Colliers, Saturday Evening Post,* and *Ladies' Home Journal* when he begins to write plays.

CHAPTER 8

The Plays

I   *Harold Ryan: The Hero in an Unheroic Age*

*H*APPY *Birthday, Wanda June* (1970) is a revision of a play
Vonnegut had written fifteen years earlier — after he had
attended a Great Books course with his wife and had become interested in Odysseus. Vonnegut confesses that "Odysseus the hero
coming home from the wars really got to me. The hero-warrior. He
seemed so preposterous in modern terms. Hemingway was alive then
and he was going around shooting lions and tigers between the eyes
and stuffing them and then encouraging other people to do the
same. I didn't like that. So I sat down and wrote a play partly out of
exasperation, partly because I wanted to try my hand at a new form.
I called the play Penelope."[1]

The revised play opened off Broadway on October 7, 1970, at the
Theatre de Lys; it had a successful run of 142 performances; the
movie version was released a year later by Columbia Pictures starring
Rod Steiger and Susannah York. Vonnegut calls it "one of the most
embarrassing movies ever made," and he feels quite happy that "it
sank like a rock."[2] He builds his play around the Hemingway-like
Harold Ryan, a modern-day Odysseus who returns home after eight
years in the South American jungle to discover that there is no longer
a place for him. He finds that his wife Penelope's two suitors are the
leader of the peace movement Dr. Norbert Woodly and the vacuum-
cleaner salesman Herb Shuttle. Moreover, his son Paul disappoints
Harold because he scorns contact sports that could injure him.

The blue soup that Harold and his companion Looseleaf Harper
were forced to drink during the time they were captives of the Lupi-
Loopo Indians had much the same effect as lotus on Odysseus' companions; it made them feel happy and slothful and filled them with
love for all living things. Despite the blue soup, Harold hated the

peaceful Indians; he butchered them before he left the jungle. Still disliking peace, he wants to fight Dr. Norbert Woodly with his bare hands or with any weapon of the doctor's choice, but Woodly prefers to flee to East St. Louis with his crippled mother. An exasperated Harold tells Penelope that "there are great issues to be fought out here — or to be argued at least" (176), and she tells him that the "old heroes are going to have to get used to this . . . the new heroes who refuse to fight. They're trying to save the planet, there's no time for battle, no point to battle anymore" (176). Because of such a change in heroes, Paul's English teacher described Harold as a legendary hero out of the Golden Age of Heroes. Ironically, Harold returns from the jungle virtually unscathed; but the teacher is murdered in broad daylight in the city's park while returning from a meeting of the African Violet Society. Crime in the streets and pollution are problems that Harold cannot solve with a gun or with his fists, and no one is more aware of her husband's inadequacy than Penelope.

One of the major themes in *Happy Birthday, Wanda June* is Vonnegut's criticism of the traditional Western conception of heroism and the concomitant stereotyped male and female roles. Traditionally, men must never weep or show emotion; and women must not only remain at home but be domesticated and uneducated. In an earlier version of the play, Penelope becomes Eve; seduces Adam; and provokes God into banishing them from the Garden of Eden. God tells Eve that, because of her sin, he "will greatly multiply thy sorrow and thy conception; in sorrow thou shalt bring forth children; and thy desire shall be to thy husband, and he shall rule over thee" (Act I, Sc. x).[3] Vonnegut suggests that the Fall has traditionally been used as evidence that women are innately inferior, and Harold tells Penelope that he expects her to be "the nigger" no matter how she feels because that is her appropriate role. He tells his son Paul that women are incomplete without men; they are only half a personality and half a soul. While women "are chemical experiments with mad scientists in charge, . . . men are men. . . . They're the ones who give society stability and common sense" (Act I, Sc. ix).

Vonnegut appears to feel that it is women who provide the stability and common sense. Penelope learns from Woodly that heroes like Harold really do not like home and "make awful messes while they're there" (131). They like war because it permits them to capture enemy women and "not have to make love to them slowly and gently" (131). Woodly is a healer who preaches gentleness and love, and he stands in obvious contrast to Harold Ryan, the killer who preaches violence and rape. But even Woodly cannot escape entirely from the traditional responsibility of the Western hero; and, when he returns to confront Harold, the gentle Penelope is horrified. Woodly tells her that he has returned because of honor — the same honor that for the past two years has compelled him to walk through the park each night at midnight to prove his masculinity. Penelope tells him she hates him for acting like a federal marshal in a Western — "high noon in the Superbowl" (185).

Vonnegut confesses in his introduction to the play that he did not have the courage to make even Harold Ryan a villain; and, by the same measure, Woodly is not a hero. His return invalidates all the pacifistic philosophy he has professed to Penelope. He returns to destroy Ryan by revealing that the modern-day Ulysses is nothing more than pathetically comic; he manfully tells Ryan that he will not beg for mercy; yet, while seemingly eager to live by Ryan's rule, the Hemingway code of "Grace under pressure," he is sickened when he realizes that Ryan is going to kill him. As a result, Woodly asks if he can beg for mercy on his knees, pleads for his life, and even thanks Ryan when the disgusted big game hunter fails to pull his trigger. Woodly's actions are inconsistent with his speeches, and they reveal his weakness. Shortly afterward, Vonnegut also deflates any trace of Ryan's heroism by having him go into another room to shoot himself in much the same way that Hemingway's death occurred. Unlike Hemingway, though, Ryan misses at point-blank range.

II *Penelope and Vonnegut's Revisions*

The very fact that Vonnegut originally entitled his play *Penelope* and not *Ulysses* is one more indication that his heroine serves as his spokeswoman and represents values Vonnegut himself holds sacred. She prefers the peacemaker to the warrior, and she tells Harold at one point that she needs gentleness from a man and not bravado. Unfortunately, she is a more fully developed character in earlier versions of the play than in the final script. Among her many speeches that Vonnegut deleted is her conversation with Paul early in the first act which contains the following lines:

PENELOPE
Then imagine what it's like to be a woman. It's time. If you can't imagine that, then think of loneliness — about a lonely human being, an isolated, friendly human being . . . For eight years I've been faithful to a man who was not here. That's not a world record, I know — but it feels like one.

Another Penelope, the wife of the wandering Odysseus, was faithful to a void for twenty years. She knitted. I took correspondence courses, which earned me my high school diploma. I went on from that to a bachelor's and a master's degree. I've knitted myself a mind of sorts. When your father disappeared

(pointing to her head)

there was nothing up there. I was little more than a child myself — your dopey older sister — Harold would not know me now. I could continue to pursue my education, as they say — but, when your father was declared legally dead, my mind and body sang in two-part harmony that I cannot be cured by a Ph.D.

(an afterthought)

— unless the Ph.D. happens to be a man. Have I made myself clear? (Act I. Sc. i).

She confesses to Paul that, while the mind she "knitted" rejects men like Harold, her body demands that she find a man. When Paul scornfully asks how she could date a homosexual dandy like Doctor Woodly, the amused Penelope replies that her son's dismissal of Woodly as "a fairy" is an interesting piece of information. At this point Vonnegut reveals parenthetically that Penelope certainly can verify Woodly's virility. In a scene deleted from later versions of the play, Penelope telephones Woodly to express her anxiety over his safety and to tell him that Harold has destroyed the doctor's prized violin, his most precious possession. This scene helped to develop the relationship between Penelope and her lover, and its deletion makes both characters less real.

In earlier versions of the play, Penelope served even more as a spokeswoman for Vonnegut's view about heroism and about the dangers inherent in Harold's view of glory and death. At one point she tells Paul that she no longer wants the kind of man Harold was: "I would have to hang around a Marine barracks or a gymnasium to find one. I could go to a bowling alley, I suppose, and sip Budweiser until your idea of a real man came along. . . . I don't want a man like your father anymore" (Act I, Sc. ii). Thus Harold is shown to be crude, insensitive, and concerned only with the physical and not with the spiritual side of life.

Later, when Harold asks how she could love a coward like Norbert Woodly, she extols pacifism because "It's a dreadfully dangerous country still. It kills and kills every day — from the sky mostly. It counts bodies, publishes the body count, a number thought to be pleasing to all lovers of freedom around the world. And all of our treasures going into reliable old killing machines and fantastic dreams of better ways to kill and kill — from the sky mostly. Oh God — if only this country would drink the blue soup!" (Act II, Sc. vii). The bitter tone of Penelope's speech is lost in the final version of the play where she becomes less shrewish and more resigned. In earlier versions she refers to her husband as a hairy tumor; but, in the final revision, she is more refined and more helpless — less an individual and more a subordinate character to her husband. Perhaps this explains why most reviewers ignored the role of Penelope and concentrated on the heroism that Harold Ryan represents.

III   The Minor Characters

The minor characters in *Happy Birthday, Wanda June* are closely linked thematically to the struggle between Harold and Woodly. Looseleaf Harper, Ryan's pilot and constant companion, was a test pilot who later flew the bomber that dropped an atomic bomb over Japan. Good natured and childlike, his answer to most questions is "I dunno." When he returns with Harold, he is overwhelmed by the short skirts and by the new sexual freedom that he observes in magazines and in conversation. When he tells Harold that something mighty important must have happened while they were gone, he is correct: the American hero has become less like John Wayne's Green Beret and more like Joseph Heller's Yossarian in *Catch 22*.

Looseleaf breaks with Ryan when he confesses that the bravest thing he could have done was to have refused to drop the bomb when ordered to do so: ". . . wars would be a lot better, I think, if guys would say to themselves sometimes, 'Jesus — I'm not going to do that to the enemy. That's *too* much.' . . . I could have been the father of all those people in Nagasaki, and the mother too, just by not dropping the bomb" (162). Looseleaf wheels around and leaves while Harold ignores him, but Penelope kisses him, evidence that he has joined Woodly's camp. Looseleaf's actions are consistent with Vonnegut's concept of what heroism should be, for he has remarked that his play's original "germ" was "about our need for heroes and our fear of death. . . . But now it's also about a new kind of American hero — the hero who refuses to kill."[4]

When Herb Shuttle expresses admiration for Looseleaf's heroic actions as a test pilot, the new hero places his job in proper perspective: "You put her into a dive, and everything starts screaming and shaking, and maybe some pipe breaks and squirts oil or gasoline or hydraulic fluid in your face. You wonder how the hell you ever got in such a mess, and then you pull back on the controls, and you blank out for a couple of seconds. When you come to, everything is usually okay — except maybe you threw up all over yourself" (151 - 52). Vonnegut's new hero does not kill, and he does not like to risk life or limb in the pursuit of something as illusory as honor or glory.

Looseleaf is counterpointed by Penelope's unsuccessful suitor, Herb Shuttle, who likens winning Penelope to making a sale and who resembles at times a much younger version of Arthur Miller's Willy Loman. Shuttle's values are portrayed as completely material, and it comes as no surprise that Harold Ryan has always been his idol. Throughout the play he functions as a surrogate Harold Ryan; but he is obviously greatly diminished in scope and in grandeur. When he takes Penelope to a boxing match, one of Hemingway's favorite forms of entertainment, she wears the jaguar coat which she used to wear when Harold Ryan took her to the fights.

Major Siegfried Von Konigswald is another minor character who serves a thematic purpose. While trying to impress his son, Harold Ryan boasts about how he killed Von Konigswald who was "one of the most hateful men in all of history — The Beast of Yugoslavia" (73). Yet Von Konigswald is in Heaven playing shuffleboard with little Wanda June. At one point he tells the audience:

I am Major Siegfried Von Konigswald. They used to call me "The Beast of Yugoslavia" on account of all the people I tortured and shot — and hanged. We'd bop-em on the head. We'd hook 'em up to electricity. We'd stick 'em with hypodermic syringes full of all kinds of stuff. One time we killed a guy with orange juice . . .

. . .

That Harold Ryan — he says he spoke to me in perfect German. He talks German like my ass chews gum. I'm glad to hear the wonderful thing he said before he killed me. I sure didn't understand it the first time around. . . . All I knew was that he was very proud about something, and he had a machine pistol and it was aimed at me (76 - 7).

The Nazi S. S. officer is a human and not a beast, and he is one more indication of Vonnegut's firm belief that there are no pure villains or pure heroes. Von Konigswald's description of the atrocities he committed loses much of its horror because of its colloquial language. He seems as much a victim of his environment as Harold Ryan since he apparently died without ever really knowing why he was to be executed. He confesses that he was just one small cog in the war machine — just a soldier following orders.

IV *Flaws in* Happy Birthday, Wanda June

As Walter Kerr has pointed out, the play is structurally ambivalent about death.[5] Heaven is described as a gigantic playground where little Wanda June, a girl who was run over by an ice-cream truck, plays shuffleboard with the Nazi "Beast of Yugoslavia," with Judas, and with Jesus Christ. Wanda June loves it there, and the Nazi finds it almost worth the trip. If death is not so terrible, then why is Harold Ryan's record of human carnage so terrible in Vonnegut's eyes? One answer is that Heaven is not idyllic since it is static, much like Wallace Stevens' picture of Heaven in "Sunday Morning." Even when a tornado whips through Heaven, it does not change or damage anything. As Harold's former wife Mildred points out, "nobody got killed. Nobody ever gets killed. They just bounce around a lot. Then they get up — and start playing shuffleboard again" (145). Heaven may be fine for a young girl like Wanda June, but it is really a Black Humor version of Jean Paul Sartre's room in *No Exit*. Hell, instead of being portrayed as a room in a third-rate hotel, becomes an intolerably boring shuffleboard game that will last forever. Vonnegut's use of a game metaphor to describe Heaven is particularly appropriate in any satire of Ernest Hemingway since he frequently used this image in his novels; in *A Farewell to Arms*, life is described as a game where "they threw you in and did not tell you the rules and the first time they caught you off-base they killed you."[6]

Vonnegut's fuzzy concept of death is not, however, the only problem with *Happy Birthday, Wanda June;* for Vonnegut, who has always hated endings, in various earlier versions of his play, experimented with other endings; and he has admitted that "we had various people shoot Harold, including children. We had Harold shoot various people, including children. We had Harold do the world the favor of shooting himself" (ix). No matter who is killed, Harold's philosophy prevails; and it is only by showing him mishandle his suicide that Vonnegut can ridicule everything the modern hero has come to represent. Harold begins the play as a ranting parody of Hemingway at his very worst, but Vonnegut's deflation of Woodly changes his audience's perspective so that the big game hunter's mismanaged suicide attempt becomes pathetic rather than comic.

Happy Birthday, Wanda June could be subtitled "A Play without a Hero," for Vonnegut believes that the traditional Western concept of the hero is now obsolete. No longer is there a place for a cult of masculinity that places a premium on courage, brutality, and stamina but ignores gentleness, love, and wisdom. During the course of the play, Harold's rival, Woodly, feels the need to prove to himself that he is brave by facing Harold and by walking through a park at midnight. Though Woodly preaches pacifism and love, he has been conditioned by American social values to act very much like Harold Ryan. While Vonnegut's play reveals the necessity for Americans to disregard the outdated concepts about stereotyped male and female roles, it also demonstrates the difficulty of changing such deeply rooted American values.

V   Between Time and Timbuktu

Between Time and Timbuktu or Prometheus-5 was a National Educational Television production that was aired March 13, 1972. In 1971 Vonnegut was hired as consultant for the script which in reality was a collage of several seemingly unrelated incidents and characters from Vonnegut's novels, short stories, and plays. Vonnegut has commented that "This script, it seems to me, is the work of professionals who yearned to be as charming as inspired amateurs can sometimes be. True, we hired the finest actors and technicians we could find. As for the meaning of the show, though, we left that to Lady Luck. She was good to us this time" (xvi). While this television play satirizes Vonnegut's favorite targets and re-emphasizes his favorite themes, the skillful juxtaposition of early and later stories clarifies many points.

In the play, the young poet Stony Stevenson is chosen the winner of a breakfast-cereal contest to determine who will be launched through the Chrono-synclastic Infundibulum; and newsman Walter Gesundheit and ex-astronaut Bud Williams, Jr., follow Stevenson's adventures through time and space. When Neil Armstrong first walked on the moon, a nationally televised show featured a panel of scientists and experts in related fields who commented on the meaning of this achievement. Vonnegut, as a science-fiction writer, seemed unawed; and he suggested that more pressing problems at home needed solution.[8] In his play he parodies many of the excesses found in network coverage of the many space shots of the early 1970's.

When ex-astronaut Williams asks Mrs. Stevenson if there were any indications when Stony was a child that her son would become an astronaut she replies that "He used to be interested in the pressure cooker. He would get it out and play with it, seal it up tight, and then unseal it again . . . put different things in it . . . marbles, his toy fire engine . . ." And she then notes, "Now they got him all sealed up" (23). Travelling in an Apollo spaceship loses much of its grandeur when it is likened to being trapped in a pressure cooker. Similarly, rather than having a "typical" astronaut family background that has been carefully investigated by government officials, Stony's mother reveals that her family had lived for a while in a Holiday Inn at government expense while welfare officials had searched for a suitable home.

Stony Stevenson discovers that his voyage through the Chrono-synclastic Infundibulum is really a journey through inner rather than outer space; for his trip traces Vonnegut's major theme from his earlier novel, *Player Piano*, through his latest play, *Happy Birthday, Wanda June*. Vonnegut once again expresses his hostility toward the blind worship of technology and his concern about the apparent meaninglessness of the universe; but, significantly, no ideas from *Slaughterhouse-Five* are included since Vonnegut apparently chose deliberately not to exorcize that Dresden demon again. Since Stony is unable to control where he will next be thrust in time and in space, he becomes a symbol of modern man's helplessness to control his own identity.

In *The Sirens of Titan* Stony Stevenson taught Malachi Constant the importance of the human imagination and instilled a sense of human dignity in his friend, but he remained a shadowy and un-developed character. In *From Time to Timbuktu* he remains un-developed and serves mainly as a Vonnegut spokesman. At one point he is contrasted to ex-astronaut Bud Williams who suffers from such a lack of imagination that, when he landed on Mars, he likened the Martian landscape to his driveway in Dallas; and he spends much of his commentary trying to remember the first words spoken by Neil Armstrong when he first stepped on the moon. In contrast to Williams, Stony as a man of imagination must grapple with the same problems Joseph Conrad probes in *Typhoon* and in *Lord Jim:* is imagination desirable or is it debilitating?

Although one of the unresolved problems in *Happy Birthday, Wanda June* is Vonnegut's treatment of Heaven, in *Between Time and Timbuktu* Stony discovers that Wanda June's Heaven is the product of a child's limited imagination. He surveys Heaven and discovers it is his "childhood dream of how God might try to make everybody happy when they were dead" (257). Stony feels

frightened when he meets Adolph Hitler in Heaven; for since he
realizes that Hitler was his childhood dream of the most terrible possible creature, he is horrified when Hitler declares

> I am death, and I am final
> (Aside, awed by himself)
> God, am I ever final.
> (To Stony)
> When I say the magic word to all these people,
> they will vanish forever. I will then say the
> magic word to you, and you, too, will vanish —
> never to be seen again.
> (to the crowd, horrifyingly)
> There is no heaven!
> When you are dead, you are dead. That's all there is to it.
> There is no afterlife in any way. . . (258).

In Stony's struggle between death and imagination, he triumphs
because he realizes that man can use his imagination to create his
own destiny; therefore, he tells Hitler that "There *is* an afterlife, if I
create one up here. I can create anything up here . . ." (262).

Between Time and Timbuktu is a tribute to Vonnegut's imagination. The very fact that the play ranges from the sunny mythical
island of San Lorenzo to the cold Schenectady laboratory of Dr. Felix
Hoenikker illustrates Vonnegut's scope. At one point Stony finds
himself a part of a scene from "Welcome to the Monkey House"
when he brings a last meal to Lionel J. Howard in an ethical suicide
parlor. Howard's question "What are people for?" is immediately
followed by a scene from *Cat's Cradle* that contains the parable from
The Books of Bokonon in which man asks God what the purpose of
life is; and God replies, "I leave it to you to think of one," and goes
away. The question has fascinated Vonnegut for many years, and the
conclusion of *Between Time and Timbuktu* suggests a Black Humor
solution. Because Stony cannot make sense of his adventures, he
seeks an answer to the meaning of his life but concludes by shrug-
ging his shoulders as a band plays

> What's the use of worrying? It never was worthwhile . . .
> So pack up your troubles in an old kit bag,
> And smile . . . smile . . . smile . . ." (277).

As the later *Breakfast of Champions* suggests, too much introspec-
tion can be dangerous, even suicidal. Perhaps the best man can do is

to accept his fate and try to make the best of life no matter how absurd it may appear to be.

VI   Fortitude

Fortitude (1968), Kurt Vonnegut's parody of the Frankenstein story written especially for a *Playboy* audience, is a comical play that illustrates Vonnegut's intense distrust of technology when it is not tempered with Humanism. Vonnegut's Doctor Frankenstein obtained his medical degree and then spent six long years studying mechanical, chemical, and electrical engineering so that he could conquer death. When the rich widow Mrs. Lovejoy gave him the funds to try to save her from death, he began to replace all her defective parts with automated equipment. As a result, Mrs. Lovejoy is reduced to a head with electrical attachments that are monitored by Frankenstein and his assistant, appropriately named Tom Swift.

While "Fortitude," the play's title, refers to the characteristic of Mrs. Lovejoy that enables her to survive, her Faust-like desire to live forever is shown to be mere vanity and not something noble. Indeed, Mrs. Lovejoy's beautician likens her to some "horrible machine in a penny arcade"; but she also explains that she still likes the woman because she occasionally "sees a tiny spark of what she used to be" and this spark cries "For the love of God — somebody get me out of here!" (106). Vonnegut structures his entire play around the beautician's growing disillusionment over Frankenstein's experimental efforts that leads her to shoot him and causes him to become also a head attached to machinery. The result is an echo of a shaggy-dog story popular during the mid-1960's that concludes with the punchline — "quit while you're a head."

VII   *The Legacy of the Plays*

Vonnegut has admitted that he knew almost nothing about writing plays when he began constructing *Happy Birthday, Wanda June*, and his plays exhibit major flaws. His underdeveloped characters resemble those found in his short fiction; for, unable to employ indirectly the narrative voice that controls *Slaughterhouse-Five*, he frequently slows the action to use a character for preaching Vonnegut homilies to his audience. While both *Happy Birthday, Wanda June* and *Between Time and Timbuktu* contain hilarious scenes, they lack the structure and the depth of characterization necessary to make them more than polemical exercises. Ultimately, *Happy Birthday, Wanda June* is an overstated polemic against the virility cult;

Between Time and Timbuktu is a nostalgic look backward that adds little to the Vonnegut canon. As Vonnegut himself has admitted, these plays lack that most important character who appears in all Vonnegut's novels — the novelist himself.

While the plays themselves are not literary monuments, they are an important stage in Vonnegut's artistic development; for they reflect his growing concern with speaking directly to his readers about subjects of importance to him. Immediately after *Breakfast of Champions,* Vonnegut published a collection of his nonfiction in which he admitted that he has drifted toward the "New Journalism." Rather than contrive to write sugar-coated, thinly veiled diatribes for a theater audience, Vonnegut discovered it was far more expedient to communicate his thoughts by writing nonfiction that utilized these technical qualities that had made him a successful novelist.

CHAPTER 9

The Public Man

I The Growth of Vonnegut's Reputation

FOR twelve years Kurt Vonnegut, Jr., was ignored by reviewers and literary critics, and he responded with feelings of resentment and self-doubt. As he recalled recently to an interviewer, ". . . I was also noticing the big money and the heavy praise some of my contemporaries were getting for their books and I would think, '. . . I'm going to have to study writing harder, because I think what I'm doing is pretty good, too.' I wasn't even getting reviewed. *Esquire* published a list of the American literary world back then and it guaranteed that every living author of the slightest merit was on there, somewhere. I wasn't on there . . . the list had made me sick, . . . it had made me feel subhuman."[1] As many chroniclers of Vonnegut's career have indicated, the publication of *Cat's Cradle* began the reader support that culminated with the publication of *Breakfast of Champions* as a monthly selection by a number of major book clubs.[2] With Vonnegut's recent appointment as a member of the prestigious National Institute of Arts and Letters, he has finally achieved the position he sought in vain for so many years.

Vonnegut's misfortune has been, however, to be summarily categorized and quickly dismissed by a whole generation of American critics. *Player Piano* contained Vonnegut's Foreword warning that "This book is not a book about what is, but a book about what could be." Despite the novel's emphasis on the very real psychological and political problems concomitant with automation, critics dismissed the book as mere science fiction. In an essay written for *The New York Times*, an angry Vonnegut lashed out at such categorizing and asserted that "The way a person gets into this drawer, apparently, is to notice technology. The feeling persists that no one can simultaneously be a respectable writer and understand how a refrigerator works, just as no gentleman wears a brown suit in the city."[3] *The Sirens of Titan* reinforced the critics' conviction that Vonnegut was not a serious writer, and the book was ignored in the reviews of virtually all major magazines and newspapers.

With the publication of *Mother Night* and *Cat's Cradle*, Vonnegut escaped the science-fiction label only to be immediately shelved with Thomas Pyncheon, John Barth, and Bruce Jay Friedman as a Black Humorist. In a perceptive essay written for *The Hollins Critic*, Robert Scholes proclaimed that Kurt Vonnegut, Jr., was a master of Black Humor and also a major figure in contemporary American fiction.[4] By establishing the relationship between Vonnegut's sardonic humor and the dark comedy of earlier masters such as Aristophanes and Jonathan Swift, Scholes made Vonnegut academically respectable. He began to be invited to various academic forums and asked to appear at writers' workshops. At one such gathering of writers, he noted that he was listed on the program as "the foremost black humorist in American fiction."[5]

While Vonnegut's critical reputation has grown slowly, he has been popular with college students ever since the publication of *The Sirens of Titan*. With the publication of *Cat's Cradle*, this following grew to cult-like proportions on some campuses; and the students used the private terminology associated with Bokononism. Among the critics who investigated this phenomenon with mixed results and with varied conclusions, Leslie Fiedler wrote a lengthy essay for *Esquire* entitled "The Divine Stupidity of Kurt Vonnegut: Portrait of the Novelist as Bridge Over Troubled Water."[6] He saw Vonnegut essentially as a transitional figure between High-Art and New Pop fiction; for, with the demise of the values of Modernism associated with T. S. Eliot's conception of "Culture" as an elite group capable of appreciating highly allusive, symbolic art, Pop Art represented, especially to young people, the storehouse of fantasy and the guide to preparing to live in the twenty-first century. Moreover, Fiedler explained that Vonnegut was also transitional because, although he utilized many Pop Art techniques in his novels, he still yearned to be considered a serious writer. As a result, many of Vonnegut's novels dealt with artists in much the same way that earlier Modernist writers such as James Joyce and D. H. Lawrence had concerned themselves with art in *Portrait of the Artist as a Young Man* and in *Sons and Lovers*, respectively. With Fiedler's bias for Pop Art, he not surprisingly considered *The Sirens of Titan* and *Cat's Cradle* to be Vonnegut's major achievements.

Unlike Leslie Fiedler, who saw Pop Art as an important cultural barometer, Benjamin Demott studied the Vonnegut cults and concluded that college students read his novels because he provided them with precisely the harmless, pleasant bromides for which they yearned. Students found in Vonnegut's fiction the same escape from reality that made the Beatles' *Yellow Submarine* such a successful movie. Another aspect of Vonnegut's work that is associated with what Demott calls "Youthcult" is his concern with major issues; and Eliot Rosewater praises science-fiction writers for "guts enough to *really* care about the future — *really* notice what machines do to us, what wars do to us, what cities do to us, what big, simple ideas do to us, what tremendous misunderstandings, mistakes, accidents and catastrophes do to us."[7]

Vonnegut also provides Youthcult with justification for its hatred of the work ethic and of moral and intellectual rigidity. Demott summarized his argument by proclaiming that "the dogmas just summarized aren't highly supportive to careerists, lads on the way up, pushers, drivers, scrappers. Instead of toughening wills, they foster softness, acquiescence, an indisposition to stamp your mark on life. And the general thrust, furthermore, like that of hundreds of writers from Blake to Hesse, is 'anti-intellectual': don't burn the books, but don't crack them either."[8] Though Demott labeled much of Vonnegut's work as esthetically displeasing, he still felt that it was fortunate for mainstream society that Youthcult had adopted Vonnegut since his Humanistic fiction preached kindness and contained no viciousness.

Though Demott saw Vonnegut's novels as a simplistic philosophy of kindness packaged in sophomoric tales that catered to the whims of unsophisticated readers, many critics found that the simplicity of his novels was deceiving. While Vonnegut's prose style is terse, his narrative techniques are experimental and often highly complex. As a result, critics began to suspect that Vonnegut assumed many different masks in his novels; and they sought to learn as much as they could about Vonnegut by interviewing him and by studying his non-fiction essays.

II   The Man and the Masks

When *Slaughterhouse-Five* became a best seller, Richard Todd decided to write an article about the latest literary phenomenon for *The New York Times Magazine*. He began following Vonnegut on his daily rounds of cocktail parties and lectures at Harvard in an attempt to gauge the man and to discover what lay behind the complex masks he wore. For a number of reasons, it was as difficult to discern the real Vonnegut behind his nonfiction as it was in his novels. While he had often been applauded for his candor, he so frequently undercut what he said that it was difficult to determine whether he was sincere or merely ironic. When Todd asked him what New York was going to "do" to him, Vonnegut replied angrily, "I'm not going to perform for you anymore."[9] But he continued to perform on such widely diverse occasions as New York City's celebration on Earth Day and as the commencement-day speaker at Bennington College.

The effect of Vonnegut's sardonic style is illustrated by a lengthy article he wrote for *Life* entitled "There's a Maniac Loose Out There." Although the narrative was advertised as a leading novelist's account of a series of brutal slayings of coeds that had taken place on Cape Cod, it was not a typical mass-circulation magazine account of rape and murder. In likening the unknown murderer to the Boston Strangler, Vonnegut suggested that "The strangler was another New England specialist in killing women, as opposed to men. Women are so easy to kill — so weak and friendly, so fond of new people and places, of dates. And what symbols they are."[10] Symbols for whom? Vonnegut implied that this type of crime was precisely what whetted the appetite of the reading public. Later, he revealed in a curious aside that

If I wanted to see the official color photographs of what was left of the women, I could probably get them from somebody — if I were willing to pay.

I might even be able to buy a piece of the rope — *after* the trial. Business is business, after all, and always has been. There is money to be made on the fringes of famous murders. For instance: I am being paid.[11]

Even though Vonnegut seemed genuinely upset at one point in his article when he revealed that the suspected killer had once threatened his own daughter, he personally entered his article just as he had so many of his novels; and he consequently shifted attention away from the brutal murders. The maniacal slayings of these coeds are reduced by Vonnegut until they become merely an integral part of the free-enterprise system that encourages magazines such as *Life* to offer sensationalism to readers.

In a similar vein, Vonnegut once reviewed for *Life* Beth Kaufman's *Up the Down Staircase*. Entitled "Second Thoughts on a Teacher's Scrapbook," his review consisted of a number of letters

supposedly written to Kaufman. Vonnegut parodied the book's for-
mat and provided letters from such characters as "Nudist" and
"Your Replacement at Calvin Coolidge High."[12] The difficulty with
this approach is that his letters present seemingly conflicting views of
the book. While Vonnegut appears to have liked it, the effect of his
remarks creates doubt as to whether or not he wholeheartedly en-
dorsed it.

With the publication of *Breakfast of Champions,* Vonnegut
decided to eliminate many of the ambiguities that have been such an
integral part of his prose style. As he confessed to an interviewer, "As
I get older, I get more didactic. I say what I really think. I don't hide
ideas like Easter eggs for people to find. Now, if I have an idea, when
something becomes clear to me, I don't embody it in a novel."[13]
Perhaps this new attitude reflects Vonnegut's new-found confidence
and his realization that he will now be listened to without the necessity of coating his messages in more palatable forms.

III   *"To Face an Audience of Strangers"*

When Kurt Vonnegut, Jr., lectured to college writing classes, he
often stressed the need for a writer to realize that he was writing to
communicate with an audience of strangers. Vonnegut himself
believes that his audience always has for the most part been much
like himself — middle-class Americans.[14] Many of his short stories
are set in small towns; and they feature heroes with such occupations
as real-estate agents, high-school teachers, and toilet-seat salesmen.
His nonfiction is also directed to a Middle-American audience that
has little trust for intellectuals, and Vonnegut even entitled his
review of the 1966 O. Henry Prize Winning collection of short stories
"Don't Take it Too Seriously." In it he clearly drew the line between
Middle-American sensibility and an *avant garde* audience in describing a John Updike story: "As for Updike's 'The Bulgarian Poetess': it
is beautiful. It may also help to explain why so many intelligent people outside of English departments and the Authors League feel that
really excellent stories aren't for them. Here is Updike's prize hero:
'He was, himself, a writer, this fortyish young man, Henry Bech,
with this thinning curly hair and melancholy Jewish nose, the author
of one good book and three others, the good one having come first.
By a kind of oversight, he had never married.' Delicious. You bet,
but Harry Truman won't get it."[15]

The implication is that Vonnegut and his readers also find Updike's mannered prose too cute and too much the product of an "art-

for-art's-sake" philosophy. After attending a Writer's Conference at Western Illinois University, Vonnegut revealed that he had met a writer named Harry Mark Petrakis and that they had admitted to each other "that we had never been published in *The New Yorker*, and probably never would be because we lacked that certain something . . . that they didn't like Greeks and Germans. . . ."[16] Veiled behind his sarcasm is the implication that, if *The New Yorker* and its editors and readers do not want Vonnegut's work, then he really does not want to have anything to do with them either.

Concerned with much the same Middle-American audience that scorns *The New Yorker*, Vonnegut once wrote a lengthy essay on his brief exposure to Transcendental Meditation for *Esquire*. In "Yes, We Have No Nirvanas," he carefully explained just how expensive it was for a middle-class novelist with a wife and daughter anxious to be schooled in meditation. He decided that "This new religion . . . offers tremendous pleasures, opposes no existing institutions or attitudes, demands no sacrifices or outward demonstrations of virtue, and is absolutely risk free. It will sweep the middle classes of the world as the planet dies — as the planet is surely dying — of poisoned air and water."[17] Even though the Maharishi struck Vonnegut as an innocuous public-relations man, he realized that the religion offered to the middle class had just the right mixture of personal and financial commitment — without any at all too controversial issues such as ecology. He concluded that "It seems like a good religion for people who, in troubled times, don't want any trouble. . . ."[18]

IV *The Public Man*

Kurt Vonnegut's soaring reputation as a novelist has provided him with numerous opportunities to air "in troubled times" his political and social viewpoints in a variety of forums ranging from *The New York Times* to *McCalls*. He summarized many of his beliefs in the address he delivered to the 1970 graduating class at Bennington College in which he declared that "The arts put man at the center of the Universe, whether he belongs there or not. Military science, on the other hand, treats man as garbage — and his children, and his cities, too. Military science is probably right about the contemptibility of man in the vastness of the Universe. Still — I deny that contemptibility, and I beg you to deny it, through the creation and appreciation of art."[19] In much the same way that Bokonon urged his followers in *Cat's Cradle* to accept truthful lies, Vonnegut felt that artists must be Humanists even though the horrors of war might suggest that the universe was more absurd than man-centered. In delineating his personal movement toward pessimism, Vonnegut offered the graduation class's entire generation the motto "To weep is to make less the depth of grief."[20] And he stated at that moment the point of view he had adopted in his nonfiction statements about both Vietnam and Biafra.

The war in Vietnam tormented Vonnegut more and more as the casualties and the tales of atrocities grew. He declared on many occasions that, while he had trained his sons to be pacifists, he resented the efforts of self-styled patriots to accuse an entire generation of cowardice. In his introductory remarks to a collection of essays from underground, high-school newspapers, he explained his view "So I've taken this space in the front of John Birmingham's good book to record something which I've wanted to record somewhere for a long time, something easily forgotten: My generation was raised to be pacifistic, but it fought well in a war it felt was just. This is sure true of the pacifists in the present high school generation: They aren't cowards, either."[21] In Vonnegut's efforts to raise a public clamor that would help to end the American commitment to Vietnam, his approach varied from outraged declarations to simple understatement. In an essay written for *The New York Times*, he compared American bombing with the ill-fated Spanish Armada that had sailed completely stocked with a number of torture devices. Vonnegut rhetorically asks, "One wonders now where our leaders got the idea that mass torture would work to our advantage in Indochina. It never worked anywhere else. They got the idea from the same childish fiction, I think, and from a childish awe of torture."[22]

In *Slaughterhouse-Five* he created Roland Weary, an unpopular soldier with a love for gruesome torture devices. From Vonnegut's point of view, the former Assistant Secretary of Defense John Mc-Naughton was as misguided as Weary when he referred to the bombing of North Vietnam as "one more turn of the screw."[23] While American participation in the Vietnam war drew Vonnegut's outraged essays and speeches, his personal visit to Biafra during its struggle for independence left him numbed after he had spent six days in the breakaway republic and before he had left on the last plane that was not fired upon. When Vonnegut was given a tour of the area by a Biafra supporter named Miriam Reik, he admitted that "Miriam was annoyed by my conversation at one point, and she said scornfully, 'You won't open your mouth unless you can make a joke.'

It is true. Joking was my response to misery I couldn't do anything about."[24]

Vonnegut's report of the tour was written for *McCall's,* but his emotional response to the human devastation he had witnessed left him unable to write what some editors and readers might have expected. He confessed that

. . . My aim will not be to move readers to voluptuous tears with tales about innocent black children dying like flies, about rape and looting and murder and all that. I will tell instead about an admirable nation that lived for less than three years.

De mortuis nil nisi bonum. Say nothing but good of the dead.[25]

Vonnegut kept his word, for he stressed the courage and endurance he observed although he did mention casually the children who died from lack of protein and the soldiers he observed who were preparing to battle Russian fighter planes and sophisticated tanks without any bullets for their rifles. No jokes appear in his long obituary of Biafra, only Vonnegut's prosaic descriptions of laudable individuals who he realized would disappear from history shortly after he had left.

V   *Vonnegut's Priorities*

While many of Vonnegut's essays have illustrated his attitude toward war, he has also written substantially about his concern for ecology and about his awareness of the loneliness and the despair that cloud the lives of millions of Americans. In an essay entitled "Excelsior! We're Going to the Moon. Excelsior!," he informed readers of the *New York Magazine* that the space program was a colossal boondogle that was worthwhile only to a few scientists like Arthur C. Clarke and to the countless engineers employed in the projects. In many ways, the maximum effort America made to reach the moon is viewed by Vonnegut as a deliberate attempt to avoid the far more difficult problems on and of Earth: "Earth is such a pretty blue and pink and white pearl in the pictures NASA sent me. It looks so *clean.* You can't see all the hungry, angry earthlings down there — and the smoke and the sewage and trash and sophisticated weaponry."[25] Because of such problems, Vonnegut agreed with Isaac Asimov that American science fiction had passed through adventure and technology phases but that it was now concerned primarily with sociology. Vonnegut expressed the hope that such an outline was prophetic of "earthling history, too. I interpret 'sociology' broadly —

as a respectful, objective concern for the cradle natures of earthlings on Earth."[27]

In a review of Eric Berne's *Games People Play* written for *Life*, Vonnegut emphasized the value of such a book for people "in their anguished need for simple clues as to what is *really* going on."[28] His own novels, particularly *God Bless You, Mr. Rosewater*, graphically depict the plight of the people nobody loves. Indeed, Vonnegut decries the hopelessness in people's lives — educated people's. "We all need a lot more fun and excitement and theatricality."[29] Vonnegut views the recent upsurge of interest in astrology and in the occult as one more search for excitement and theatricality that people can no longer find in their own lives. His lengthy article about the life of Madame Blavatsky, the Theosophist leader and a Spiritualist, illustrates his impatience with frauds; however, he indicates his realization that Spiritualism might very well serve as a necessary crutch for some people as they face a world that is much too rational and too coldly scientific.

In describing how Madame Blavatsky was converted to Spiritualism by the American medium William Eddy, Vonnegut matter-of-factly lists the seven visible spirits that Eddy summoned, including the last one:

> Finally, he materialized an old man who wore around his neck the Russian decoration of Saint Ann . . . This last spook was her [Blavatsky's] uncle.
> This happened over a period of fourteen days. It was a splendid show, and I do not propose to reveal how the swindle was perpetrated.[30]

Vonnegut's disbelief is apparent in his debunking use of *spook* to describe the uncle and in his reduction of this séance to a side show. But Vonnegut is also aware that Madame Blavatsky was not a simple fraud and that her believers were not simple dupes:

> At a minimum: Madame Blavatsky brought America wisdom from the East, which it very much needed, which it very much needs. If she garbled or invented some of that wisdom, she is doing no worse than other teachers did. The only greed I can detect in the woman is a greed to be *believed*. . . .
> . . . Bizarre as she may have been, she was something quite lovely: she thought all human beings were her brothers and sisters — she was a citizen of the world.[31]

As is clear, this description of the Spiritualist aptly describes Vonnegut himself. In his latest book, a collection of essays entitled

Wampeters, Foma, & Granfalloons, Vonnegut confesses in his Preface that he finally realizes that ". . . public speaking is about the only way a poet or a novelist or a playwright can have political effectiveness in his creative prime. If he tries to put his politics into a work of the imagination, he will foul up his work beyond all recognition."[32]

In the final analysis Vonnegut's fiction and his nonfiction reflect his love for all humanity and his belief that both war and pollution are obscene — are far worse than the simple bittersweet-lies that bring temporary happiness and amelioration of pain. His recent plays and essays and the polemical nature of *Breakfast of Champions* illustrate Vonnegut's movement from novelist to public man. In his efforts to change his country's direction he apparently has abandoned fiction because of the communication barriers inevitable between readers and novelist. By abandoning his narrative masks to speak directly to his audience, Vonnegut appears to be moving on the same path that Norman Mailer has traveled. *Breakfast of Champions* serves as Vonnegut's version of Mailer's *An American Dream,* for both feature their creators as heroes whose lives illustrate the course of action that Americans must pursue if they desire to prevent the American dream from becoming an American nightmare.

Notes and References

Chapter One

1. This account of Vonnegut's background is drawn from the unsigned essay, "An Account of the Ancestry of Kurt Vonnegut, Jr., by an Ancient Friend of His Family," *Summary*, I (1971), 76 - 118.

2. Robert Scholes, "Chasing a Lone Eagle: Vonnegut's College Writing," in *The Vonnegut Statement*, ed. Jerome Klinkowitz and John Somer (New York: Seymour Lawrence, 1973), p. 47.

3. "Science Fiction," *New York Times Book Review*, September 5, 1965, p. 2.

4. See particularly H. Bruce Franklin, "Fictions of Science," *Southern Review*, N. S. III (Autumn, 1967), 1036 - 49.

5. "Science Fiction," p. 2.

6. Ibid.

7. John Casey, "Interview with Kurt Vonnegut, Jr.," in *Apocalypse: Dominant Contemporary Forms*, ed. Joe David Bellamy (Philadelphia: Lippincott, 1972), p. 382.

8. David Standish, "*Playboy* Interview: Kurt Vonnegut, Jr.," *Playboy*, XVIII (July 1973), 68.

9. Perhaps the most informative study of recent anti-utopias is found in Chad Walsh's *From Utopia to Nightmare* (New York, 1962). See also Stanley Schatt, "O Brave New Nightmare: Time in Contemporary Dystopic Fiction," *English in Texas*, IV (Summer 1973), 88 - 90.

10. David Standish, "*Playboy* Interview: Kurt Vonnegut, Jr.," p. 68.

11. Roger Henkle, "Wrestling (American Style) with Proteus," *Novel: A Forum on Fiction*, III (Spring 1970), 198.

12. Robert Scholes, "A Talk with Kurt Vonnegut, Jr.," in *The Vonnegut Statement*, pp. 93 - 4.

13. I am indebted to Ms. Lynn Buck of the State University of New York at Stony Brook for first pointing out this significant theme in Vonnegut's work. Much of the material in this section is drawn from her unpublished paper which she read at the 1972 Modern Language Association seminar about Vonnegut, J. B. Cabell, and John Barth.

14. "Science Fiction," p. 2.

15. Peter Reed, *Kurt Vonnegut, Jr.* (New York, 1972), p. 29.

16. James M. Mellard, "The Modes of Vonnegut's Fiction: Or, *Player Piano* Ousts Mechanical Bride and *The Sirens of Titan* Invade the Guttenberg Galaxy," in *The Vonnegut Statement* (New York, 1973), p. 180.

17. Reed, *Kurt Vonnegut, Jr.*, p. 47.

18. John Casey, "Interview with Kurt Vonnegut, Jr.," pp. 383 - 84.

19. John Somer, "Quick-Stasis: The Rite of Initiation in Novels of Kurt Vonnegut, Jr.," Ph.D. Dissertation, Northern Illinois University, 1971, pp. 106 - 12.

20. James Mellard, "The Modes of Vonnegut's Fiction," p. 197.

21. John Somer, "Quick-Stasis: The Rite of Initiation in the Novels of Kurt Vonnegut, Jr.," p. 130.

22. David Ketterer, *New Worlds for Old: The Apocalyptic Imagination, Science Fiction, and American Literature* (Garden City, N.Y., 1974), p. 321.

23. Ibid.

24. Theodore Rozak, *The Making of a Counterculture* (Garden City, N.Y., Doubleday, 1969).

25. Ibid., p. 260.

Chapter Two

1. As a science-fiction writer, Vonnegut was well aware of John W. Campbell, Jr., the editor of numerous science-fiction magazines. Vonnegut's schizophrenic Nazi lives in a fantasy world as cut off from reality as the exotic creatures found in *Galaxy* or in *The Magazine of Fantasy and Science Fiction*.

2. For the most complete account of this part of Vonnegut's life, see the unsigned "An Account of the Ancestry of Kurt Vonnegut, Jr., by an Ancient Friend of His Family," *Summary*, I (1971), 76 - 118.

3. Tony Tanner, "The Uncertain Messenger: A Study of the Novels of Kurt Vonnegut, Jr.," *Critical Quarterly*, XI (Winter 1969), 303.

4. L. J. Clancy, "Kurt Vonnegut: 'Running Experiments Off,' " *Meanjin Quarterly*, XXX (Autumn 1971), 49 - 50.

5. "Schizophrenia," in *International Encyclopedia of the Social Sciences*, Vol. XIV, ed. David L. Sills (New York, 1968), p. 1045.

6. Francis J. Braceland and Michael Stock, *Modern Psychiatry: A Handbook for Believers* (New York, 1963), p. 127.

7. Ibid., p. 129.

8. Van A. Harvey, *A Handbook of Theological Terms* (New York, 1964), p. 200.

9. Erich Fromm, *You Shall Be As Gods* (New York, 1966), p. 161.

10. William James, *Pragmatism* (New York: William Longmans, Green, 1907), p. 246.

11. Andrew J. Reck, *Introduction to William James* (Bloomington, Indiana: Indiana University Press, 1967), p. 76.

12. Henry Alonzo Myers, *Systematic Pluralism: A Study in Metaphysics* (New York: Cornell University Press, 1961), p. 181.

13. T. S. Chang, *Epistomological Pluralism*, trans. C. Y. Chang (New York: World Book Company, 1932), p. 25.

14. Jerome Klinkowitz, "Kurt Vonnegut and the Crimes of His Times," *Critique*, XII (1971), 45.

15. Robert Scholes, " 'Mithridates, He Died Old': Black Humor and Kurt Vonnegut, Jr.," *The Hollins Critic*, III (October 1966), pp. 3 - 4.

16. Bruce Jay Friedman, Foreword, *Black Humor*, ed. Bruce Jay Friedman (New York: Bantam, 1969), p. x.

17. Ibid., p. xi.

18. Max F. Schulz, "Towards a Definition of Black Humor," *Southern Review*, N. S. IX (Winter 1973), 120.

19. L. J. Clancy, " 'Running Experiments Off,' " 54.

20. Ibid., p. 48.

21. Vonnegut may very well be punning on "bad Doestoevsky," to indicate that the Russian plagiarist falls far short of the master.

22. Jerome Klinkowitz, "Kurt Vonnegut, Jr., and the Crime of His Times," *Critique*, XII (1971), 40.

23. Robert Scholes, "A Talk with Kurt Vonnegut, Jr.," in *The Vonnegut Statement*, p. 108.

Chapter Three

1. Glen Meeter, "Vonnegut's Formal and Moral Otherworldliness: *Cat's Cradle* and *Slaughterhouse-Five*," in *The Vonnegut Statement*, p. 209.

2. Vonnegut has confessed that he learned that "Irving Langmuir, a Noble Prize winner in chemistry, told H. G. Wells an idea for a science fiction story about a form of ice that was stable at room temperature. Wells wasn't interested. I heard the story and as Langmuir and Wells were both dead, considered it my legacy, my found object." (John Casey, "Interview with Kurt Vonnegut, Jr.," in *Apocalypse: Dominant Contemporary American Forms*, ed. Joe David Bellamy (Philadelphia: Lippincott, 1972), p. 384.

3. W. H. Auden, "Numbers and Faces," in *Selected Poetry of W. H. Auden* (New York: Random House, 1958), pp. 128 - 29.

4. Jerome Klinkowitz, "Kurt Vonnegut, Jr. and the Crime of His Times," p. 50.

5. Kurt Vonnegut, Jr., letter to Stanley Schatt dated May 20, 1969.

6. Andrew J. Reck, *Introduction to William James*, p. 81.

7. Two fine studies of this subject are Frank Kermode, *The Sense of an Ending: Studies in the Theory of Fiction* (New York: Oxford University Press, 1967), and Rudolf Bultmann, *The Presence of Eternity: History and*

Eschatology (New York: Greenwood Press, 1957). The various ways American writers have treated the idea of an apocalypse in recent fiction are considered in Stanley Schatt, "Waiting for the Apocalypse: Eschatology in Recent American Fiction," *Journal of the American Studies Association of Texas*, IV (1973), 102 - 08.

8. John May, *Toward a New Earth: Apocalypse in the American Novel* (Notre Dame, Indiana: Notre Dame University Press, 1972), p. 197.

9. Robert Scholes, " 'Mithridates, He Died Old': Black Humor and Kurt Vonnegut, Jr." This essay is reprinted with a lengthy Afterword in *The Sounder Few*, ed. R. H. W. Dillard, *et al.* (Athens, Georgia: University of Georgia Press, 1971), pp. 173 - 91.

10. John Casey, "Interview with Kurt Vonnegut, Jr.," in *Apocalypse: Dominant Contemporary Forms*, p. 384.

11. Kurt Vonnegut, Jr., letter to Stanley Schatt dated May 20, 1969.

12. This idea is developed at length by Leonard J. Leff, "Utopia Reconstructed: Alienation in Vonnegut's *God Bless You, Mr. Rosewater*," *Critique*, XII (1973), 29 - 37.

13. Matthew 7:6. I am indebted to Max F. Schulz for first pointing out this passage to me.

Chapter Four

1. David Standish, "*Playboy* Interview: Kurt Vonnegut, Jr.," *Playboy*, XVIII (July, 1973), 70.

2. Wilfred Sheed, "Requiem to Billy Pilgrim's Progress," *Life*, LXVI (March 21, 1969), 9.

3. Ibid.

4. Elizabeth Wright, *The Pilgrim's Progress: Chapter Notes and Criticism* (New York: Monarch Press, 1966), p. 16.

5. Van A. Harvey, *A Handbook of Theological Terms* (New York: Macmillan, 1964), p. 200.

6. Keats's friend Woodhouse wrote to John Taylor that the young poet believed that the highest order of poet will be "able to throw his own soul into any object he sees or imagines, so as to feel . . . all that the object itself would see, feel, be sensible of or express . . . his own self will with the exception of the Mechanical part be 'annihilated' . . . See Walter Jackson Bate, "Negative Capability," in *Keats: A Collection of Critical Essays*, ed. Walter Jackson Bate (Englewood Cliffs, N.J.: Prentice Hall, 1964), p. 66.

7. Dayton Kohler, "Time and the Modern Novel," *College English*, X (October 1948), 16.

8. David Irving, *The Destruction of Dresden* (New York: Holf, Rinehart and Winston, 1963).

9. David Standish, "*Playboy* Interview: Kurt Vonnegut, Jr.," 68.

10. Peter Scholl, "Vonnegut's Attack Upon Christendom," *Newsletter of the Conference on Christianity and Literature*, XXII (Fall 1972), 11.

11. David J. Greiner, "Vonnegut's *Slaughterhouse-Five* and the Fiction of Atrocity," *Critique*, XIV (1973), 43.

12. Raymond Olderman, *Beyond the Waste Land: A Study of the American Novel in the Nineteen-Sixties* (New Haven: Yale University Press, 1972), p. 211.

Chapter Five

1. L. J. Clancy, "Kurt Vonnegut, Jr., 'Running Experiments Off,' " 49.

2. David Standish, "*Playboy* Interview: Kurt Vonnegut, Jr.," p. 214.

3. Ibid.

4. Alain Robbe-Grillet, *For a New Novel: Essays on Fiction*, trans. Richard Howard (New York: Grove Press, 1965), p. 28.

5. Marie Amaya, *Pop Art and After* (New York: Viking, 1966), p. 17.

6. Vonnegut is particularly vocal on this subject in his interview with L. J. Clancy in the *Meanjin Quarterly*, XXX (Autumn 1971), 48.

7. Richard Bridgeman, *The Colloquial Style in America* (New York: Oxford University Press, 1966), p. 12.

8. Ibid., p. 89.

9. Ibid., p. 32.

10. L. J. Clancy, "Kurt Vonnegut, Jr., 'Running Experiments Off,' " 48.

11. David Standish, "*Playboy* Interview: Kurt Vonnegut, Jr.," p. 160.

Chapter Six

1. "Slapstick," in *The Encyclopedia Britannica*, IX, 1975, p. 265.

Chapter Seven

1. *Welcome to the Monkey House* (New York, 1969), p. xiv.

2. Kurt Vonnegut, Jr., letter to Stanley Schatt dated May 20, 1969.

3. L. J. Clancy, " 'Running Experiments Off,' An Interview with L. J. Clancy," p. 51.

4. *Wampeters, Foma & Granfalloons* (New York, 1974), p. xxv.

Chapter Eight

1. Mel Gussow, "Vonnegut is Having Fun Doing a Play," *New York Times*, October 6, 1970, p. 56.

2. Patricia Bosworth, "To Vonnegut, the Hero is the Man Who Refuses to Kill," *New York Times*, October 25, 1970, Sec. 2, p. 5.

3. *Between Time and Timbuktu or Prometheus-5* (New York, 1972), p. xvi.

4. See Genesis 3:16.

5. Patricia Bosworth, "To Vonnegut, the Hero is the Man Who Refuses to Kill," p. 5.

6. Walter Kerr, "At Last, An Imaginative Mind," *New York Times*, October 18, 1970, Sec. 2., p. 1.

7. Ernest Hemingway, *A Farewell to Arms* (New York: Charles Scribner's Sons, 1927), p. 327.

8. Vonnegut developed his ideas on this subject at length in "Excelsior! We're Going to the Moon! Excelsior," *New York Times Magazine*, July 13, 1969, pp. 9 - 11.

Chapter Nine

1. David Standish, "*Playboy* Interview: Kurt Vonnegut, Jr.," p. 214.

2. Ibid.

3. Jerome Klinkowitz provides an excellent reputation study in "The Literary Career of Kurt Vonnegut, Jr.," *Modern Fiction Studies*, XIX (Spring 1973), 57 - 67.

4. "Science Fiction," *New York Times Book Review*, V (September 1965), p. 2.

5. Robert Scholes, " 'Mithridates, He Died Old': Black Humor and Kurt Vonnegut, Jr.," pp. 1 - 12.

6. "Teaching the Unteachable," *New York Times Book Review*, August 6, 1967, p. 1.

7. Leslie A. Fiedler, *Esquire*, LXXIV (September 1970), 195 - 197, 199 - 200, 202 - 04.

8. *God Bless You, Mr. Rosewater*, p. 27.

9. Benjamin Demott, "Vonnegut's Otherwordly Laughter," *Saturday Review*, XIV (May 1, 1971), p. 31.

10. Richard Todd, "The Masks of Kurt Vonnegut, Jr.," *New York Times Magazine*, January 24, 1971, p. 31.

11. " 'There's a Maniac Loose Out There,' " *Life*, LXVII (July 25, 1969), 55.

12. Ibid., p. 58.

13. "Second Thoughts on Teacher's Scrapbook," *Life*, LIX (September 3, 1965), 9 - 10.

14. David Standish, "*Playboy* Interview: Kurt Vonnegut, Jr.," 214.

15. This idea is developed in some depth by Jerome Klinkowitz in "The Literary Career of Kurt Vonnegut, Jr.," pp. 57 - 67.

16. "Don't Take It Too Seriously," *New York Times Book Review*, March 20, 1966, p. 1.

17. "Teaching the Unteachable," *New York Times Book Review*, August 6, 1967, p. 1.

18. "Yes We Have No Nirvanas," *Esquire*, LXIX (June 1968), 78.

19. Ibid., p. 179.

20. "Vonnegut at Bennington: Skylarking and Socialism," *Quadrille*, IV (July 1970), 3.

21. Ibid., p. 2.

22. Introduction in *Our Time is Now: Notes From the High School Underground,* ed. John Birmingham (New York: Praeger, 1970), p. ix.

23. "Torture and Blubber," *New York Times,* June 30, 1971, p. 41.

24. Ibid.

25. "Biafra: A People Betrayed," *McCalls,* XCVII (April 1970), 135.

26. Ibid.

27. "Excelsior! We're Going to the Moon! Excelsior," *New York Times Magazine,* July 13, 1969, p. 10.

28. Ibid., p. 11.

29. "Headshrinker's Hoyle on Games We Play," *Life* LVIII (June 11, 1965), 15.

30. Patricia Bosworth, "To Vonnegut, the Hero is the Man Who Refuses to Kill," *New York Times,* October 25, 1970.

31. "The Mysterious Madame Blavatsky," *McCalls,* XCVII (March 1970), 142.

32. *Wampeters, Foma, & Granfalloons* (New York, 1974), p. xxv.

Selected Bibliography

PRIMARY SOURCES

(Listed in chronological order by types.)

1. Novels, Collections of Short Stories, and Collected Essays (All Vonnegut
   novels are now available in hardbound editions by Delacorte Press
   and in paperbound editions by Dell Publishing Company.)
Player Piano. New York: Charles Scribner's Sons, 1952. London: Macmillan,
   1953.
The Sirens of Titan. New York: Dell Publishing Company, 1959. London:
   Victor Gollancz, 1962.
Canary in a Cat House. Greenwich, Connecticut: Fawcett, 1961. (short
   stories)
Mother Night. Greenwich, Connecticut: Fawcett, 1961. London: Jonathan
   Cape, 1968.
Cat's Cradle. New York: Holt, Rinehart & Winston, 1963. London:
   Penguin, 1965.
God Bless You, Mr. Rosewater. New York: Holt, Rinehart & Winston, 1965.
   London: Jonathan Cape, 1965.
Welcome to the Monkey House. New York: Delacorte Press, 1968. London:
   Jonathan Cape, 1969. (short stories)
Slaughterhouse-Five. New York: Delacorte Press, 1969. London: Jonathan
   Cape, 1969.
Breakfast of Champions. New York: Delacorte Press, 1973. London: Jona-
   than Cape, 1973.
Wampeters, Foma, & Granfalloons. New York: Delacorte Press, 1974.
Slapstick. New York: Delacorte Press, 1976.

2. Uncollected Short Stories
   (Limited to those stories discussed in Chapter 6.)
"Ambitious Sophomore." *Saturday Evening Post*, CCXXVI (May 1, 1954),
   31, 88, 92, 94.
"Any Reasonable Offer." *Collier's*, CXXIX (January 19, 1952), 32, 46 - 47.

"Bagombo Snuff Box." *Cosmopolitan,* CXXXVII (October 1954), 34 - 39.
"The Boy Who Hated Girls." *Saturday Evening Post,* CCXXVII (March 31, 1956), 28 - 29, 58, 60, 62.
"Custom-Made Bride." *Saturday Evening Post,* CCXXVI (March 27, 1954), 30, 81 - 82, 86 - 87.
"A Night For Love." *Saturday Evening Post,* CCXXX (November 23, 1957), 40 - 41, 73, 76 - 77, 80 - 81, 84.
"The No-Talent Kid." *Saturday Evening Post,* CCXXV (October 25, 1952), 28, 109 - 10, 112, 114.
"The Powder Blue Dragon." *Cosmopolitan,* CXXXVII (November 1954), 46 - 48, 50 - 53.
"Thanasphere." *Collier's,* CXXVI (September 2, 1950), 18 - 19, 60, 62.
"This Son of Mine . . ." *Saturday Evening Post,* CCIX (August 18, 1956), 24, 74, 76 - 78.

3. Plays

Between Time and Timbuktu, or Prometheus-5. New York: Delacorte Press, 1972.
"Fortitude." *Playboy,* XV (September 1968), 99 - 100, 102, 106, 217 - 18.
Happy Birthday, Wanda June. New York: Delacorte Press, 1971.
"The Very First Christmas Morning." *Better Homes and Gardens,* XL (December 1962), 14, 19 - 20, 24.

4. Articles and Book Reviews

(Limited to those articles and book reviews discussed in Chapter 8.)
"Biafra: A People Betrayed." *McCall's,* XCVII (April 1970), 68 - 9, 134 - 38.
"Don't Take It Too Seriously." Review of *Prize Stories of 1966: The O. Henry Awards,* edited by Richard Poirier and William Abrahams. *New York Times Book Review,* March 20, 1966, pp. 1, 39.
"Excelsior! We're Going to the Moon! Excelsior." *New York Times Magazine,* July 13, 1969, pp. 9 - 11.
"Headshrinker's Hoyle on Games We Play." Review of *Games People Play* by Eric Berne. *Life,* LVIII (June 11, 1965), 15, 17.
"Introduction." *Our Time is Now: Notes from the High School Under-ground,* ed. John Birmingham. New York: Praeger, 1970, pp. vii - x.
"The Mysterious Madame Blavatsky." *McCall's,* XCVII (March 1970), 66 - 7, 142 - 44.
"Science Fiction." *New York Times Book Review,* September 5, 1965, p.2.
"Second Thoughts on Teacher's Scrapbook." Review of *Up the Down Staircase* by Bel Kaufman. *Life,* XLIX (September 3, 1965), 9 - 10.
"Teaching the Unteachable." *New York Times Book Review,* August 6, 1967, pp. 1, 20.
" 'There's a Maniac Loose Out There,' " *Life,* LXVII (July 25, 1969), 53 - 56.
"Torture and Blubber." *New York Times,* June 30, 1971, p. 41.

"Vonnegut at Bennington: Skylarking and Socialism." *Quadrille*, IV (July 1970), 3.
"Yes, We Have No Nirvanas." *Esquire*, LXIX (June 1968), 78 - 79, 176, 178 - 79, 182.

SECONDARY SOURCES

1. Bibliographies

HUDGENS, BETTY LENHARDT. *Kurt Vonnegut, Jr: A Checklist*. Detroit, Michigan: Gale Research Company, 1972. Descriptive bibliography; includes blurbs and juvenilia as well as novels, book reviews, plays, and short stories.

KLINKOWITZ, JEROME, et al. "The Vonnegut Bibliography." In *The Vonnegut Statement*, edited by Jerome Klinkowitz and John Somer. New York: Delacorte Press, 1973. Listing of available primary and secondary material on Vonnegut.

PIERATT, ASA B. and JEROME KLINKOWITZ. *Kurt Vonnegut, Jr. A Descriptive Bibliography and Annotated Secondary Checklist*. Hamden, Connecticut: Shoe String Press, 1974. The most complete bibliography of primary and secondary sources available. Criticism is annotated and cross-indexed by subject.

2. Articles and Books

"An Account of the Ancestry of Kurt Vonnegut, Jr. by an Ancient Friend of his Family." *Summary*, I, 2(1971), 76 - 118. Detailed study of all Vonnegut's relatives and their relationship to nineteenth-century American immigration patterns.

BOSWORTH, PATRICIA. "To Vonnegut, the Hero is the Man Who Refuses to Kill." *New York Times*, October 25, 1970, Sec. D, p. 5. Background of *Happy Birthday, Wanda June* and Vonnegut's feelings about writing plays.

DEMOTT, BENJAMIN. "Vonnegut's Otherworldly Laughter." *Saturday Review*, LIV(May 1, 1971), 29 - 32, 38. Vonnegut's fiction is read by the young because it exemplifies many of the characteristics of Youthcult.

FIEDLER, LESLIE A. "The Divine Stupidity of Kurt Vonnegut: Portrait of the Novelist as Bridge Over Troubled Water." *Esquire*, LXXIV(September 1970), 195, 197, 199 - 200, 202 - 04. Vonnegut as a writer on the borderline between Old High Art and Pop Art.

GOLDSMITH, DAVID H. Kurt Vonnegut: *Fantasist of Fire and Ice*. Bowling Green, Ohio: Bowling Green University Popular Press, 1972. Analysis of Vonnegut's "cosmos" and his technique with the conclusion that his innovative technique might be more significant than his unsystematic philosophical views.

GREINER, DONALD J. "Vonnegut's *Slaughterhouse-Five* and the Fiction of Atrocity." *Critique*, XIV, 3(1973), 38 - 51. Vonnegut's treatment of the Dresden holocaust in light of his nonfiction sources.

GROSSMAN, EDWARD. "Vonnegut and his Audience." *Commentary*, LVIII (July 1974), 40 - 46. Vonnegut's gentle pessimism and Pop Art techniques are popular among the young.

HARRIS, CHARLES B. *Contemporary American Novelists of the Absurd.* New Haven: College and University Press, 1971. Vonnegut's treatment of a purposeless universe reveals his movement toward an Absurdist vision and his growing resignation.

HAUCK, RICHARD BOYD. *A Cheerful Nihilism: Confidence and The Absurd in American Humorous Fiction.* Bloomington, Indiana: Indiana University Press, 1971. While Vonnegut is only briefly mentioned, Hauck provides a useful analysis of the very humorous Nihilism that some critics call Black Humor. He suggests that the novelist's giggle is not an attempt to annihilate death but an echo of death.

KLINKOWITZ, JEROME. "The Literary Career of Kurt Vonnegut, Jr." *Modern Fiction Studies*, XIX(Spring 1973), 57 - 67. Vonnegut's growth in reputation and his maturity as an artist. *Breakfast of Champions* is seen as vindication of his position as one of the most respected innovators of the decade.

——— and JOHN SOMER, eds. *The Vonnegut Statement.* New York: Delacorte/Seymour Lawrence, 1973. A collection of essays, mostly previously unpublished, that includes comments by fans, friends, and critics. The essays consider Vonnegut in terms of his relationship to science fiction, his style, his philosophy, and his imagination.

MAY, JOHN R. "Loss of World in Barth, Pynchon, and Vonnegut: The Varieties of Humorous Apocalypse." *Toward a New Earth: Apocalypse in the American Novel*, pp. 172 - 200. Notre Dame, Indiana: University of Notre Dame Press, 1972. An analysis of *Cat's Cradle* in terms of the tradition of a humorous apocalypse in which an imagined catastrophe provokes laughter. Vonnegut is linked to such earlier apocalyptic American writers as Hawthorne, Melville, and Twain.

OLDERMAN, RAYMOND M. "Out of the Waste Land and into the Fire: Cataclysm or the Cosmic Cool." In *Beyond the Waste Land: the American Novel in the Nineteen-Sixties.* New Haven, Connecticut: Yale University Press, 1972, pp. 189 - 219. Vonnegut as a fabulist who portrays modern life in waste land terms and then offers a Cosmic Cool philosophy as a way to survive the absurdities of his Black Humor universe.

REED, PETER J. *Kurt Vonnegut, Jr.* New York: Warner Paperback Library, 1972. Discussion of Vonnegut's novels centering on his humor and on his pessimism.

RICHARDSON, JACK. "Easy Writer." *New York Times Book Review*, April 6, 1969, Sec. 7, 1, 23. Probably the most detailed attack on Vonnegut position as a major writer; sees Vonnegut as a minor satirist attacking easy targets and using allusions to add pretentiousness to his sophomoric content.

SCHATT, STANLEY. "The World of Kurt Vonnegut, Jr." *Critique*, XII(1971), 54 - 69. Vonnegut's philosophical concern with epistomology dominates many of his novels; he sees the world as pluralistic.

SCHOLES, ROBERT. " 'Mithridates, He Died Old': Black Humor and Kurt Vonnegut, Jr." *The Hollins Critic*, III(October 1966), 1 - 12. Reprinted in *The Sounder Few*, edited by R. H. W. Dillard, et al. Athens, Georgia: University of Georgia Press, 1971, pp. 173 - 185. Perhaps the single most important study of Vonnegut's novels and the first to link him to Black Humor.

SCHOLL, PETER A. "Vonnegut's Attack Upon Christendom." *Newsletter of the Conference of Christianity and Literature*, XXII(Fall 1972), 5 - 11. Vonnegut has lost his faith and repudiated Christianity, but he retains Christian ethics that he cannot justify intellectually.

SCHULZ, MAX F. "Toward a Definition of Black Humor." *The Southern Review*, IX n.s. (Winter 1973), 117 - 34. The philosophical and literary backgrounds to the Black Humor movement.

———. "The Unconfirmed Thesis: Kurt Vonnegut, Black Humor, and Contemporary Art." *Critique*, XII(1971), 5 - 28. Vonnegut's honest attempt to resist the temptation to formulate answers is seen in the context of contemporary artists such as Willem de Kooning.

TANNER, TONY. "The Uncertain Messenger: A Study of the Novels of Kurt Vonnegut, Jr." *Critical Quarterly*, XI(Winter, 1969), 297 - 315. Reprinted in *City of Words: American Fiction 1950 - 1970*, pp. 181 - 201. New York: Harper and Row, 1971. A thorough reading of Vonnegut's novels.

TODD, RICHARD. "The Masks of Kurt Vonnegut, Jr." *New York Times Magazine*, January 24, 1971, pp. 16, 17, 19, 22, 24, 26, 30. Vonnegut as a serious artist and as an entertainer. His classroom performance at Harvard as a writing teacher.

WOOD, MICHAEL. "Dancing in the Dark." *New York Review of Books*, XX (May 31, 1973), 23 - 24. Review of *Breakfast of Champions;* examines it in the context of Vonnegut's earlier work and recent criticism.

Index

173